'I am an American'

In loving memory of my aunt, Doris Fyfe Thomas

and

For my friends in Morgantown, the most ordinary and extraordinary Americans I know

'I am an American'

Filming the Fear of Difference

Cynthia Weber

intellect Bristol, UK / Chicago, USA

First published in the UK in 2011 by
Intellect, The Mill, Parnall Road, Fishponds, Bristol, BS16 3JG, UK

First published in the USA in 2011 by
Intellect, The University of Chicago Press, 1427 E. 60th Street,
Chicago, IL 60637, USA

A catalogue record for this book is available from the British Library.

Cover designer: Holly Rose
Copy-editor: Emma Rhys
Typesetting: Mac Style, Beverley, E. Yorkshire

ISBN 978-1-84150-422-3

Contents

Introduction

'I am an American'. This declaration plays a central role in US history, whether to instill a sense of civic duty in US citizens or to distinguish them from citizens of other nations. In the wake of the September 11, 2001, terrorist attacks, US advertizing executives mulled over this expression as they pondered what it is that makes America unique.[1] They concluded that the nation's celebration of diversity is the defining feature of America. Fearing a backlash against Arab and other minority Americans after the attacks, they decided to produce a Public Service Announcement (PSA) to remind US citizens 'that this was the time to unite as a country'.[2] The result was the famous 'I am an American' PSA which they shot for the American Ad Council, the leading producer of PSAs in the US.

The 'I am an American' PSA, which began airing on US television ten days after 9/11, features US citizens of various ages, races, religions, and ethnicities looking directly into the camera and declaring 'I am an American', while emotive Americana music plays in the background. To communicate that 'out of many faces, religions, geographical backgrounds, and ethnicities, we are one nation',[3] the PSA incorporates the original US motto – *E Pluribus Unum*/Out of Many, One. It ends with a little girl – possibly Arab, possibly South Asian, possibly Hispanic – smiling broadly as she waves the US flag.

The response to the PSA was unprecedented, both in terms of media donations of time to air the spot and expressions of thanks from US citizens to the Ad Council for 'bringing such an important message to the country at this time'.[4] Indeed, the PSA so enchanted US citizens that the Ad Council concluded it 'made a measurable difference in our society'[5] because it 'helped the country to unite in the wake of the terrorist attacks'.[6] These many years later, the PSA is still fondly remembered by many US citizens when they recall September 11 and the spirit of unity that embraced the country in its aftermath.

For all its good intentions, though, the 'I am an American' PSA did not prevent a backlash against minority populations in the US after the terrorist attacks. Nor did it articulate the full breadth of sentiment at play in the post-9/11 US, as President George W. Bush announced that the time for mourning was over and the time to take sides in the War on Terror was upon us.[7] For what became increasingly clear was that the 'with us or with the terrorists' War on Terror was going to be fought every bit as much on the home front as it was on the battlefields of Afghanistan and Iraq. And its fault lines were not just between US citizens and non-US citizens but between some kinds of US citizens and others.

What we US citizens witnessed after September 11 was that national unity is not as easily achieved in practice as it is in the US motto or in the idealized image of the American melting pot as it is portrayed in the 'I am an American' PSA. Instead, September 11 splintered the US along some very lamentable yet predictable lines (like when the idea of the 'clash of civilizations' pitted Christian against Muslim) and unpredictable lines (like when humanitarians, artists, and environmental activists were accused by the Bush administration of being or being associated with terrorists). As the War on Terror dragged on, what became increasingly apparent was that being a US citizen was no guarantee of being part of the 'One'. What also became apparent was that the seemingly simple declaration 'I am an American' is fraught with complications and paradoxes, particularly when it is meant to express citizenship, identity, tolerance, nationalism, patriotism and justice.

This project chronicles some of those complications and paradoxes. Part history, part cultural anthropology, part political biography, part memoir, the project is rooted in first-person interviews with US soldiers and citizens who more often than not found themselves on the wrong side of the Bush administration's interpretation of what it means to be and to act like a loyal and law-biding US citizen. Though it insistently observes the failures of the post-9/11 US to live up to its national ideals, the project is in no way meant to disparage the US for its ambition of constructing the celebration of diversity as among its claims to identity. Nor is it meant to deny the practical achievements the US has made in this direction, both before and after 9/11. Rather, by documenting the human costs of a fear-based patriotism, it is intended to serve as an intimate reminder to US citizens of just how great the gulf between lived realities and principled ideals can be, especially in the wake of national tragedy, and predominantly for those 'Many' US citizens whose differences prevent them from melting into the always changing national ideal of the 'One'. With this in mind, while this project takes September 11, 2001, as its focus, it is as much an invitation to US citizens to contemplate the history of the US that is currently being written by the administration of President Barack Obama and the history of the US that has yet to be written as it is an invitation to them to critically reconsider September 11 itself.

The project began as a series of documentary films. My struggle to write about these films has been a long and arduous one, as I grappled with how reductive yet also supplementary textual accounts of films can be. It was not until I was invited to mull my dilemma over with an extraordinary group of academics at the Institute for LGBT Studies at the University of Arizona – Laura Briggs, Adam Geary, Laura Gutierrez, Miranda Joseph, Liz Kennedy, Eithne Luibheid, Spike Peterson and Hai Ren (aka, the Clusteristas) – that I broke out of this predicament. They told me, 'Don't write about your films as a writer; write about them as a film-maker'. Their comment was foreshadowed in the phrase the sociologist Kate Nash had used a year earlier to describe my project, a phrase that became the subtitle of this book – 'Filming the fear of difference'. Between these covers is the book that resulted from the sage advice of these colleagues.

The book is organized into two parts. Part I explores how this project grew out of my encounter with the American Ad Council's 'I am an American' PSA and tells the stories of the US citizens I interviewed through my experiences of filming them. Using vignettes and images, these chapters move from showcasing the most predictable protagonists in the War on Terror (soldiers who fought in the Iraq War and their families) to the less predictable (citizens fighting the emerging War on Immigration) to the unpredictable (citizens who declared no side in these wars yet got caught up in the War on Terror as 'collateral damage'). Dispersed throughout are red, white, and blue comment cards containing anonymous public reflections on the project which I collected at public screenings and exhibitions. Part II offers a selection of academic reflections on the project.

The many images throughout the book are drawn mainly from the documentary films I produced, highlighting the filming aspect of the project, while the vignettes offer my reflections on the film-making process – sometimes as a film-maker, sometimes as an academic trained in the field of International Politics, and always as a US citizen living abroad who has returned to the US in search of a ground-level view of what it means to say, 'I am an American'. Within each chapter, these materials are not organized by character, by chronology, or by event. Instead, they are mixed together and juxtaposed to one another in ways that both mirror how these citizens and their stories were introduced to the US public, as well as how fragmented the process of filming actually is. To me, their organization highlights the ironies and illogicalities that marked post-9/11 US policies and some of the responses to them, all in the name of being 'an American'. But there is nothing essential in their ordering, so readers should feel free to engage with these materials in any order.

The fourteen films that resulted from my filmed interviews can be found in the permanent collection of the September 11 Memorial Museum located at the site of the former World Trade Center in New York City. A selection of the films can also be viewed online at the Open Democracy website at: http://www.youtube.com/user/opendemocracyteam. All but one of these films are four minute mini-documentaries in which each of the people I interviewed tell their story in the first person. The final film is my critical remix of the Ad Council's 'I am an American' PSA featuring the 'Many' US citizens I interviewed. They state not only 'I am an American' but also what kind of US citizen they are – the son of an immigrant without papers, a political refugee *from* America, a wrongly accused terrorist spy. This remixed PSA also incorporates many of the 'flag shots' that end each of the individual mini-documentaries and which are included in this book, in which each main character poses with the US flag in a way that expresses their relationship to the US state.

While I produced, directed, filmed, and edited all of the films, my Co-Director at Pato Productions Nina Clovis provided invaluable support for this project throughout and provided crucial production assistance whenever I needed it, particularly on the film featuring Greg and Glenda Avery.

The research for this project was made possible by two major grants, one from the British Academy and another from the Leverhulme Trust, which allowed me to conduct interviews in the US, Mexico and Canada, and by a Visiting Professorship in the Department of Political

Science at the University of Arizona, where I was based during some of my filming. My generous network of friends and family helped my research funds go further by providing me with accommodation, food, and transportation whenever they could. They include Lucy Suchman, Andrew Clement, Monique Fortier, Roxanne Doty, Spike Peterson, Nigel and Cheryl Clark, Larry and Connie Banta, Candy, Heather and Max Ogle, Shelia Rye, and as ever Nina, Chuck, Lindsay, and Seth Clovis. I received additional grants for the production of exhibition materials from the Lancaster University Faculty of Arts and Social Sciences and the Lancaster University Friends Association. The Department of Political Science at Arizona State University also generously contributed funds toward an exhibition in Phoenix, Arizona.

My greatest debt is to the people featured in this project – Lupe Denogean, Phil McDowell, Jamine Aponte, Fernando Suarez del Solar, Cindy Sheehan, James Yee, Chris Simcox, Elvira Arellano, Saul Arellano, Shanti Sellz, José Matus, Ofelia Rivas, Greg and Glenda Avery, Abe Dabdoub, Julia Shearson, Will Potter, and Steve Kurtz. They not only consented to multiple interviews. They each granted me 'fly-on-the-wall' status, often for days at a time as they went about their lives. Behind the scenes, numerous individuals and organizations helped me to secure these interviews – Brandon Mayfield, Lee Zaslofski, Nina Clovis, Bonnie Stewart, Barbara Griffin, Pastor Walter Coleman, Emma Lozano, Father Daniel French, Dereka Rushmore, and Roxanne Doty as well as Somos America, No More Deaths, Sin Fronteras, Alianza Indígena Sin Fronteras, Guererro Azteca Por La Paz, the Minutemen, the Council on American-Islamic Relations, and the Critical Art Ensemble.

The project has so far been shared through numerous public lectures, film screenings, and exhibitions in the United States, Canada, Mexico, England, Wales, Northern Ireland, Belgium, Denmark and Turkey. Thanks to all the organizers and audiences of those events, particularly Marianne Marchand who organized an exhibition at the University of the Andes in Puebla, Mexico; Jen Urso who curated an exhibition at the Ice House Gallery in Phoenix, Arizona; Marjaana Jauhola and Jennifer Pedersen who curated an exhibition at the University of Wales, Aberystwyth Arts Center; Leon Gurevitch who organized an exhibition at the Dukes Cinema Gallery in Lancaster, England; Christina Rowley and Elspeth Van Veeren who included the work in an exhibition they curated at the Centerspace Gallery, Bristol, England; and Jane McElhone who curated an exhibition at the Open Society in London, England. Thanks also to Bill Gamble, Kirk Woolford, Dave Blacow, Mick Bowen, Janan Yakula, Andy Sellers, Lucy Frost, Kat Stoney, and especially Chuck Clovis for their artistic and technical support and assistance with the still video portraits used in the exhibitions. A further thanks is due to Chuck for his unwavering and timely technical assistance throughout every stage of the film-making process. Robert Ransick, who I met while filming in Arizona and Mexico, has become an important sounding board for the project, both in terms of its content and its exhibition. And had I not received initial training in documentary film-making at Leeds University thanks to my colleagues in the Department of Communications Jayne Rodgers and Stephen Hay, it is doubtful this project ever would have existed. Thank you.

All exhibitions were co-sponsored by OpenDemocracy, which initially published a selection of the films on its website OpenDemocracy.net. Thanks to Sarah Lindon, Grace Davies, David Hayes, and Tony Curzon Price on these fronts. Thanks also to Jamaica Jones who upon discovering the films on the Open Democracy website invited all of the materials from the project to become part of the permanent collection of the US National September 11 Memorial and Museum at the former site of the World Trade Center.

While most of the images found in this book come from the films I shot, Jen Urso, Christy Putz, and Anne-Marie Fortier kindly granted their permission for me to reproduce their photographs documenting the project, and the American Ad Council, the Council on American-Islamic Relations, Guererro Azteca Por La Paz, Critical Art Ensemble, the Westboro Baptist Church, Greg Avery, Cindy Sheehan, James Yee, Phil McDowell, and Will Potter granted permission for additional images to be printed here. Thank you. Pastor Beti Guevara, Fernando Suarez del Solar, Marianne Marchand, and especially Luisa Fernanda Grijalva Maza assisted me with the Spanish translations of the films. Again, thank you.

I would also like to thank the editorial team at Intellect Books – my copy-editor Emma Rhys and especially my editor May Yao, who has creatively and supportively steered this book project from start to finish. Thank you both.

Returning to my academic colleagues, thanks to Jef Huysmans, Tim Luke, Alex Danchev, Roxanne Doty, Peter Nyers, and Lily Ling who reflected on this project and kindly agreed to have their commentaries reproduced here. Their commentaries originally appeared in *International Political Sociology* (2010), 4:80–103 under the title 'IPS Forum on Cynthia Weber's Multi-media Project "I am an American"'. Thanks also to Peter for allowing me to interview him about the case of Yaser Hamdi. I would also like to thank my colleagues at Lancaster University, especially Mark Lacy, for their support, enthusiasm, and constructive criticisms of this project as it developed. I am grateful to Lancaster University for providing me with a timely sabbatical during which I was able to complete my filming and begin my writing. I finished writing this book just after I began my new post at Sussex University. I am grateful to the School of Global Studies at Sussex University for contributing to the costs of printing this book in color, as showing the color images from my original color films makes an enormous difference in the telling of this image-based story. I am also appreciative of the supportive intellectual setting in the Department of Politics and International Relations at Leeds University, where I first began thinking about this project.

Having said all that, though, there has been no greater intellectual influence on me or on this particular project than that provided by Richard K. Ashley. Rick taught me that the key political move is to ask the question 'who are we?', and the key ethical move is to ask this question critically so that it can open up new possibilities for political and ethical engagements. This is in contrast to how scholars like Samuel P. Huntington ask this question and mobilize answers to it to close down political and ethical engagement. So to Rick, another heartfelt thank you.

I am particularly grateful that I was able to share this book with Professor Emeritus of Geography and Regional Planning Dr. Charles Weber (aka, my father), who not only embraced its content but provided important editorial comments. Thank you.

Finally, I wish to thank Anne-Marie Fortier, who has lived with this project nearly as long as I have and has advised me on it every step of the way. Her astute intellectual input and editorial suggestions have been invaluable. So has her graciousness in putting up with the many disruptions caused to our lives by my breakneck filming schedule and by my working on this book during our holidays. Thanks for your unwavering support of this project and of me.

Notes

1. These advertizing executives were from the Austin, Texas ad agency GSD&M. For more details about how they conceived of the 'I am an American' PSA, see http://www.adcouncil.org/default.aspx?id=141. Downloaded 8 September 2009.
2. http://www.adcouncil.org/default.aspx?id=141. Downloaded 8 September 2009.
3. http://www.adcouncil.org/default.aspx?id=141. Downloaded 8 September 2009.
4. http://www.adcouncil.org/default.aspx?id=141. Downloaded 8 September 2009.
5. http://www.adcouncil.org/default.aspx?id=61. Downloaded 8 September 2009.
6. http://www.adcouncil.org/default.aspx?id=141. Downloaded 8 September 2009.
7. President George W. Bush (2001), 'Address to a Joint Session of Congress Following 9/11 Attacks', 20 September, http://www.americanrhetoric.com/speeches/gwbush911jointsessionspeech.htm. Downloaded 8 September 2009.

Part I

'I am an American'

Chapter 1

Beginnings

Figure 1: Final shot of American Ad Council's 'I am an American' PSA. Courtesy of AdCouncil.org.

Loss and remembrance

Paramus, New Jersey: I have returned home from England to bury my favorite aunt. It is a couple of weeks after September 11, 2001. Everyone in the family is doubly shaken – by this death and by the deaths of so many others across the river and across the country.

My cousin and I head into New York City, as we do every time I'm home. We think we are wandering aimlessly, but at some level we know we are bound for what was the Twin Towers, to what is now this new place called 'Ground Zero'. We taste the smoke and dust still lingering in the air. We see missing persons flyers lining walls and shop windows. We stop at Fire Stations overflowing with wreaths. A few blocks from Ground Zero, barricades stop us. We loiter behind them with others who have wandered in this same direction. This is the quietest New York crowd I have ever been a part of.

Back in Jersey, we bury my aunt. We retire to the house where we recall her life, her spirit, her goodness, what we love most about her.

A television plays in one corner of the living room, as our attention is torn between a life that was and a War on Terror that is beginning. A commercial airs. It is a Public Service Announcement (PSA) by the American Ad Council. In it, US citizens of various ages, races, religions, and ethnicities look directly into the camera and declare, 'I am an American' while emotive Americana music plays in the background. The original US motto appears on the screen, first in Latin, then in English – *E Pluribus Unum*/Out of Many, One. The final shot is of a young girl – possibly Middle Eastern, possibly South Asian, possibly Hispanic. She rides her bike in Brooklyn Bridge Park across the river from where the Twin Towers used to be. Smiling broadly, the little girl waves a US flag.

The PSA touches a cord in me. I know my response to it is as much about the grief and mourning I feel for my aunt as it is about the grief and mourning I feel for those who died on 9/11. But even right there in that living room, I grasp the similar desires bound up in my personal grief and a broader collective grief – a desire to remember the best of what has been lost, a resistance to speak of the lost in the past tense, an attempt to rekindle a lost spirit.

The PSA recalls the best of what it means to be a US American – to be so melted into the US that differences of race and religion matter less to us than our shared identification as US Americans. This is what the PSA celebrates. This is what the PSA attempts to rekindle in us now, refusing to speak about this spirit in the past tense.

Yet I experience the PSA as a death notice, announcing the death of the melting pot myth. For if this myth were alive and well, the Ad Council would not need to remind US Americans of its existence and of their duty to act upon it in the wake of 9/11 by not, for example, targeting 'Arab-looking' and 'Muslim-looking' US Americans as the enemy. In contrast to my pessimistic reading of it, the PSA strives to be optimistic. For it suggests that by looking back at our history, we will find our common future, one in which we will put aside our petty differences and respect the Many as much as we do the One.

Looking back at our nation's history is what the PSA is calling upon us to do as US citizens. Looking back at our family's history is what my relatives and I instinctively do as we bury my aunt. For this is the best that loss and remembrance have to offer – a moment to pause, critically reflect, and come away from a painful experience stronger, smarter.

But my family's reflections about my aunt are anything but critical. As the days go on, these reflections become more and more idealized. 'She was the soul of our family'. 'She was only good'. 'She was always thus'. This is the family pact – that we agree to tell this and only this story about a complicated and surely flawed woman we love so much. No one says this is what we are doing. No one has to. We know what we are doing. We are searching for some relief from our grief by fudging the facts in favor of a more comforting fiction because this consoles us in this difficult moment.

This is what troubles me about the PSA. I see in it a call for US citizens to do the very same thing in relation to the US nation that my family is doing in relation to my aunt – remember only what is good, don't be too critical especially now, take comfort from flawed memories if these help us regroup at this difficult moment.

The PSA is as full of flawed memories about the US nation as my family is about my aunt. What it remembers and celebrates is the melting pot myth as if it were an accomplished fact, as if it were a good idea for everyone living in the US, as if indigenous and formerly enslaved US Americans were not and are not often excluded from the One forged out of the Many, as if new categories of excluded US Americans are not being invented every day.

It is this invention of new categories of excluded US Americans that the makers of the PSA were trying to address. They understood all too well that 'Arab-looking' and 'Muslim-looking' US Americans were in danger of experiencing a backlash in the wake of 9/11, as US grief turned into US rage. By making a PSA about what they believe is fundamentally good about the US, they were trying to avert such a backlash. It didn't work, but it was a laudable aim. The difficulty is that these days, some years after 9/11, few US Americans remember this PSA as representative of just this laudable aim – to present a partial truth about who we are as US Americans as if it were the whole truth so that in the aftermath of 9/11 our actions would make it completely true.

Over the years since it first aired, the PSA is still vividly remembered by countless US Americans. Some of them tell me that the PSA captures the essence of what it means to be a US American. These are the US Americans who firmly feel like part of the One. Other US Americans speak of how the PSA plays on old and emerging exclusions of the Many from the One. They point to how those who are excluded are turned into those to be feared – from 'the angry young black man' to 'the undeserving immigrant' to 'the Muslim terrorist'. This, they tell me, shows that the melting pot myth is an idealized rather than a real account of the US, especially now. If this were not the case, they point out, there would have been no backlash against 'different' US Americans after 9/11.

These US Americans remind us that we must not remember 9/11 and its aftermath simply as we wish it had been, as our individual selective memories and our collective national myths encourage us to. Nor must we forget it. Instead, we must remember 9/11 as fully as we can, including those things about it we would rather forget. For it is this more complete history that is shaping who we are and who we might become, individually and collectively, in relation to the seemingly simple declaration 'I am an American'.

A double bind

Leeds, England: I attend a Faculty Tea to welcome students back to the British University where I teach. It is some weeks after September 11. Because the British academic year begins in October, I have not seen my colleagues since before 9/11. The outpouring of good feeling toward me as a US citizen and toward the US in general because of the terrorist attacks is extraordinary. I experience this same response everywhere I go in Europe right now. This is partly why I am so taken aback when one of my colleagues expresses a very different sentiment. 'America got what it deserved,' she says.

I want to ask her – What America? Which Americans? Of course, she is referring to the United States of America and to US citizens. And she is expressing the idea that the terrorist attacks are the result of what Chalmers Johnson writes about as 'blowback', the unintended and unwelcome domestic consequences of US foreign policy.[1] But what has me fuming is how she is spinning this into a condemnation of the US nation and its people as a whole.

I want to scream at her: Did the grieving families I just saw in New York get what they deserved on September 11? Did all those students who enlisted in the Military Reserves to pay for their education and who will soon find themselves going off to war get what they deserved? Did the US citizens who voted *against* George W. Bush for president and now find themselves in a 'with us or with the terrorists' War on Terror get what they deserved? Did the US citizens who voted *for* George W. Bush for president and will soon find themselves as appalled by the Bush Administration's responses to the September 11 terrorist attacks as they were to the attacks themselves get what they deserved?

Here's the problem, I want to tell her. You have just equated all US citizens not only with the policies of their government but with their state itself, as if each individual US citizen were the symbolic equivalent of 'The US State'. So if someone has a problem with 'The US State', then on your thinking this is a justification for them to attack a symbol of 'The US State' – whether this is an inanimate object like the World Trade Center or an animate subject like a US civilian. All are equally justifiable targets. The problem with this logic is not only that it justifies the murder of US civilians on September 11; it justifies the violent killing of anyone who could be conceived of as a symbolic enemy of anyone with a political cause. And since we are all potential political symbols – whether as 'citizens' or 'terrorists' or other engaged or even disengaged political actors – 'humanity' (with all the complications that term implies)[2] becomes the necessary casualty of oppositional politics. For me, that's a serious problem.

I also want to challenge her comment in a British context. As a British citizen, would she allow her students to make such blanket statements about 'the British'? Would she condone equating all British citizens with the policy decisions of 'The British State' and transforming them into symbols of 'The British State'? Would she condone denying the humanity of British citizens based on nothing more than the accident of their birth? I don't think she would. Instead, I think she would lecture her students on their laziness in relying upon national stereotypes that rarely if ever make sense when applied to real, living human beings and that may be a lot more reactionary than they intend them to be. Yet somehow she feels OK about applying these sorts of stereotypes herself to US citizens.

I understand that my colleague's quip 'America got what it deserved' is grounded less in her British citizenship than it is in her distain for much of US foreign policy. This foreign policy supports US hegemonic power often to the detriment of other states and peoples, even when it understands itself to be helping them. In uttering this quip, she is acknowledging a point I very much agree with – that there is a history to September 11. September 11 is not some isolated instance in US history when 'evil terrorists' came out of nowhere and attacked 'the innocent USA'. Rather, September 11 is a moment that sits within a wider US history. This history should sometimes be celebrated, sometimes be criticized, and always be debated. But it should never be allowed to use September 11, 2001, as an exceptional moment that justifies all US policy decisions in its aftermath. But that does *not* mean 'America got what it deserved on September 11'. It means things are a lot more complicated than that. And that means that blanket condemnations of the US and its citizens that understand everything the US does as 'bad' and everything opposed to the US as 'good' are not only smug; they are stupid.

But the truth is I don't say anything to my colleague. I remain silent because of the double-bind I find myself in as a US citizen living abroad. If I say anything in defence of the US, I am written off as a stereotypical unthinking American. Yet if I make a balanced comment that is at all critical of US policy, I am read as inviting others to trash the US as a whole. Either way, I fail to convey my point because of how my point is interpreted through my citizenship. Working my way out of this bind takes on a new urgency for me in light of this conversation. But the best I can do today is project a disagreeing silence and then walk away.

Two years later during the morning rush hour in London, terrorists opposed to British involvement in the wars in Afghanistan and Iraq blow up trains, a bus, and mostly British passengers. At work, no one says Britain got what it deserved.

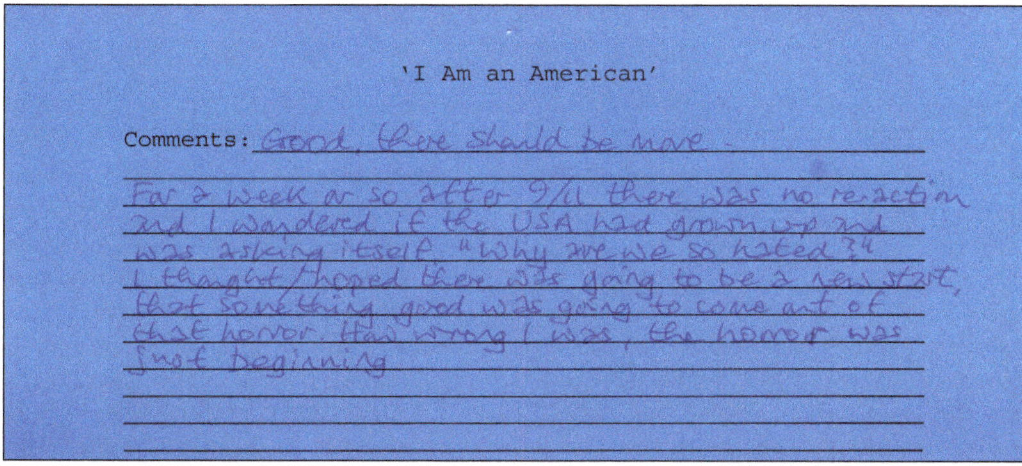

'I Am an American'

Comments: Good, there should be more.

For a week or so after 9/11 there was no reaction and I wondered if the USA had grown up and was asking itself, "Why are we so hated?" I thought/hoped there was going to be a new start, that something good was going to come out of that horror. How wrong I was, the horror was just beginning

Figure 2: Anonymous comment.

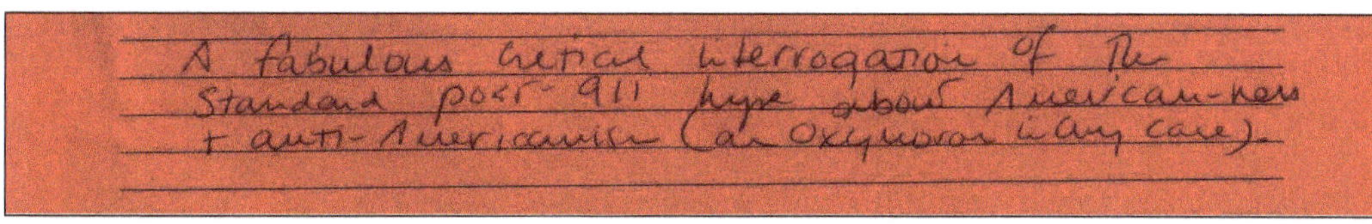

A fabulous critical interrogation of the standard post-911 hype about American-ness + anti-Americanism (an oxymoron in any case).

Figure 3: Anonymous comment.

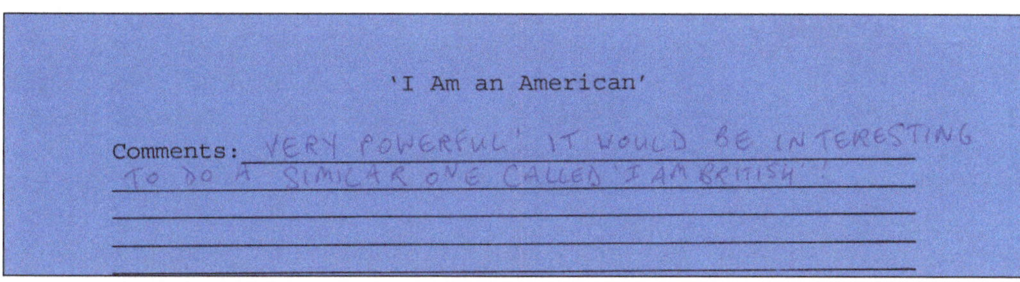

'I Am an American'

Comments: VERY POWERFUL! IT WOULD BE INTERESTING TO DO A SIMILAR ONE CALLED 'I AM BRITISH'!

Figure 4: Anonymous comment.

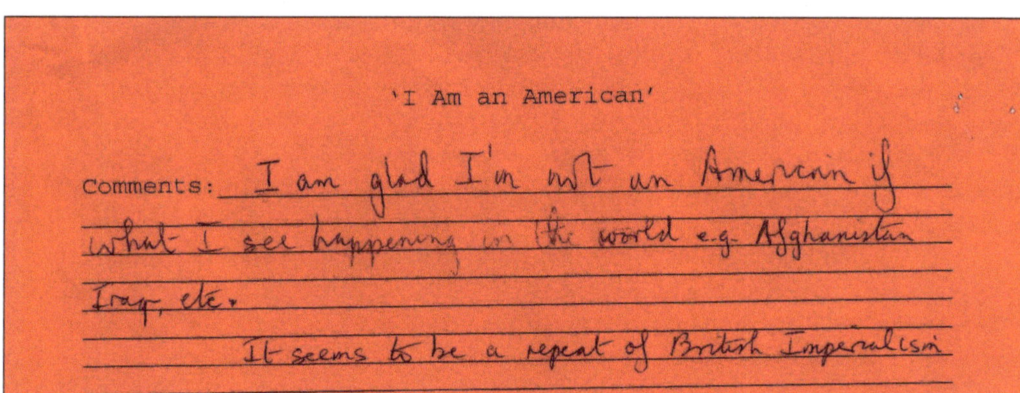

'I Am an American'

Comments: I am glad I'm not an American if what I see happening in the world e.g. Afghanistan Iraq, etc.

It seems to be a repeat of British Imperialism

Figure 5: Anonymous comment.

Unknown Americans

Lancaster, England: I can't stop thinking about the American Ad Council's 'I am an American' PSA.

Much time has passed since I first saw it, and yet the PSA regularly haunts me with some nagging questions: Who were the people featured in the PSA? Did they all feel like they were part of the 'One' that the PSA celebrates when they agreed to be in it? What are their post-9/11 experiences? How might each of them interpret the declaration 'I am an American' in light of those experiences? Would they all agree on what it means to be a patriotic US citizen in the post-9/11 US? Do their post-9/11 ideas about patriotism and justice differ from their pre-9/11 ideas about patriotism and justice? Do they believe that tolerance is a fundamental US value? Do they believe the US is as tolerant of difference as the PSA suggests, especially now? Do they think the PSA was a success, even though it did not prevent a backlash against 'different' US citizens after 9/11? Were any of them subjected to a backlash in the aftermath of 9/11? Did any of them take part in such a backlash? How do they feel about how US Americans experienced the PSA immediately after 9/11 and how US Americans experience it now?

I will never know the answers to these questions, as the individuals featured in the PSA are unknowable beyond their apparent race, sex, gender, ethnicity and US citizenship. I think about trying to find them, to ask them my many questions, but I am sure that they are largely untraceable because their names are not listed in the PSA's credits.

Their anonymity intrigues me. On the one hand, it means that viewers of the PSA are not distracted by the individual stories of the US citizens featured in the PSA, with the PSA directing them to focus only on how these US citizens look and sound, what they say, and where they say it (often in front of US national landmarks). But on the other hand, it means that viewers of the PSA lack any additional context or content through which to relate to the people in the PSA. All viewers have are faces and flags, Americana monuments and music, and one simple sentence, 'I am an American'. And what the PSA's particular staging of the sentence 'I am an American' creates is a sentimental yet rather empty sense of patriotism and national unity, even though it is anchored in the idea of the American melting pot.

It is all reminiscent of how countries around the world memorialize 'the unknown soldier'. The unknown soldier is always an anonymous, unidentifiable individual who was sacrificed for a national cause and who is celebrated after his[3] death as a reminder to all citizens that national purpose trumps individuality, especially in times of national crisis. The unknown soldier can serve as a national emblem of unity and patriotism only because his individuality is erased. For it is his anonymity that allows him to be nothing more and nothing less than a soldier, with no personal history and no personal political views. This is vital to unifying the nation, for if the unknown soldier's backstory were known it would surely detract from if not raise uncomfortable questions about how this particular entombed individual fits into the seemingly universal idea of the nation.

I expect the situation would be the same if the people featured in the 'I am an American' PSA were not anonymous. For if we knew more about them – if they seemed more real to us because they were something more than just unknown Americans – these US citizens would surely complicate if not shatter our collective national ideals about what it means to be an American.

I put these thoughts aside and get on with my work as an academic, which begins each day with reading online newspapers. Today, as on many other days since 9/11, I am struck by the numerous accounts about the 'Many' US citizens whose experiences put into question the post-9/11 US national ideal of the 'One'. These 'Many' US citizens cross all segments of US society, not only in terms of race, class, religion, ethnicity, gender and sexuality. They are also as likely to be soldiers charged with fighting in foreign US wars in Afghanistan and Iraq as they are to be civilians caught up in domestic US wars over public policies like immigration that resonate differently during the War on Terror, or to be innocent bystandards who one way or another have become entangled in these wars even though they took no sides and made no public declarations. What I've noticed about these stories is that they break as spectacular headlines, then fade away so thoroughly that these 'Many' US citizens seem to be every bit as ethereal as the US citizens featured in the Ad Council's PSA. Maybe this is why, as time goes on, I find myself haunted by them as well.

Who are we?

Lancaster, England: What does it mean to be an American after 9/11? Or, to borrow Samuel Huntington's famous question about US national identity, 'Who are we?'

I know this is an unanswerable question because it is impossible to reduce the identities of all US citizens into one collective national identity and because the 'we' that stands for 'America' and 'Americans' changes all the time. Yet this question intrigues me. The more I think about it, the more I realize that I'm less interested in coming up with some definitive answer to this question than I am in exploring how US citizens are working out answers to this question themselves. How would they answer the question, 'What does it mean to you to be an American?'

I expect their answer would help to dispel some of the stereotypes about US citizens and the US nation, whether these are the glorious images of the melting-pot Americans circulated in the Ad Council's PSA or the inglorious images of US Americans that make expressions like 'America got what it deserved on 9/11' possible.

I think back to the long list of questions I wanted to ask the US citizens featured in the Ad Council's PSA, mindful of the fact that I'll never be able to ask these US citizens my questions. And then an unusual thought occurs to me. Why not put my long list of questions about core American values around citizenship, patriotism, tolerance, and justice to the 'Many' US citizens I've read about whose post-9/11 experiences defy both positive and negative stereotypes about America and Americans? And instead of presenting these US Americans as anonymous, why not take pains to contextualize them so they are as 'real' as possible?

I could make a series of films about them, I think to myself, in which each of these citizens begins by saying their name and what they do and then goes on to narrate their story. And while I could ask each of them to reflect on what it means to them to be 'an American' and to responsibly enact their US citizenship in a post-9/11 context, I could let their personal stories and how they tell them provide the answers.

I decide to return to the US as soon as possible, to pursue this project. I have no idea if any of the 'Many' US citizens I've read about or seen on television will talk to me, much less consider being part of this project. Nor do I have any idea how they would tell their personal stories in light of my many questions. But because I believe their reflections are key to a fuller understanding of what it means to be a US citizen now and in the future, I pack my bags and head to the States.

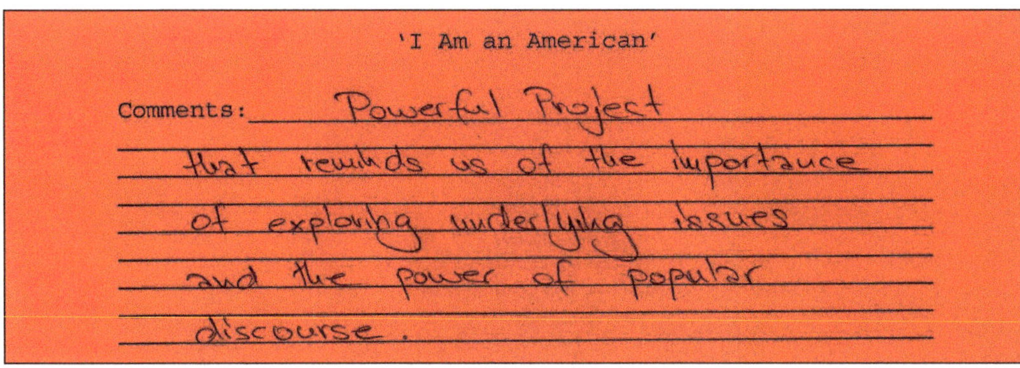
'I Am an American'

Comments: Powerful Project that reminds us of the importance of exploring underlying issues and the power of popular discourse.

Figure 6: Anonymous comment.

Notes

1. Chalmers Johnson (2000), *Blowback: The Costs and Consequences of American Empire*, New York: Metropolitan/Owl Books.
2. 'Humanity' is a tricky term, as at times it is taken for granted that there exists some essential notion of humans as a force of humanity in the world who use reason or science to progress toward bettering themselves. I reject this sense of humanity for the same reasons that John Gray does, because, as he puts it, '"humanity" is itself a myth, a dusty remnant of religious faith. In truth there are only humans, using the growing knowledge given to them by science to pursue their conflicting ends' (John Gray [2007] *Al Qaeda And What It Means To be Modern*, London: Faber and Faber, p. 4. Having said that though, this does not mean that one cannot mobilize a critically-contested rather than an essentialized notion of humanity for political purposes. That is how I am using the term here. I use the term humanity throughout this book and in my wider project on citizenship as a category that in this case can help us to critically engage with representations of citizenship politically, sociologically, morally and ethically, all the while accepting that 'humanity'

itself is an unstable, not-necessarily progressive, and always political representation. This use of the category of humanity has a long tradition in the writings of people like Michel Foucault ('Face aux gouvernements, les droits de l'Homme' [translated sometimes as 'Facing Governments: the Rights of Man' or as 'Confronting Governments, Human Rights'], *Liberation*, June 30–July 1, 22, 1984) and more recently in the work of Jens Bartelson ('Is There a Global Society?', *International Political Sociology*, 3:1, 2009, pp. 112–15) and Siba Grovogui ('Counterpoints and the Imaginaries Behind Them: Thinking Beyond North American and European Traditions', *International Political Sociology*, 3:3, 2009, pp. 327–31). Also see Cynthia Weber (2010) 'Citizenship, Security, Humanity', *International Political Sociology*, 4:1, pp. 80–85.

3. I use the pronoun 'his' here because the one thing we know about the unknown soldier is that he is male.

Chapter 2

Soldiers

Featuring Guadalupe Denogean, Phil McDowell, Jamine Aponte, Jesus Suarez del Solar, Fernando Suarez del Solar, Casey Sheehan, Cindy Sheehan, James Yee

Sueños Americanos

Twentynine Palms, California: I have come to the US to begin my interviews with US citizens who in one way or another have become embroiled in the US War on Terror. I am driving through a desert that is littered with abandoned shacks. Every few miles, I glimpse another one, then nothing. There are no stores, no gas stations, no rest stops, no trees. Just shrubs, empty road, and eerily empty houses. Did I take a wrong turn? Am I in Nevada, driving through an old nuclear test site? Or am I really where I'm supposed to be, on the edge of the largest US military base in the world? I don't remember crossing into Nevada. And anyway, these dilapidated dwellings are much smaller than the test site homes, with just a single room and a few add-ons. When I see a sign welcoming me to Twentynine Palms, California, I relax. This is my destination.

I'm here to interview Guadalupe 'Lupe' Denogean, a retired Marine who became the Iraq War's first 'fast-tracked' US citizen. I'd read about Lupe in the newspaper. A legal US resident and Mexican citizen, Lupe was one of the first casualties of the Iraq War. In the hospital recovering from his injuries, he was asked if he had any requests. He asked if he could become a US citizen. Lupe's request was 'fast-tracked', and three days later President Bush visited him in the hospital to attend his swearing in as a US citizen. This was the start of the fast-track citizenship program for legal resident aliens fighting honorably for the US in the War on Terror.

You won't find a more good natured or grateful man than Lupe. Yes, he's been through hard times, having suffered severe physical injuries that left him unable to continue his military career. But by the time I meet him, he has recovered his body, his spirit, and his livelihood. He loves the US, and he loves being a US citizen. As he tells me, 'Being a citizen of the United States is the greatest thing. I *am* the American Dream'.

This is a dream Lupe is keen to protect. He granted permission for our interview on the condition that I did not say anything bad about the US in my film about him. I explained to him that all of my films are narrated by the person I'm interviewing, and that I edit each film so it is representative of that person's perspective in the context of my project.

We go through the initial interview and meet up the next day to do some atmospheric shots. On our drive through town, I learn the history of the abandoned shacks. After World War I, many veterans suffering the effects of mustard gas came to Twentynine Palms to recuperate and take advantage of the US government homesteading program. Launched under the slogan, 'The government bets you 160 acres of desert that you can't survive on it

Figure 7: Lupe and Jeri Denogean under 'Mi Casa Es Mi Casa'/My House is My House sign.

for three years', homesteaders got to keep the land if they improved the property every year.[1] This explains the oddly shaped add-ons to these buildings – one room, then a porch or a windmill, then a second room, and so on.

Lupe and I return to his house to shoot more atmospherics. His wife Jerri joins us. Lupe and Jerri sit on their front porch. I'm searching for something with clear, sharp edges to correct my focus. I see a fuzzy sign above them. I focus and read, 'Mi casa es mi casa' (My house is my house).

I reframe the image to show Lupe, Jeri, and their dog sitting on their porch swing under this sign. The final shot uncannily captures the essential elements of Lupe's American Dream – immigrating to the US, becoming a US citizen, landing a good job, and owning a piece of the US he can call his own. As I reflect on Lupe's realization of his American Dream in the context of US military service, I realize that the image also suggests how military service, survival and compensation are being remixed in the War on Terror.

The wrong war

Tijuana, Mexico/San Ysidro, California: When Jesus Suarez del Solar was a boy living in Tijuana, Mexico, he dreamed of fighting the War on Drugs because he saw how destructive drugs were in his community. Some years later while in a US shopping mall just across the US-Mexico border, his dream seemed to be within reach. For here Jesus met a recruiter for the US Marine Corp who told Jesus that if he joined the Marines, after two years of service he could transfer into the US Drug Enforcement Agency (DEA).

Although it might seem strange that a US Marine recruiter would be interested in Jesus – a Mexican citizen – it is not. For like the militaries of many other countries, the US military has a large number of non-citizens among its ranks. In the US military, these are predominantly Mexican and Pilipino youth, many of whom were raised in the US.

Jesus persuaded his father Fernando to move the family to California because the recruiter told Jesus he would have an easier time getting into the Marines if he graduated from a US high school. Fernando moved the family to California, and when Jesus finished high school, he joined the Marines.

But Jesus never got to fight the War on Drugs or join the DEA. On a visit home after boot camp, Jesus told his father, 'The recruiter lied. I cannot transfer from the Marines into the DEA.' Instead, after 9/11 Jesus was sent to Iraq to fight the War on Terror. There he stepped on an unexploded US cluster bomb and died.

Figure 8: Jesus Suarez del Solar as a young boy. Photo provided by Fernando Suarez del Solar.

Figure 9: US Marine Jesus Suarez del Solar. Photo provided by Fernando Suarez del Solar.

'No!'

Escondido, California: Fernando Suarez del Solar stands on the tiny porch between his trailer and its attached carport, smoking a cigarette. Below him is a red van adorned with stickers that announce his political views – 'Support our troops, Bring them home NOW!', 'Bush Lies, Who Dies?', 'I Support Iraq Veterans Against the War' and several more colorful slogans.

Fernando was an anonymous cashier at a local 7-Eleven when his US Marine and Mexican citizen son Jesus Suarez del Solar was killed in the early days of the Iraq War. But once the US government offered to make Jesus a posthumous US citizen – an honor occasionally

Figure 10: Fernando Suarez del Solar.

bestowed upon non-US citizens who die fighting for the US – Fernando came to national attention for uttering one single word, 'No!'

At the funeral, Jesus' coffin was draped with the US flag. Before burying Jesus, Fernando replaced this flag with the Mexican flag. With his hand over his heart, Fernando stood next to his dead son and his grieving wife and sang the Mexican National Anthem.

Fernando tells me how proud Jesus was to be a Mexican citizen and of his lack of interest in and need for US citizenship. Jesus did not need US citizenship to join the US Marines, and Jesus refused his father's offer to help him apply for US citizenship some years earlier, when Fernando himself became a US citizen. And so to change Jesus' citizenship after his

Figure 11: Fernando Suarez del Solar hangs the Mexican and US flags outside his home.

death without his consent seems like a grave injustice to Fernando. As Fernando tells me, 'Jesus needs US citizenship now less than ever'.

Even so, Jesus did become a posthumous US citizen. Jesus' wife decided to accept US citizenship on her husband's behalf because she feared that the military might one day change the laws to make their son ineligible for military benefits if his father was not a US citizen.

Fernando accepts his daughter-in-law's decision, but Fernando's family has never come to terms with Fernando's on-going protest – of posthumous citizenship for Jesus specifically but also of the War in Iraq and the recruitment of Hispanic youth to fight in that war. And so, Fernando is now divorced and estranged from some of his children and grandchildren.

Fernando puts out his cigarette, goes inside and re-emerges on his front porch. He is holding two large flags – one US, one Mexican. He carefully hangs one on one side of the porch and one on the other side. This is his daily ritual. Standing between them, Fernando smokes another cigarette.

Give us your tired, your poor, your huddled masses yearning to be free…

Toronto, Canada: Phil McDowell is giving his very first interview as an Iraq War Resister. Phil and his wife Jamine Aponte, both US citizens, arrived in Canada a month earlier seeking political asylum. Phil and I sit in the basement apartment they are fixing up in exchange for rent while they await work permits. Phil is a well-educated, articulate, confident 20-something. But he is clearly nervous when our interview begins. For every one of the questions I put to him is new. And so every one of his answers is raw, edgy, saturated with deep feeling – hurt, betrayal, defiance, wonder, disappointment, hope.

Phil is one of many Iraq War Resisters I've interviewed in Canada. I am particularly drawn to his story because it is the one that I think US Americans will best be able to relate to. Phil tells of how as a college senior, he was inspired by 9/11 to enlist in the Army to defend his country. 'At the time', Phil tells me, 'I thought the US was a beacon of light in the world, and that we were a good society'.

Upon graduation, Phil was posted to Iraq, the new frontline in the War on Terror. It was in Iraq where Phil started to question the war, after no weapons of mass destruction or pre-existing links to al-Qaeda were found. When Phil observed 'the common everyday Iraqi being treated like an enemy combatant', he also lost faith in his superior's new explanation for why the US was in Iraq – to help the Iraqi people.

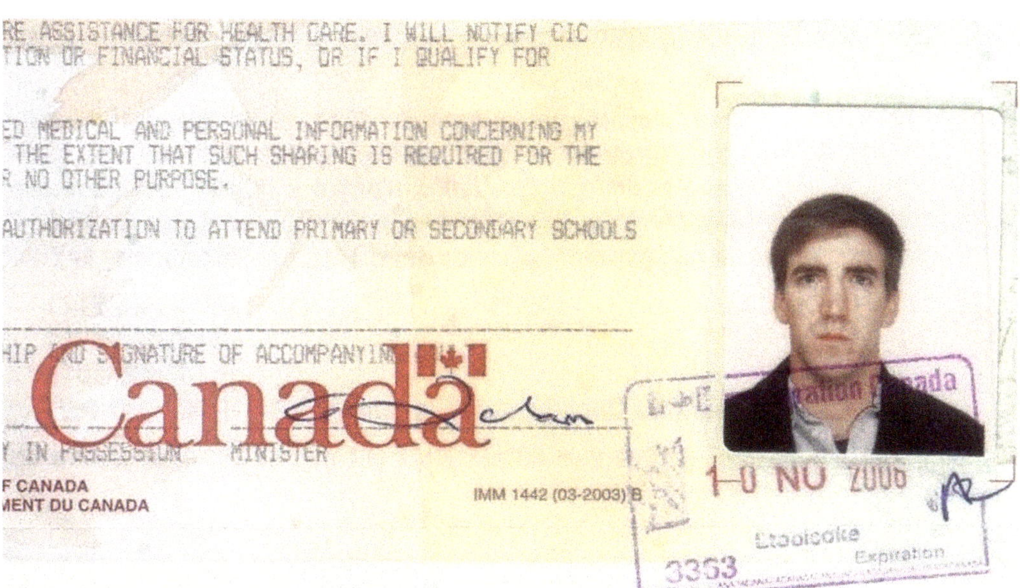

Figure 12: Political refuge to Canada Phil McDowell. Document provided by Phil McDowell.

As Phil's service in the Army was coming to an end, he decided he no longer believed in this war. He served out his time, got his separation papers, and cleared base some days early because he had vacation time saved up. Five days before his vacation expired, Phil received a letter telling him he was 'stop-lossed' – that due to a shortage of troops, he had to return to the Army for redeployment in Iraq. Failure to do so would put him in AWOL status.

Feeling like he had effectively been drafted, Phil returned to base, trying to find a way to serve his stop-loss time stateside. But when his commander told him definitively he was going back to Iraq, Phil made the decision to leave the US and seek political refugee status in Canada. He did so on the grounds that the Iraq War was illegal and immoral and that his continued military service violated international law.

Phil's conclusions about the war have no legal standing, either with the US government or with the Canadian government. And Phil's decision to apply for refugee status in Canada means his own legal status is in limbo, with the duration of his stay in Canada yet to be determined. If Phil returns to the US – either voluntarily or as a result of being deported by the Canadian government (something that has happened to other Iraq War Resisters) – he will likely be court marshaled and face a prison term.

Thoughtfully, but also with a tone that betrays a sense of being initially overwhelmed by the magnitude of his new realities, Phil tells me, 'I never thought I'd be a political refugee from the United States'.

The greatest place in the world

Toronto, Canada: I am interviewing Iraq War Resister Jamine Aponte. Jamine is one of the most spirited, even 'chipper', people I have ever met. Like her husband, Phil McDowell, Jamine is instantly likeable. Also like Phil, she is a thinker.

I ask Jamine if her experience of becoming a political asylum seeker in Canada has changed how she thinks about the US.

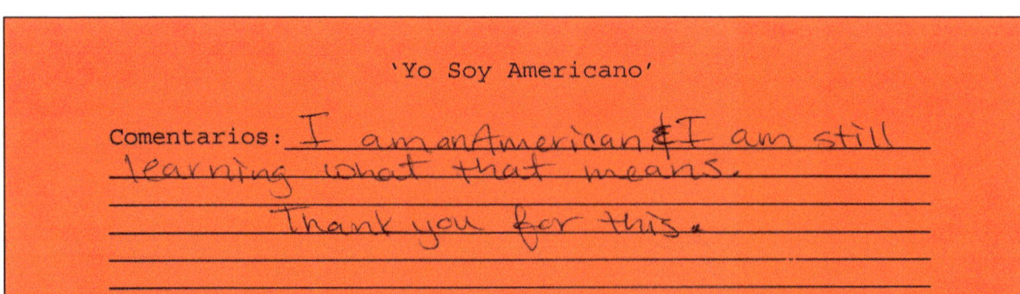
'Yo Soy Americano'

Comentarios: I am an American & I am still learning what that means.

Thank you for this.

Figure 13: Anonymous comment.

Figure 14: Iraq War Resister Jamine Aponte.

Her answer begins lightly, 'I don't know how I feel about being American anymore'. Almost jokingly, she continues, 'I used to think it was the greatest place in the world'. She takes a long pause. Her mood changes, her eyes drift off into space. 'I don't know if I believe that anymore'.

Jamine tells me, 'I feel like I've been handed something that's broken'.

Casey

San Francisco, California: I'm reading Cindy Sheehan's book in preparation for our interview tomorrow. In it, she describes her surprise when her 21-year-old son Casey announced he had joined the Army. A deeply religious young man, Casey was about to graduate from college, so his parents were shocked that he'd chosen to join the military instead of pursuing some other career path. When they pressed him for an explanation, Casey 'looked briefly confused' and told them 'I thought I was supposed to'.[2] Yet neither of his parents had ever encouraged him to do so.

Cindy speculates about what made Casey join up – the military service of his grandfathers, the fact that the Sheehans lived in a military town, or the idea that the Boy Scouts (in which Casey excelled) 'is just another organization that trains young men to be "good soldiers"'.[3] Whatever the underlying reason, the immediate reason Casey enlisted was because his recruiter promised him he would become a chaplain's assistant and never see battle. But in 2004, Casey was assigned to combat duty in Iraq, where he died five days into his tour.

Upon Casey's death, Cindy received the traditional Gold Star metal awarded to the families of those who die in US wars. Cindy writes that 'I had already decided by then, even in my deep shock and absolute pain, that I wasn't going to be a "good soldier"', and that 'a Gold Star is not a fair trade for a son's life'.[4]

Figure 15: Casey Sheehan. Photo provided by Cindy Sheehan.

Figure 16: Camp Casey outside President George W. Bush's Crawford, Texas ranch. Image provided by Cindy Sheehan.

Multitasking

San Francisco, California: I'm filming Cindy Sheehan as she gives a live radio interview. Cindy is the typical American housewife turned 'Peace Mom' who, upon the death of her son Casey in the Iraq War, famously set up Camp Casey outside President George W. Bush's Crawford, Texas, ranch where she waited in vain for the President to answer her question, 'For what noble cause did my son die?' This bold, desperate gesture brought Cindy to US national attention and provided US television viewers with a powerful image of a grieving mother that could be substituted for the banned footage of US soldiers returned home from the war in caskets.

In the course of the interview, Cindy passionately delivers her views on the war, on the economic recession, on peace and its connections to economic activism, and on her disillusionment with the US government on all of these scores.

As I follow Cindy with my microphone and camera lens, I imagine a listener following Cindy's voice with only their ears. I wonder how this listener pictures Cindy – perhaps

Figure 17: Cindy Sheehan at home.

smartly dressed and seated in a posh radio studio or instead decked out in 'intellectual causal' while secluded in the quiet study of her home.

Cindy *is* giving this interview from home, but there is no quiet study in the tired tower block apartment she shares with her daughter Callie. And if there were, Cindy would have little time to escape to it, as Callie tells me her mom averages three such interviews a day.

Instead, Cindy's reality is quite different. Wearing a simple house dress and comfortable slippers, Cindy gives the interview from her kitchen while cradling the phone with her neck so she can get on with chopping the dinner vegetables.

This is what it looks like to be a Peace Mom.

God and country

Lancaster, England: Former US Army Muslim Chaplain Captain James Yee addresses an audience of students, faculty, and townspeople at Lancaster University. He tells of his pride in becoming one of the first Muslim Chaplains in the US military and how his exemplary service in this capacity lead him to be hand-picked to serve at Guantanamo Bay, Cuba, where 'enemy combatants' in the War on Terror – all of whom are Muslims – are detained.

The rest of James' story is well-known in the US. After serving at Gitmo for several months, James was given two weeks of R&R to return to the States to see his wife and daughter. But James never made it home. For as soon as he landed on US soil, he was arrested on suspicion of aiding the Taliban and al-Qaeda. The supposed evidence against James was his Master's thesis on Syrian Foreign Policy that he was carrying in his backpack, which was compiled from publically available books and articles and had nothing to do with the Taliban or al-Qaeda. In spite of his protests, James found himself suited up in an orange jumpsuit just like the ones worn by inmates at Gitmo, fitted with sensory-deprivation devices, and shipped off to a US Naval Brig where he spent 76 days in solitary confinement. Here, military prosecutors threatened him with the death penalty.

Figure 18: James Yee reading the Holy Quran.

But because James had done nothing wrong, there was no case to be made against him. And so the charges against him were dropped, and James was released. James tried to resume his military career but found his position untenable, mainly because the military refused to close its case against James and continued to investigate him. And so, reluctantly, James resigned his post and received an honorable discharge.

Becoming one of us

Washington, DC: Since becoming a fast-tracked US citizen, Lupe Denogean regularly turns up in the speeches of President George W. Bush. In an address on immigration, this is what President Bush had to say about Lupe.

> We will always be proud to welcome people like Guadalupe Denogean as fellow Americans. Our new immigrants are just what they've always been – people willing to risk everything for the dream of freedom. And America remains what she has always been: the great hope on the horizon, an open door to the future, a blessed and promised land. We honor the heritage of all who come here, no matter where they come from, because we trust in our country's genius for making us all Americans – one nation under God.[5]

If that's what you've gotta do

Twentynine Palms, California: I ask Lupe Denogean about his road to citizenship. I'm surprised to learn that this national exemplar of 'fast-tracked' citizenship had applied for US citizenship many times over the past two decades, but none of his applications were successful. Lupe explains this was because the military reassigned him every couple of years. And with every reassignment, his citizenship application was invalidated because his address had changed.

The fast-track citizen program that Lupe inspired ironed out that wrinkle in soldier's citizenship applications. Thanks to this program, the application processing time for US soldiers serving honorably in the War on Terror was reduced from approximately three years to six months, making the success of their applications much more likely. Still, this program would not have existed at all had Lupe not been seriously wounded in Iraq and if Lupe had not responded to the routine question put to wounded soldiers, 'Do you have any requests?', by answering that he wanted to become a US citizen.

'Friends say it's ironic that I had to get injured to become a citizen', Lupe tells me. Laughing, he continues, 'Getting blown up is a heck of a way to become a citizen, but if that's what you've gotta do, that's what you've gotta do'.

Figure 19: Lupe Denogean at his Citizenship Ceremony congratulated by President George W. Bush. Photo provided by Lupe Denogean.

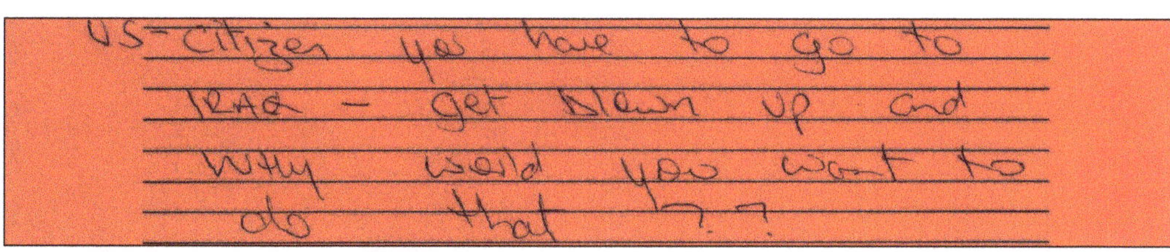

US-Citizen you have to go to IRAQ - get blown up and why would you want to do that ??

Figure 20: Anonymous comment.

Next Page – Figure 21: Fernando Suarez del Solar at his son Jesus' grave.

'He died in Iraq, and he became an American.'

– Fernando Suarez del Solar, resisted posthumous US citizenship for his Mexican son, US Marine Jesus Suarez del Solar.

Video Portraits of Post-9/11 US Citizens Series I by Cynthia Weber © Pato Productions 2008.

The wrong side of mourning

Escondido, California: We almost didn't go there. But as Fernando Suarez del Solar and I were returning from filming him at a small monument he made to his son Jesus, Fernando suggested that we stop at Jesus' grave.

At the cemetery, Fernando is on auto-pilot, going through a ritual no father should ever have to go through. His feet lead him to his son's grave. Bending down, Fernando tapes a poster onto the back of the headstone. On it is an image of Jesus in his US Marine uniform and messages about the futility of war. Facing this poster and the back of Jesus' grave, Fernando silently kneels for a very long time.

As I zoom in to film Fernando from a respectful distance, my camera does not pick up the poster Fernando insistently fixes his eyes upon, only what he refuses to acknowledge – a headstone that celebrates the sacrifice of a young life for a national cause, Operation Iraqi Freedom. Positioned as he is, Fernando is not only on the wrong side of Jesus' grave. He is on the wrong side of national mourning.

Patriotism and justice

Toronto, Canada: I have asked Iraq War Resister Phil McDowell how he squares his sense of himself as a patriot with the reality that he is a deserter from the US Army.

'I did desert the Army, but I don't feel like I deserted my country', Phil explains. 'Being a soldier, you have the obligation to make the right decision. When you're faced with a moral decision such as participating in an illegal war which misrepresents everything the United States is about, then saying "no" is one of the most patriotic things you can do'.

I push Phil further. What about those people who agree with you – that saying 'no' to the Iraq War is a patriotic decision? Many of them would still object to the fact that you fled the US and the US Army for Canada, rather than stayed in the Army and accepted a court marshal.

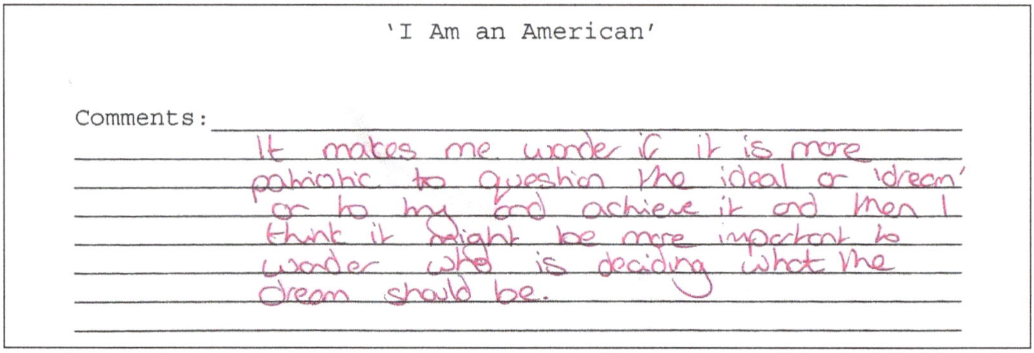
'I Am an American'

Comments: It makes me wonder if it is more patriotic to question the ideal or 'dream' or to try and achieve it and then I think it might be more important to wonder who is deciding what the dream should be.

Figure 22: Anonymous comment.

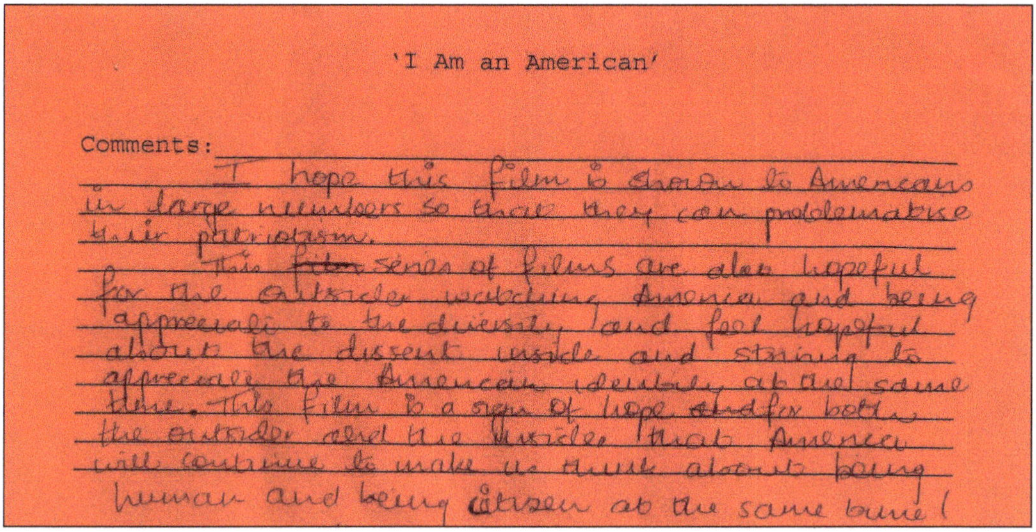

'I Am an American'

Comments: I hope this film is shown to Americans in large numbers so that they can problematise their patriotism.

This ~~film~~ series of films are also hopeful for the outsider watching America and being appreciate the diversity and feel hopeful about the dissent inside and striving to appreciate the American identity at the same time. This film is a sign of hope ~~and~~ for both the outsider and the insider that America will continue to make us think about being human and being citizen at the same time!

Figure 23: Anonymous comment.

Phil accepts this criticism, understands it, but still rejects it. He tells me, 'I really believe that nobody should go to prison because they don't want to participate in an illegal war'. But there's more to it than that. Phil explains, 'If I go to prison, I'm just going to be in a prison and that's it. I can't do anything about the war. Coming to Canada gives me a voice, gives me an outlet to speak out against it, to help other people who are coming up here leaving the Army. It gives me an opportunity to do something rather than just sit in a cell'.

Writing on the flag

Various Locations: I've started showing my 'I am an American' project publicly. Whenever I do, I invite audience members to share their thoughts about the project on comment cards. Patrons leave their comments on bits of red or white or blue paper, then tack them up with other bits of paper in a pattern that resembles the US flag.

Comments range from superficial to serious. Topics cover everything from artistic form to political content to personal histories. Themes vary depending on where the work is exhibited. In Latin America, most patrons mention immigration. In Europe, they remark on the shared predicaments faced by US and European citizens. And in the US, there is often surprise at the many things 'I am an American' now means. Overall, they are a hodgepodge that mimic the content of the show, the contradictions in what appears to be a simple statement 'I am an American'.

A selection of these public comments is scattered throughout this book.

Figure 24: Gallery patrons posting their comments on the 'flag'.

Figure 25: The 'US flag' made out of gallery patron comments.

Matriotism

San Francisco, California: It has recently occurred to me that I should ask my interview subjects if they would be willing to write a comment about the project on one of the bits of red, white, and blue paper that compose the US 'flag' at exhibitions of this project. And so, during one of our interviews, I ask Cindy Sheehan for her comment.

Cindy writes, 'Matriotism not Patriotism!' and signs it 'Peace Mom'.

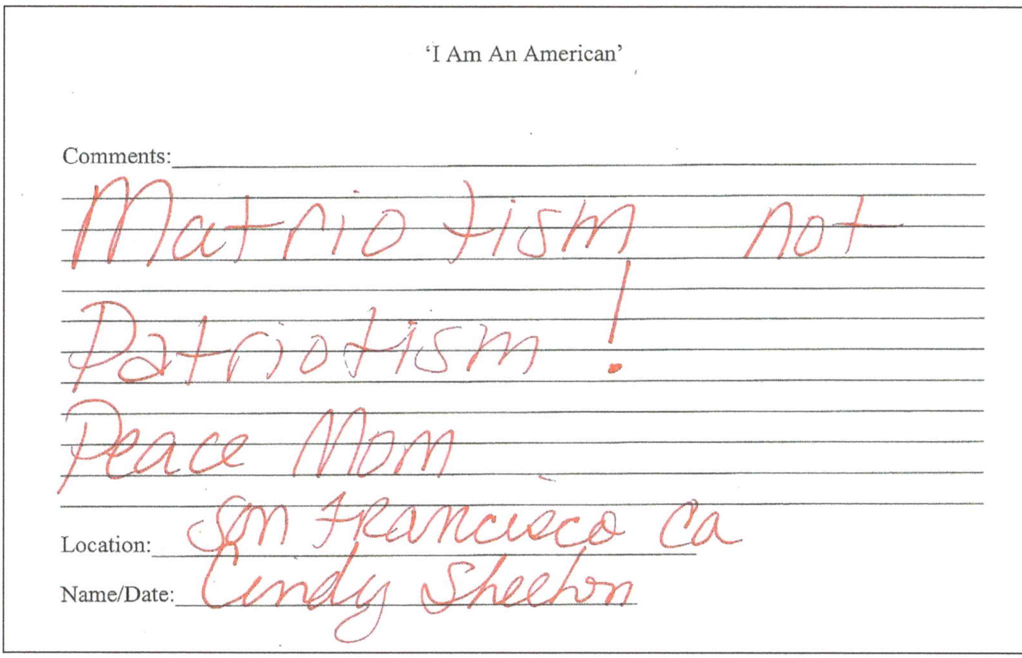
'I Am An American'

Comments: Matriotism not Patriotism! Peace Mom

Location: San Francisco Ca

Name/Date: Cindy Sheehan

Figure 26: Cindy Sheehan, 'Matriotism Not Patriotism!'

Cindy's comment echoes an argument she has been making for some time now – that matriotism ought to replace patriotism as the foundation upon which decisions about waging war are made. As a 'fierce pacifist', Cindy believes that all wars are wrong, and that patriotism is among those things that makes wars possible. For her, patriotism does not just describe a citizen's love of country to the point that the citizen is willing to die for their country. It also means 'exploiting others' love for country by sending them to sacrifice for my bank balance!'[6]

Cindy believes that 'matriotism is the opposite of patriotism [...] not to destroy it, but to be a yin to its yang and to balance out the destructive militarism of patriotism'.[7] As its name implies, matriotism is based on motherhood or the 'matria' rather than fatherhood or the 'patria' as patriotism is. Cindy explains of matriotism, 'Not everyone is a mother, but there is one universal truth [...] Everyone has a mother! Mothers give life, and if the child is lucky, mothers nurture life. And if a man has had a nurturing mother, he will also already have a sound basis for matriotism'.[8] Based upon this nurturing by mothers rather than the false nurturing of the state/the patria, Cindy claims that a true matriot 'knows that her country can do a lot of things right' but that she 'would never drop an atomic bomb, carpet bomb cities and villages, or control drones from thousands of miles away to kill innocent men, women, and children'. Nor, claims Cindy, would a matriot ever 'send her child or another mother's child to fight nonsense wars [...] and would herself march into a war that she considered just, in order to protect her child from harm'. 'Matriots', Cindy concludes, are unlike patriots who 'hide behind the flag and eagerly send young people to die in order to fill their pocketbooks'. Instead, 'matriots would fight their own battles, but take a dim view of having to do so, and they would seldom resort to violence to solve conflict'.[9]

I'm not a fan of either patriotism or matriotism, both because I am aware of the abuses of patriotism and because I agree with the argument Jean Elshtain makes in her book *Women and War* that neither the myth of men as the 'Just Warriors' of patriotism nor the myth of women as the 'Beautiful Souls' of matriotism holds up in practice, as many fathers/men oppose wars and many mothers/women support them. [10] Even so, I appreciate how Cindy is struggling to find some ground upon which to oppose not just the US wars in Afghanistan and Iraq themselves but to oppose how people like President Bush and Professor Elshtain herself characterized these wars as just wars that the US has a moral imperative to fight, which is among the many points where I, too, part company with President Bush and Professor Elshtain.[11]

As I sit in Cindy's apartment thinking these thoughts, I am struck by how different Cindy's and Professor Elshtain's feminist readings of the US War on Terror are. I am also struck by how unlikely it is that the views of the housewife turned Peace Mom Cindy Sheehan are, for a little while at least, getting as much attention in the US media as the views of Jean Bethke Elshtain who is the Laura Spelman Rockefeller Professor of Social and Political Ethics at the University of Chicago Divinity School.

The face of despair

Escondido, California: I am in a hotel room reviewing Fernando Suarez del Solar's personal footage of his 2003 trip to Iraq. Fernando's trip was part humanitarian relief effort, part fact-finding mission, part a final goodbye to his son Jesus.

Most of the footage is unusable. It is unsteady, out of focus, and improperly exposed. But as a chronicle of this father's lone quest to place a cross in the field where his son was killed, it is deeply touching.

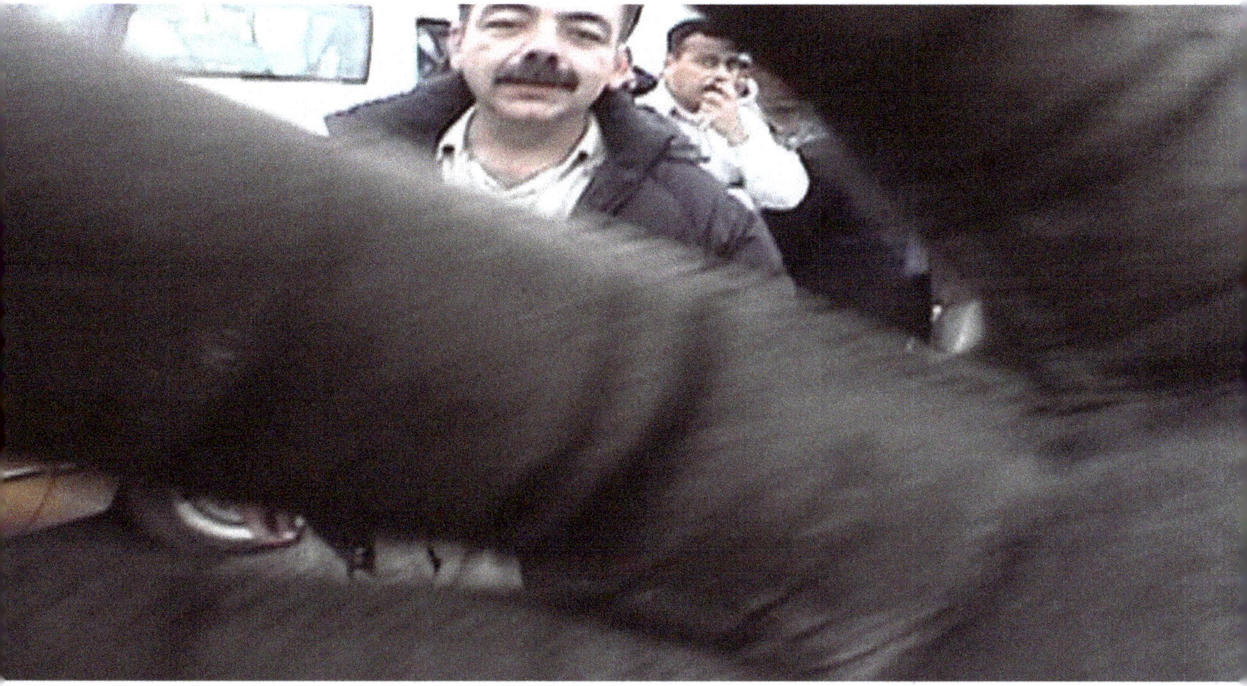

Figure 27: Fernando Suarez del Solar in Iraq. Footage provided by Guerrero Azteca Por La Paz.

As the video rolls, I find myself watching a scene of Fernando stopped at a checkpoint by a group of US soldiers. Fernando is trying to explain himself to a soldier, but the soldier's attention is on the fact that his discussion with Fernando is being filmed. The soldier moves toward the camera with an outstretched hand. As he places his hand over the lens, I glimpse Fernando's despondent face through the soldier's fingers. And then he's gone.

'I Am an American'

Comments: I thought that the video was very moving. I had not heard stories like these before. I wasn't aware that it was this difficult to become a citizen. The one that hit me hardest was the Marine who was killed in Iraq. I think it's horrible that he had to die to be considered a citizen. i would love more than anything for this to be easier.

Figure 28: Anonymous comment.

Finding the form

Toronto, Canada: I have been filming for about a year, collecting stories that express the often uneasy relationship between the One US nation and the Many US Americans who don't fit comfortably into the specific post-9/11 US ideal of unity. Yet in all this time, I have yet to settle on a structure for my films. While interviewing Iraq War Resisters Phil and Jamine, I figure it out.

What if I use my interviews with US Americans caught up in the crossfire of the War on Terror not only to produce a series of individual short films about each of them but also to produce a remixed version of the American Ad Council's 'I am an American' PSA? What if I ask them to say not only 'I am an American' (as US Americans do in the original PSA) but also what kind of US American they are? And what if I end this remixed PSA and each of the individual films as the Ad Council's PSA ends – with a flag shot, in which each of these US Americans uses the flag to express their post-9/11 relationship to the US state?

I pitch the idea to Phil and Jamine. They instantly get it, understanding how their American experiences and those of other US Americans I'm interviewing expose the complications inherent in the ideals enshrined in the Ad Council's PSA.

In my remixed PSA, Phil stands on the Canadian side of the US-Canadian border and says, 'I am an Iraq War Resister, and I am an American'.

Jamine says, 'I am a political refugee *from* America'.

Figure 29: Phil McDowell, 'I am an Iraq War Resister, and I am an American'.

Peace Mom

San Francisco, California: It's 4 am San Francisco time. I've been tossing and turning for hours because I'm unsatisfied with Cindy Sheehan's flag shot, and the first thing I have to do when I meet her in a few hours is see if she's willing to reshoot it.

Yesterday, I asked Cindy if she would reproduce the pose that is on the cover of her book *Peace Mom* for my film. In that pose, Cindy stands facing the camera while joyfully hugging a picture of Casey dressed in his military uniform, the US flag behind him. This shot was staged in front of the White House, to reference Cindy's on-going dispute with President George W. Bush over the war in Iraq. We restaged the shot in Cindy's living room. On her empty white wall, we hung a large US flag. Cindy stood in front of it, hugging a similar picture of Casey.

All night I've wondered what it is about this shot that bothers me. Now, at 4 am, I've figured it out. The image clearly references Cindy as a loving mother, Casey as her absent son, and Casey's military service as that which is responsible for their separation. But the image does not reference peace. Without the book title *Peace Mom*, neither the book's cover shot nor my restaged version of it say 'peace' to anyone unfamiliar with Cindy's story. And because my flag shots are intended for the initiated *and* uninitiated, it must be reshot. But how?

I consider replacing the US flag with a peace flag, and when the shops open, I go from store to store in search of one. But in the course of shopping, I reject this idea because my objective is not to replace one flag and its representative ideals with another, but to show both visions simultaneously so that the potential tensions and contradictions between them are evident in my shot. Then I consider asking Cindy to write the word 'peace' across the US flag, an act that would not only express both sets of ideals at once but would also gesture toward Cindy's protest politics with her writing on the flag as a sort of writing back to the US state. As I entertain this idea, I switch to shopping for chalk. But I quickly reject this idea, too, because it fails as both a still image (because the still would be shot after Cindy had written 'peace' across the flag, thereby making it unclear if Cindy had written this word or if I had) and as a filmic image (because it violates the first rule of film-making – show it; don't say it).

With time running out before our next shoot, the solution comes to me. I go to Cindy's apartment, apologetically explain why we need to reshoot her flag shot, and pitch her my idea. Cindy is quiet for a long five seconds and then very happily says 'OK'. Relieved, I dig into my camera bag for the red duct tape I always carry with me. Over the white stars outlined in blue, I tape a large red peace sign and mount this US flag onto the wall. Standing in from of this 'peace flag', Cindy again hugs Casey's picture while I film.

Finally, the image says what Cindy's 'I am an American' line says, 'I am a Peace Mom, and I am an American'.

Next Page – Figure 30: Cindy Sheehan's flag shot.

'I am a Peace Mom, and I am an American.'

– Cindy Sheehan, peace activist who camped outside President George W. Bush's Crawford, Texas, ranch waiting for the President's response to her question, 'For what noble cause did my son Casey die in Iraq?'

Video Portraits of Post-9/11 US Citizens Series I by Cynthia Weber © Pato Productions 2009.

The hero shot

Twentynine Palms, California: Fast-tracked US citizen Lupe Denogean takes me for a tour of the US Marine Corp base. He inspects a line of tanks and points out those similar to the one he was shelled in while in Iraq. On base, retired Master Gunnery Sergeant 'Deno' (as his men call him) is revered. Everyone knows him and respects him, and his every request for impromptu filming is graciously granted.

What is more impressive, though, are Lupe's interactions with people off base. Like when we stop outside a ranch house flying the US flag and the US Marine Corps flag so we can use the flags as background in our shot. When Lupe introduces himself to the rancher to ask his permission to film, the rancher breaks into a big grin, says 'I know about you', and extends his hand out to Lupe, less as a greeting than as an expression of thanks as well as congratulations.

As I absorb this scene, I decide to change my shot – to shoot Lupe as all those we've met see him. I position Lupe close to the flag, standing in profile for the camera. Crouching low and close, I shoot Lupe from below as he surveys the horizon, the flags flying large and proud behind him.

This is the hero shot. But this is not how Lupe sees himself, and so it is not the flag shot he chooses to end his film. Instead, when we return to his house, Lupe stages his own flag shot. He picks up two small flags mounted side-by-side on a wooden platform. One is the US flag; the other is the US Marine Corp flag. Flanked by both flags, Lupe says, 'I am a fast-tracked citizen, and I am an American'.

Figure 31: The hero shot.

Figure 32: Lupe's flag shot.

The distance between us

Toronto, Canada: Phil McDowell and I are in his basement apartment shooting his video portrait. As a prop, we have a small US flag, but otherwise there isn't much available to us to convey Phil's attachment to and distance from the US. In place of some dramatic backdrop – the US-Canadian border or Niagara Falls – we have a brown sofa and an off-white wall.

So I ask Phil to put on his Iraq War Resisters T-shirt and hold the US flag in front of him. The flag covers most of Phil's shirt, but as Phil stretches his arms in front of him, the tops of three-white letters printed on his black T-shirt seem to swim right next to the flag, as if they are Phil's unconscious yet insistent thought. This is the word these three letters spell out – 'war'.

Next Page – Figure 33: Phil McDowell's flag shot.

'I am an Iraq War Resister, and I am an American.'

– Phil McDowell, seeking political asylum in Canada in protest of US Army 'stop-loss' order to return to Iraq.

Video Portraits of Post-9/11 US Citizens Series I by Cynthia Weber © Pato Productions 2008.

Cultural expert

Springfield, New Jersey: James Yee and I are wrapping up our first interview about his experiences as a US Army Muslim Chaplain at Guantanamo Bay, Cuba, his arrest on suspicion of aiding the Taliban and al-Qaeda, and his subsequent release.

James has explained that while his case is extreme, he was not the only US Muslim Chaplain to experience harassment. He tells of how one of the Muslim Chaplains to Gitmo was called in for questioning after James' arrest and how this Chaplain resigned from the military because of what he saw at Gitmo. He tells of how another Muslim Chaplain at Gitmo warned him of the hostility he would experience on base. And he tells of how yet another Muslim Chaplain who was on a military ship when the US attacked Afghanistan was restricted to his quarters the day of the attack.

In light of all of this, I ask James what the situation has been at Gitmo for the Muslim Chaplain assigned there after James' arrest. James explains that the military decided not to replace him with another Muslim Chaplain. Instead, the military hired a 'Cultural Expert', a civilian employee who according to James is 'not in a position to have any valuable input to make sure that prisoners are religiously accommodated in accordance with the values of this country'.

Figure 34: US Army Muslim Chaplain James Yee in Guantanamo Bay, Cuba. Photo provided by James Yee.

Humanism in the strangest places

Toronto, Canada: I'm wrapping up my shoot with Iraq War Resisters Phil and Jamine. The interviews are finished, the staged shots have been captured from a multitude of angles, and I've got a CD full of stills and videos of Phil's military service in Iraq.

I ask them if there is anything else I should film before putting my camera away. They can't think of anything, but they let me wander around the apartment just in case. On the wall in a laundry room/back closet/study is a poster supporting the War Resisters' cause. Below it is a bumper sticker that reads, 'I love my country, but I think we should start seeing other people'.

Figure 35: 'I Love My Country' bumper sticker.

I am a patriotic American Muslim

Lancaster, England: James Yee and I are watching the American Ad Council's 'I am an American' PSA play on my computer. James doesn't remember seeing this PSA before. What impresses him most is the PSA's representation of US diversity. James remarks on how 'America is made up of so many ethnicities, nationalities, colors, races' and how his Chinese American heritage 'falls right into that whole mix of diversity'. When I ask him why he thinks the PSA was made, he remarks that 'the Ad Council was anticipating that others would try to redefine what patriotism is, and their goal was perhaps trying to show that being a patriotic American is about promoting one's individual identity'.

'Why patriotism?', I ask him.

'Because I see the young child at the end waving the flag', he tells me.

I ask James to watch the PSA a couple more times while I film him, getting long, medium, and close-up shots of him from various angles.

Afterwards, James reflects further on the PSA. 'There's nothing that specifically defines [anyone in the PSA] as a person of a specific faith. There's one short glimpse of a woman wearing a head covering, but you can't tell if it is religious. The Ad Council is pointing out diversity of race, ethnicity, color, not religion or faith'.

What James has observed is what Evelyn Alsultany writes about as the 'limits to American cultural citizenship'.[12] She points out that after 9/11, statements by President Bush, US government practices like racial profiling, and US media representations all 'defined US citizens as diverse and united in the "War on Terror", over and against Arabs and Muslims, who were represented as un-American, terrorists, enemies'. One of Alsultany's key examples is the American Ad Council's 'I am an American' PSA.

Alsultany notes that the PSA is a celebration of US American difference to the point that '[d]ifference is identified as defining the nation'. To celebrate this 'diversity-patriotism', as Alsultany calls it, the PSA 'promotes what appears to be an inclusive and diverse United States', but it does this by being ambiguous about its inclusion of Arabs and Muslims and by being unambiguous about its exclusion of any markers of Muslim identity. For example, the one person in the Ad Council's PSA who might be Arab is the one who has the most difficult time getting the words 'I am an American' out of his mouth. There is also an African American man who might be Nation of Islam because he is wearing a suit and bowtie. But it is just as likely that he is not. Beyond these two individuals, the PSA includes 'no visible markers of anything Arab, Muslim or Sikh [which is misread as Muslim by some US Americans] [...] no veil, no mosque, no turban, no beard; no distinctive Arab, Muslim or Sikh clothing; and no Arab accent'. In these ways, Alsultany concludes, 'the Ad Council affirms the binary between "the citizen" and "the terrorist"'.

James tells me to check out the Council on American-Islamic Relations' (CAIR) Ad that was made in response to the American Ad Council's PSA. In the CAIR Ad, James tells me, there are a diverse range of US Americans who say 'I am an American Muslim', making it clear that there is no contradiction between being a US American and being a Muslim.

I've seen and read about the CAIR ad. It does do what James suggests. But how it does this is by playing off of the 'good Muslim/bad Muslim' dichotomy. This is the idea that good Muslims are those who not only embrace US American values and assimilate into US American culture but *can be shown to be doing so*. For it is only these shows of patriotic belonging to the US nation that prevent the rest of 'us' from confusing 'them' with terrorists, traitors, or other 'bad Muslims'. This is a point Alsultany makes. In the American Ad Council's PSA, she notes, it is enough for presumably non-Arab and non-Muslim US Americans to say 'I am an American' to be accepted as 'good Americans'. But in the CAIR ad campaign, Muslim US Americans always also must *show* themselves to be enacting their 'good citizenship', by serving in the US military or the Girl Scouts or pledging allegiance to their country.

Figure 36: 'We're American Muslims' CAIR ad. Reproduced with permission from the Council on American-Islamic Relations.

Figure 37: James Yee, 'I am a wrongly accused terrorist spy, and I am a patriotic American'.

James is all too aware of the dilemma he faces as a Muslim and as an American, of how his religion is increasingly read during the War on Terror as cancelling out his patriotism and his right to fully belong within the ideal of national unity. This seems to explain why James chose to stage his 'I am an American' line at the Veterans Memorial Park in his hometown next to a row of US flags. James decided to say, 'I am a wrongfully accused terrorist spy, and I am a *patriotic* American'.

Of course, James' case marks another limit to 'American cultural citizenship'. This is because James' service to his country is ironically what got him accused of being a terrorist spy in the first place. And although the charges against him were dropped, the US government refuses to close the case against James or apologize for the unsubstantiated accusations they made against him that ruined his military career.

Like most of the others I interviewed, James is among the Many who cannot fully be part of the One, no matter what he says or does right now, no matter how 'good' he is.

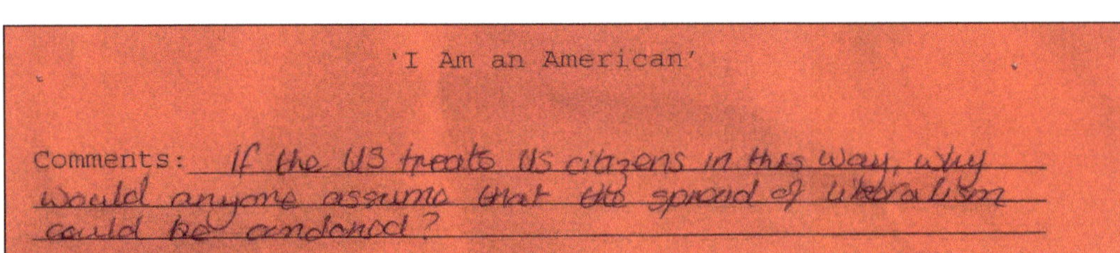
'I Am an American'

Comments: If the US treats US citizens in this way, why would anyone assume that the spread of liberalism could be condoned?

Figure 38: Anonymous comment.

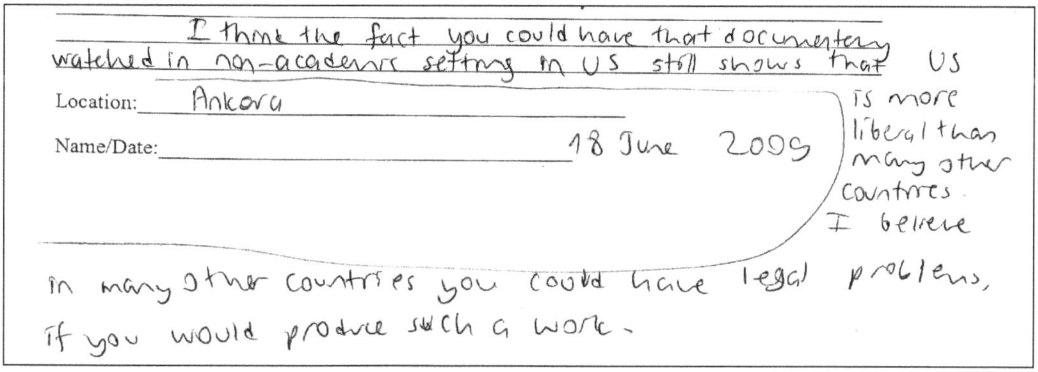
I think the fact you could have that documentary watched in non-academic setting in US still shows that US is more liberal than many other countries. I believe in many other countries you could have legal problems, if you would produce such a work.

Location: Ankara

Name/Date: 18 June 2009

Figure 39: Anonymous comment.

Live terrorist acts

Phoenix, Arizona: An exhibition of my 'I am an American' project is hosted by the Ice House Gallery in Phoenix, Arizona. The curator of the exhibition, Jen Urso, brings to my attention a review of the exhibition that appears in a local paper. The reviewer writes that the exhibit embodies H.L. Mencken's famous quote that radicals are not bad citizens who hate their country but good citizens who so love their country that they are driven to despair. This is a powerful reading of the work, for which I am grateful. Yet the title of the review troubles me, 'God Bless Americans: The ones that aren't terrorist spies, that is'. Is this meant to be ironic? It would seem so. But because of the way the review begins, there is room for doubt. 'For the past few weeks, Valley schoolchildren have taken perhaps the first field trip in history to feature the phrase, "I am an accused terrorist spy and I am a patriotic American"'.

This line is a reference to the film about US Army Muslim Chaplain Captain James Yee. But it is an incorrect reference. The line James says in his film is, 'I am a *wrongly* accused terrorist spy, and I am a patriotic American'. I consider writing a response, especially since the review's misquoted first line coupled with its title could be read as claiming that 'an accused terrorist spy' could never be 'a patriotic American', as if an accusation were enough to prove guilt and 'bad citizenship'. But I decide it is best to leave these things alone.

Some days later, I find I have become blog fodder. Based on this review, a blogger posts his conclusion that my exhibition is an example of 'skewed, anti-American multiculturalism'. As evidence, he reproduces the review minus the quote by Mencken. What infuriates the blogger is that I am leading Phoenix schoolchildren astray by exposing them to my exhibition, an exhibition that might enable them to 'confuse' an accused terrorist spy with a patriotic American.

The blog entry is entitled 'Poisoned Fruit', but it could just as easily be called 'Live Terrorist Acts', in a play on Lauren Berlant's article 'Live Sex Acts (Parental Advisory: Explicit

Figure 40: James Yee in front of the Statue of Liberty. Photo by Anne-Marie Fortier.

Material)'.[13] For the blog entry enacts the same moral panic and rushed cry to protect the innocence of children from discourses about terrorism as Berlant claims US national culture more generally enacts about discourses on sex.

As I think about all this, I have to wonder why there is a moral panic around the possibility of Phoenix school children seeing my exhibition and not around the US government's decision to designate an innocent Muslim American who served honorably in the US military a 'terrorist'.

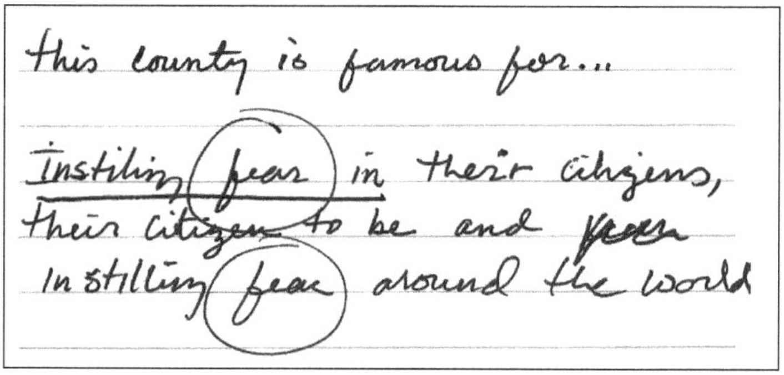

Figure 41: Anonymous comment.

Notes

1. http://www.globalsecurity.org/military/facility/29palms.htm.
2. Cindy Sheehan (2006), *Peace Mom: A mother's journey from heartache to activism*, New York: Atria Books, p. 11.
3. Sheehan, op cit., p. 14.
4. Sheehan, op. cit., p. 14.
5. President George W. Bush (2006), 'President Bush Addresses the Nation on Immigration Reform', May 15, http://georgewbush-whitehouse.archives.gov/news/releases/2006/05/20060515-8.html. Downloaded 12 September 2009.
6. Sheehan, op. cit., p. 212.
7. Sheehan, op. cit., p. 213.
8. Sheehan, op. cit., p. 213.
9. Sheehan, op. cit., p. 214.
10. Jean Bethke Elshtain (1987), *Women and War*, Chicago: University of Chicago Press.
11. Jean Bethke Elshtain (2004), *Just War Against Terror: The Burden of American Power in a Violent World*, New York: Basic Books.
12. Evelyn Alsultany (2007), 'Selling American Diversity and Muslim American Identity Through Nonprofit Advertizing Post-9/11', *American Quarterly*, 59:3, pp. 593–622.
13. Lauren Berlant (1995), 'Live Sex Acts: (Parental Advisory: Explicit Materials)', *Feminist Studies*, 21:2, pp. 379–404.

Chapter 3

Civilians

Featuring Chris Simcox, Elvira Arellano, Saul Arellano, Shanti Sellz, José Matus, Ofelia Rivas

The other War on Terror

Tucson, Arizona: If you ask a US citizen where the War on Terror is being fought, most tell you in Afghanistan or Iraq or anywhere there is a suspected al-Qaeda cell. Occasionally, they'll tell you at Gitmo or in the United States over issues of surveillance, racial and religious profiling, and civil liberties. It is very rare, though, to be told that the US War on Terror is being fought on the US-Mexico border through US immigration policies. Yet this is precisely what human rights activist and No More Deaths volunteer Shanti Sellz is telling me now.

'It is a low intensity war zone,' Shanti says about this border region, 'and it is seen and felt by every person who interacts with this border, whether it's ranchers [...] [or the indigenous] people in the Tohono O'odham Nation' that straddles the US-Mexico border. An infrastructure of war is 'dominating their communities,' Shanti explains. 'Walls going up in the middle of communities, the search lights, the helicopters, the roads Border Patrol rips through'.

Figure 42: Border Patrol vehicle at US-Mexico border.

After 9/11, the War on Terror redefined immigration as once again a national security issue, with illegal immigrants this time viewed as potential terrorists. From this perspective, anyone who assists illegal immigrants in any way – even if only by providing lifesaving food, water, and medical care – could easily find themselves on the wrong side in the 'with us or with the terrorists' War on Terror.

This is what happened to Shanti and to Daniel Strauss, two volunteers for the humanitarian aid organization No More Deaths, when they tried to assist three seriously ill migrants they found in the Arizona desert. Border Patrol officials arrested Shanti and Daniel on charges that they were smuggling undocumented migrants into the US. In actuality, Shanti and Daniel were following a procedure well known to Border Patrol of transporting the ill migrants who had already crossed into the US to the hospital.

At their hearing, the Prosecutor asked Shanti, 'Did you ask those men if they were terrorists before you put them in your car?' Shanti recalls, 'I was like, "Ma'am, they're not terrorists." And she was like, "How do you know? Are you psychic?" And then our lawyers objected, and it was over'.

Figure 43: Border fence at International Road at the US-Mexico border.

Figure 44: May Day march in Tucson, Arizona.

But Shanti realizes that things might have been different. 'If we were in a jury trial and she said that, just bringing out the terrorist card, she knew that that could change the entire course of the discussion, just plant the seed in the jury's mind, playing on the fear of the 9/11 attacks'.

This is the new challenge human rights activists working on immigration issues face – preventing a conflation of 'terrorists' with 'undocumented immigrants' and with themselves. For Shanti, the stakes of maintaining this distinction are not just about her personal freedom versus her potential sentence of fifteen years in prison. They are about the implications of how all of us respond to 'the terrorist card'. As she puts it, 'If you take out the terrorist card, people's rationale goes out the window' and 'we lose our humanity through it'.

Crossing

US-Mexico Border: The year is 1997. A young Mexican woman whose father is ill and who cannot find gainful employment at home makes the difficult decision to leave Mexico for the US, where she can earn enough money to send funds home to her family. She lacks the necessary documents that would allow her to legally live and work in the US, as well as the necessary funds to pay a coyote to illegally guide her across the border. Knowing how dangerous it is to cross the desert unguided, she decides to walk up to the US border check point and pass over the border with the many other Mexican citizens who legally enter the US each day.

On her first attempt, she is turned back by immigration officials. But on her second attempt, no one challenges her. And so 22-year-old Elvira Arellano pushes through the turnstile to begin her life as an undocumented worker in the US.

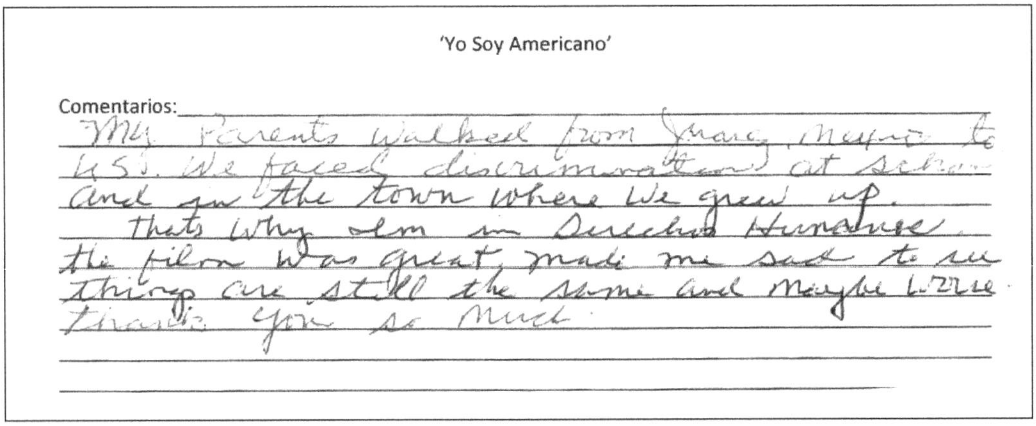
'Yo Soy Americano'

Comentarios: My Parents walked from Juarez, Mexico to US. We faced discrimination at school and in the town where we grew up. Thats why I'm in Derecho Humanos. the film was great, made me sad to see things are still the same and maybe worse. thanks you so much.

Figure 45: Anonymous comment.

The power of art

A ranch south of Three Points, Arizona: The modern-day Minutemen hold a Muster along the US-Mexico border. They do so not to re-enact history, as Musters often do. They do so to make history. Led by Chris Simcox, who founded the Minutemen Civil Defense Corps in response to 9/11, these civilian volunteers patrol the border to prevent drug dealers, terrorists, and migrants from entering the US illegally. For now that individuals passing through US border check points are more strictly monitored, an increasing number of undocumented people are crossing at unmonitored sites into Texas, New Mexico, Arizona and California. Like the original Revolutionary War Minutemen who fought the British to

Figure 46: Modern-day Minutemen on patrol.

form this new nation, the modern-day Minutemen see themselves as an elite force willing to risk life and limb in defense of their country.

I film an orientation session, a camp set-up, a night patrol. The Minutemen take all of these activities very seriously, yet I find it difficult to take the Minutemen seriously. For as hard as I try to see them as they see themselves, to me the Minutemen do not resemble an elite defense force. Yes, they have codes and codenames, a central command structure and standard operational procedures, all borrowed from the US military. But the Minutemen I observe are either senior citizens or Wild West enthusiasts or military wannabes.

The seniors look as though they would be equally at home in an RV Park as at a Minutemen Muster, with their comfortable chairs, flasks of hot coffee, and sensible clothes. The Wild West enthusiasts look like they just walked off a film set, thanks to their fancy cowboy boots, handlebar mustaches, and leather vests. It is the military wannabe Minutemen who come closest to looking like proper troops. Yet they are so over-accessorized – wearing desert camouflage and flak jackets and carrying multiple weapons – that they seem more like actors or extras than they do elite defenders of the nation, especially when on patrol with the senior citizens who compose the vast majority of the Minutemen I meet.

The whole affair reminds me of Allison Smith's public art project, 'The Muster', in which Smith invited people to declare their cause by creating campsite-installations in response to her organizing question, 'What are you fighting for?'[1] That's how I see this Minutemen Muster – as an artistic campsite installation where a battle is being staged against illegal immigration but not really fought.

Simcox is no fool. He understands this and, at times, admits as much. This is why he goes back and forth in his interview between, on the one hand, recounting impressive statistics of how many IA's (illegal aliens) the Minutemen have sighted and, on the other hand, pointing out that the Minutemen cannot solve the problem of illegal immigration with their patrols. The best they can do is bring attention to this problem by showing the commitment of everyday US Americans to 'do the job the government won't do,' as Simcox puts it.

That's what these seniors and soldiers and cowboys are doing. They are bringing attention to their cause by bringing attention to themselves. This is what ultimately makes me take them seriously – not just the national and international attention they are receiving but the way this attention is affecting US history.

A day in the life

Humbolt Park, Chicago, Illinois: It's February. My hands are protected by gloves covered by a pair of mittens. I shed these coverings and begin fumbling with the buttons and switches on my camera. My camera is so cold, it is painful to touch. I focus and frame a shot of the storefront church where Elvira Arellano is in sanctuary. I direct my hands not to drop the camera that I can barely feel. I will my body to stop shaking from the cold long enough to get a stable image.

Figure 47: Window of church where Elvira Arellano is in sanctuary.

Elvira and her 8-year-old son Saulito have been living in a small apartment above this church for months now. As an undocumented immigrant from Mexico, Elvira (now a single mother) had been working illegally as a cleaner at Chicago's O'Hare Airport to support herself and her son and to contribute to supporting her family back in Mexico. She was arrested as part of Operation Tarmac, a post-9/11 government initiative to ensure that no terrorists were working at US airports. Instead of picking up terrorists, the Operation led to the arrest and deportation of many illegal immigrants who, like Elvira, were using false social security numbers to obtain jobs. Elvira received a deportation order, but instead of reporting for deportation, Elvira sought sanctuary in this Chicago church. She did so on the grounds that deporting her effectively meant the US government would be deporting Saulito, a US citizen who was born and raised in the US.

I ring Elvira's number again. Again, no answer. Elvira does not answer this telephone, ever. It is only answered if another member of the organization supporting Elvira, Sin Fronteras/ Without Borders, is in the church. I have been waiting 45 minutes in the street for access to the upstairs apartment, for access to Elvira. It was all prearranged, but no one answers the door, the phone, my shouts up from the street. I'm not surprised, as I could be one of the many Minutemen who occasionally protest in front of Elvira's apartment or an immigration official seeking access to Elvira.

Then I see Flor, a member of Sin Fronteras who shares the apartment with Elvira, coming down the street carrying several large bags of clothes. Flor was scheduled to let me into the apartment earlier, but it is laundry day, and the laundromat was busier than expected.

Flor and I enter the apartment. Elvira is vacuuming. This is one of her jobs at Sin Fronteras, to be responsible for keeping the inside space clean. Elvira finishes her work, then sorts through the clothes with Flor, putting her and Saulito's things in the small room they share with another woman.

I run my frozen fingers under cold, then warm, then hot water.

We settle down for an interview.

National Security

Tohono O'odham Nation, US-Mexico Border: The siren behind me starts suddenly. Startled, I look in my rearview mirror. I see a Border Patrol vehicle with red and blue flashing lights in hot pursuit. I look for a place to pull over so the BP agent can pass me. And then it dawns on me. He isn't going to pass me. He is going to pull me over. I am who he is pursuing.

The BP agent questions me and my passenger José Matus, a Yaqui Nation member and Director of Alianza Indigena Sin Fronteras/Indigenous Alliance Without Borders. 'Who are we? What is our citizenship? Why were we at the border? What were we doing? Did we have permission to be there?'

I explain that I've come to the border with José to film a segment of my film on US citizens. I explain that we were already questioned and cleared by a Tohono O'odham Nation member monitoring the border. I also explain that José picked this site because he thought it would be a quiet spot to work.

This, of course, is why we have been stopped. It turned out that this was not a quiet spot to work. For what José and I unwittingly stumbled upon was the US National Guard constructing a vehicle barrier along the border to stop unauthorized vehicles from transporting undocumented people into the US. Even though we set up well away from the construction, our filming was constantly interrupted by massive trucks travelling up and down the border road.

As we were leaving, I asked the Commander of the National Guard unit if I could film their activities, on the promise that I would not put any people in my shots. He agreed without any hesitation, and he and I and a number of other Guardsmen had a friendly chat as I filmed. About a 100 yards away, the BP agent who stopped us was watching this scene from his truck.

Figure 48: José Matus waves to National Guard building border fence.

When he later stops us, I explain to this Border Patrol agent that I had permission from the National Guard Commander to film. His reply is, 'The National Guard is not in charge. We are in charge'. He reminds me that this is a matter of national security, but he also admits that 'we don't want these pictures to end up on Fox News'. I assure him that I have no intention of supplying Fox News with my footage.

Within half an hour, it is all over. We are free to go on our way.

On the drive off the Nation lands, José explains to me that prior to 9/11, 'things were good on Indian lands. But after 9/11, things got worse'. He tells me how Border Patrol regularly stops, detains, and harasses Nation members because of the 'hysteria' about 'anti-immigration, terrorism, and drugs'. 'It's escalated to the point that people are afraid to come out of their houses and travel on their own land because they don't want to be hassled, and they don't want to be stopped and questioned'. José explains, 'That's what happened to us today. We were harassed more than anything because of national security [...] It's done in the name of national security'.

A nation divided

Tohono O'odham Nation, US-Mexico Border: I am interviewing Ofelia Rivas at her home on the Tohono O'odham Nation, a mere quarter mile from the US-Mexico border in Arizona. Our interview is interrupted by the sound of a helicopter flying low across the property. 'Can you hear them?' Ofelia asks me. This, she explains, is the National Guard patrolling the border.

Since 9/11, this border has been increasingly militarized, making National Guard flyovers and Border Patrol stop and searches daily occurrences for the people who live on the Nation. For years now, there has been some sort of fence or wall demarcating US territory from Mexican territory. But in 2003, the US government began the construction of a vehicle barrier wall right through the middle of the Tohono O'odham Nation, a Nation that extends well into Mexico.

Figure 49: Ofelia Rivas with her only form of ID.

For people like Ofelia who regularly cross the US-Mexico border to attend religious O'odham ceremonies in one part of the Nation or another, this border fence means longer distances travelling to official US border crossing checkpoints and increased delays at these checkpoints. For Ofelia, these delays occur because, like many other indigenous Americans, Ofelia has no passport because she has no birth record. She doesn't know the exact day she was born, nor is she certain of the year. Ofelia just knows that she was born during a particular ceremonial season in the mud house on the property where we are filming. Instead of a passport, Ofelia has a Tohono O'odham Nation member card. This is her only official form of identification, and it does not mention her US citizenship.

O'odham is Ofelia's heartfelt identification, even though she and her mother were born in the US and her father was born in Mexico. She explains that her O'odham identification is less and less tolerated because of the stricter division of Tohono O'odham lands into US and Mexico.

As an example, Ofelia tells a story about being stopped by a Border Patrol agent on Nation lands. 'I was told to say that I was a US citizen or a Mexican citizen. And I said I was an O'odham. And he proceeded to clip his handgun, and he pointed it at my head. And he told me to say that I was either a US citizen or a Mexican citizen or he would throw me on the pavement, handcuff me, and deport me. And I said, "Where are you going to deport me to? Mexico is also my land."'

Ofelia and I set up her final shot. 'My nation is divided by an international border', she says. 'And I am an O'odham American'.

Fiesta Binacional

Naco, US-Mexico Border: International Road runs between Naco, Arizona and Naco, Sonora. These two communities used to be one, with people passing freely across International Road. But that all changed when a roughly 13-foot-high border fence formally split Naco's US and Mexican sides.

A few miles out of town, this impassible structure gives way to a waist-high assemblage of poles and slats that anyone could easily pass over, under, or through. It is here where the Fiesta Binacional/Bi-national Festival is being staged. This annual gathering of residents from Naco and Naco defies enforced division by temporarily reuniting the communities through a celebration of art, music, dance, games and food, transforming the fence into a point of connection rather than a security barrier. Picnic tables jut up against it, small children paint a rainbow mural through it, and a group of boys play volleyball over it.

One boy hops back and forth across the fence. 'I'm Mexican. I'm American. I'm Mexican. I'm American,' he exclaims each time he crosses.

A Border Patrol vehicle creeps past. The boy ends his game. He picks a side and knows he must stick to it.

Figure 50: Volleyball game over US-Mexico border fence. Photo by Anne-Marie Fortier.

O Canada

A ranch south of Three Points, Arizona: Chris Simcox gives me a tour of Minutemen Operations at the US-Mexico border. We agreed to meet here because this is where Simcox first organized civilian border patrols and where most Minutemen activities are still based.

I ask Simcox about Minutemen patrols on other US borders. He informs me about teams guarding the Northern border with Canada, about maritime patrols working the St. Lawrence River in upstate New York, and about finding boatloads of Chinese nationals trying to enter the country illegally. Then, without prompting, he volunteers, laughing, 'We were finding more people entering Canada illegally than we did finding people going the other way'.

I know those leaving the US for Canada are more likely to be economic or health care refugees than political refugees. Still, I think of those I know who have made this journey – Phil McDowell, Jamine Aponte, and the many other Iraq War Resisters I met in Canada. My thoughts turn to a short film Phil showed me called 'Asylum'. It is a fictitious story about *Canadian* Minutemen-like civilians patrolling the US-Canadian border. Set in the not-too-distant future, the film shows Canadian Minutemen apprehending a young US man who has crossed into Canada to avoid a new US policy of compulsory military service.

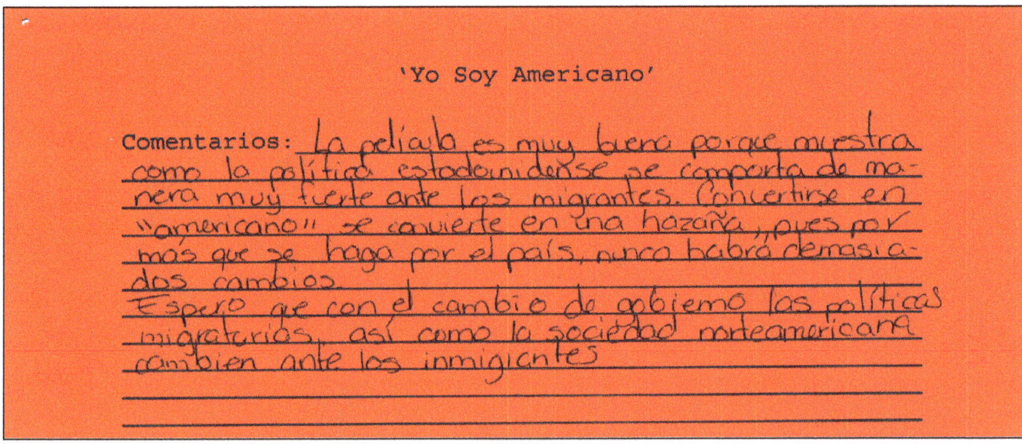
'Yo Soy Americano'

Comentarios: La película es muy buena porque muestra como la política estadounidense se comporta de manera muy fuerte ante los migrantes. Convertirse en "americano" se convierte en una hazaña, pues por más que se haga por el país, nunca habrá demasiados cambios.
Espero que con el cambio de gobierno las políticas migratorias, así como la sociedad norteamericana cambien ante los inmigrantes

Figure 51: Anonymous comment. Translation: The film is very good because it shows how US politics has become very anti-immigrant. Becoming American has been converted into a major feat, because the more one does for the country, there are never enough changes.

The Wall

The Ice House Gallery, Phoenix, Arizona: Shanti Sellz' 'I am an American' film is projected onto the largest wall in the gallery. Shanti tells of her arrest with another No More Deaths volunteer while they were transporting three ill undocumented migrants to Tucson to receive medical care. What is shocking about this incident is that No More Deaths and Border Patrol had worked out a protocol for such transports, so Border Patrol knew exactly what these No More Deaths volunteers were doing and why they were doing it. Yet the case went on for a year and a half before a judge dismissed the charges.

A healthcare worker and life-long resident of Phoenix watches the film. Afterwards, she comments on the contradiction in US policy on this issue. She tells me hospitals have a legal obligation to provide care for everyone – no matter their legal status – if they present themselves for treatment. But transporting undocumented migrants to a hospital where they can legally receive care is illegal.

Of course, the ideal scenario for Border Patrol is not so much to stop people like Shanti from transporting illegal migrants to US hospitals. It is to keep illegal migrants from entering the United States altogether. One of the ways the US government is trying to accomplish this is by building a border fence along the US/Mexican border.

The wall, the healthcare worker reflects. It isn't stopping illegal immigration or helping to solve the US healthcare crisis. It is making matters worse, she tells me. Because of the wall, our hospital treats *more* undocumented migrants now than it did before because more of them are getting injured as they cross the border, as they fall off of the wall.

Figure 52: Shanti's film in gallery exhibition.

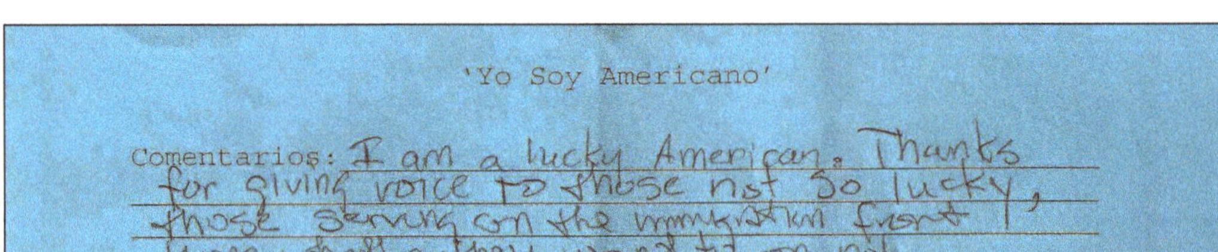

'Yo Soy Americano'

Comentarios: I am a lucky American. Thanks for giving voice to those not so lucky, those serving on the immigration front lines whether they want to or not.

Figure 53: Anonymous comment.

Shadows and light

Arizona Desert, US-Mexico Border: My camera burns my hands, as there is no protection from the sun, the heat, the light. I overexpose my shot, letting the light pour into my lens so I have a bright image on my side display panel. This is the only way I can see what I'm filming, to get a focus and frame, because my glasses prevent me from looking through the viewfinder. I adjust the exposure, switching on every one of my camera's built-in filters. The image on my display is now so dark, I am watching shadows perform. I will only see the images as the camera has captured them when I review them in playback.

My technological estrangement from the scene I'm filming is welcome. Chris Simcox is telling me why he founded the Minutemen Civil Defense Corps, a 9/11-inspired group of civilian volunteers who patrol the US border to prevent 'drug dealers, terrorists and IAs (illegal aliens)' from entering the US illegally. We get into his car for a reconnaissance tour of the ranch, looking for IAs and evidence of IAs.

Simcox tells me of his frustration with the US government over immigration. He speaks from a rage that seems contained for the camera. '[…] Every poll in this country regardless of what side of the issue you're on, everyone is demanding that the federal government do something. And they're drawing this out and dragging their feet as long as they can. Why? […] You know why – cause they're making money off of it'. He continues, 'I think the President, President Bush, and all four Southern border state Governors should be under federal investigation for potential ties to drug cartels and the money somehow that they're making on this. There can be no other reason that they're allowing this to happen'.

If this didn't all sound so 'US talk radio', Simcox' rant would shock me, not just because it lacks any evidence to support his allegations but also because of how out of touch with political reality it is. For instead of the President and these Governors being involved in some grand conspiracy involving 'drug cartels and money', the fact of the matter is that their positions on illegal immigration are complicated because they recognize just how dependent the US domestic economy is on cheap, undocumented labor. But Simcox never mentions facts such as these. Instead, he relies on this common tactic of the far right – to make serious, unsubstantiated public claims to rally his base around the cause of stopping illegal immigration.

Simcox concludes solemnly, 'I just had to stand up and do something for my country. This was just my calling'.

After the interview, I review my footage and see lighted images for the first time. My eyes focus on something I shot out of Simcox's car window. It is a simple shot of the car chasing the sun as it sits high over the desert. But seen through my filters, the light streaks across the frame in six directions. It looks like the holy Christian star leading the Three Wise Men to the Baby Jesus. My camera pans across the frame, out the car's side window. Two Minutemen are standing patrol. Stopping his car at the side of the road, Simcox makes three.

Figure 54: A view from Chris Simcox' car window.

Proud to be an American

Santa Rosa Learning Center, Tucson, Arizona: Ofelia Rivas and I are in a local library doing her voice-over interview. Our conversation turns to September 11, 2001, and what changes the events of that day have brought to the Tohono O'odham people.

'The thing that happened in New York,' Ofelia begins. 'They said that in this country there was never any terrorist attack on this land. But as indigenous people and as O'odham and tribal people, we know that terrorism happened when foreign people came into our lands and killed villages and people by the hundreds and introduced diseases into our lands. And we were forced into these concentration camps that are called reservations'.

Ofelia explains that while most US citizens know this history of indigenous Americans, they think life on the reservations has improved. But Ofelia points out that there is abject poverty on the reservations still today and that the rights of indigenous people are regularly violated.

She tells me several stories – about how at last year's traditional deer hunting ceremony 'men were surrounded by Border Patrol and held at gun point until someone arrived to tell the Border Patrol these were traditional hunters', about the Border Patrol agent who entered her best friend's house allegedly looking for undocumented people but instead of searching the house 'held a flashlight to my friend's breast while she was breastfeeding her baby', and about a young O'odham man coming from the Mexican side of the Nation to receive medical care for severe burns who was denied entry into the US even though he was entitled to enter and receive care as a member of the O'odham Nation. 'And the young man died at the border in Mexico'.

'We seem to be so subhuman these days that we feel no one has listened to our issues', Ofelia tells me. 'It's an outrage. I call it an atrocity that these things still continue today,' Ofelia says angrily. 'We are without rights [...] These kind of things happen all the time on the Nation'.

'There's so many people who are so proud and so very patriotic in this America and don't realize that these violations still occur'. She tells me, 'We want to be proud of America, but how can we when they continue to violate our rights?'

Figure 55: Stop Terrorizing Our Human Rights.

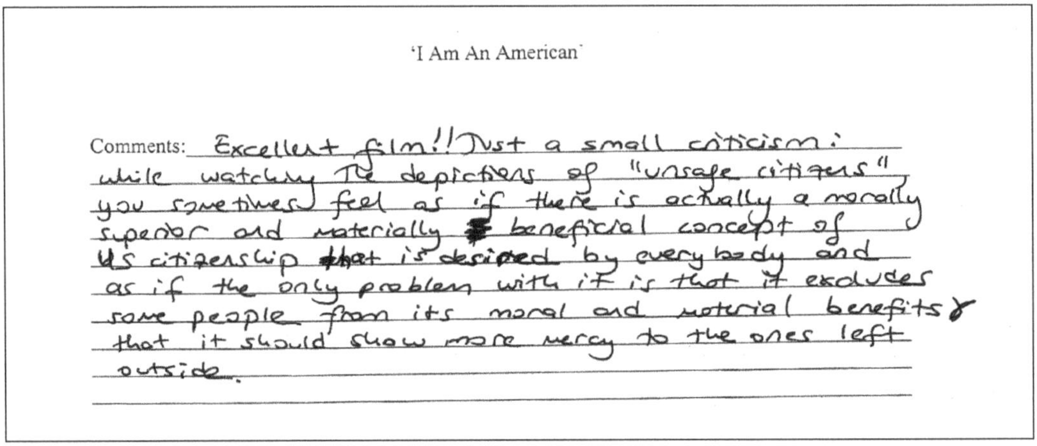

'I Am An American'

Comments: Excellent film!! Just a small criticism: while watching the depictions of "unsafe citizens" you sometimes feel as if there is actually a morally superior and materially beneficial concept of US citizenship that is desired by everybody and as if the only problem with it is that it excludes some people from its moral and material benefits & that it should show more mercy to the ones left outside.

Figure 56: Anonymous comment.

Madonna and Child

Humbolt Park, Chicago, Illinois: Images of the Virgin of Guadalupe are common sights in churches with Hispanic congregations. The Aldaberto United Methodist Church where Elvira Arellano is in sanctuary is no exception. The classic image of the pregnant Madonna supported by a winged angel adorns the wall behind me as I interview Elvira.

A Mexican icon, the Virgin of Guadalupe symbolizes not only an indigenous Mother Mary bringing her son into the New World as flesh and blood of that New World but also motherly protection for all those who believe in her. According to the Miracle of Tepeyac where the Virgin revealed herself to Juan Diego, the Virgin's promising words are:

> My little son. Do not be distressed and afraid.
> Am I not here, she who is your Mother?
> Are you not under my shadow and protection?
> Am I not the fountain of your joy?
> Are you not in the fold of my mantle, in the cradle of my arms?

Elvira and I move into an adjoining room, where my eye is drawn to a very different representation of Madonna and Child. It is on a large black and white poster that Sin Fronteras uses in political rallies. The image reminds me of a widely circulated photograph of Elvira and Saul. In that photo, Elvira stands behind Saul, her head bowed, her chin just touching his hair, her arms gently wrapped around her son. Melted into his Mother, Saulito holds the arms that hold him.

Figure 57: 'Don't Let the Migra Take My Mommy Away'.

But in this poster-sized image, what we see is not Elvira but her haunting absence, symbolized by a dotted line outlining the blank space next to Saul. This space is labeled, 'Elvira Arellano. Under Deportation'. The poster's caption reads, 'Don't let the Migra (Spanish for immigration authorities) take my Mommy away'.

'I am not a terrorist'

Humbolt Park, Chicago, Illinois: I have asked Elvira Arellano to pose for a 'video portrait'. I am making video portraits of all the major characters in my films to display in gallery exhibitions, and Elvira is certainly a major character. That she is not a US citizen but a continental American makes her portrait all the more poignant, as it poses questions about how a term that designates all peoples from the Americas has come to refer exclusively to US citizens.

She stands in the badly lighted kitchen wearing a black T-shirt that asks in white lettering, 'Who would Jesus deport?' Looking directly into the camera, she says the only words she has spoken to me in English, 'I am not a terrorist'.

Next Page – Figure 58: 'Who Would Jesus Deport?'

'I am not a terrorist.'

– Elvira Arellano, undocumented immigrant and mother of US son Saul Arellano arrested in post-9/11 security sweeps, pictured here in sanctuary in a US church before her deportation to Mexico.

Video Portraits of Post-9/11 US Citizens Series I by Cynthia Weber © Pato Productions 2008.

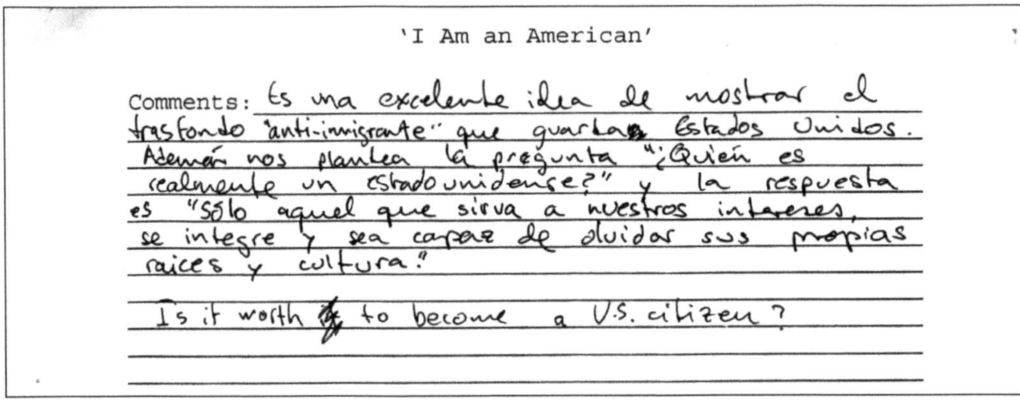

'I Am an American'

Comments: Es una excelente idea de mostrar el trasfondo "anti-inmigrante" que guarda Estados Unidos. Además nos plantea la pregunta "¿Quién es realmente un estadounidense?" y la respuesta es "Sólo aquel que sirva a nuestros intereses, se integre y sea capaz de olvidar sus propias raíces y cultura."

Is it worth ~~it~~ to become a U.S. citizen?

Figure 59: Anonymous comment. Translation: It is an excellent idea to show the anti-immigrant background that secures the US. It makes us ask, 'Who really is a US citizen?' and the answer is 'only those who serve US interests, who integrate, and who are able to forget their own roots and culture. Is it worth to become a US citizen?

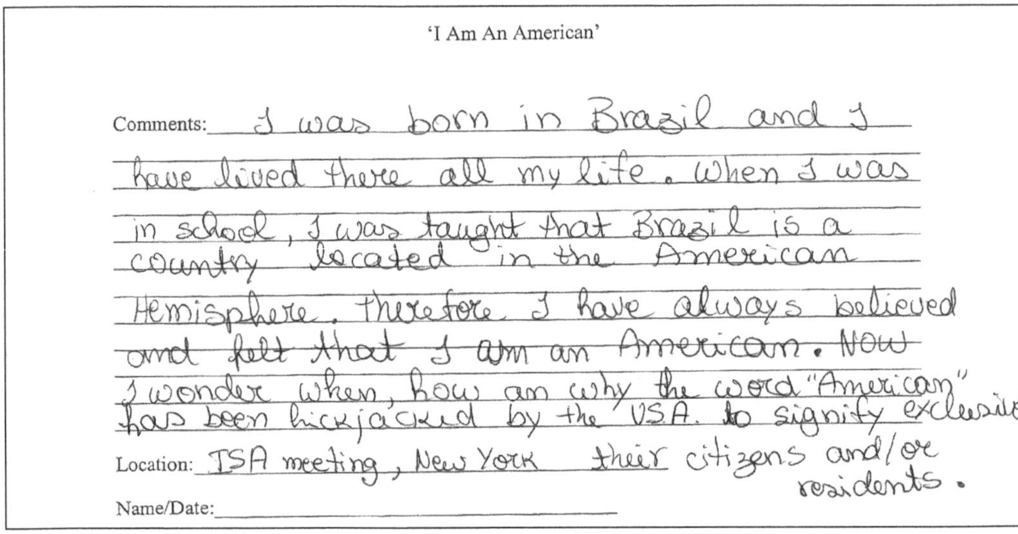

'I Am An American'

Comments: I was born in Brazil and I have lived there all my life. When I was in school, I was taught that Brazil is a country located in the American Hemisphere. Therefore I have always believed and felt that I am an American. Now I wonder when, how an why the word "American" has been hickjacked by the USA. to signify exclusivid their citizens and/or residents.

Location: ISA meeting, New York

Name/Date:

Figure 60: Anonymous comment.

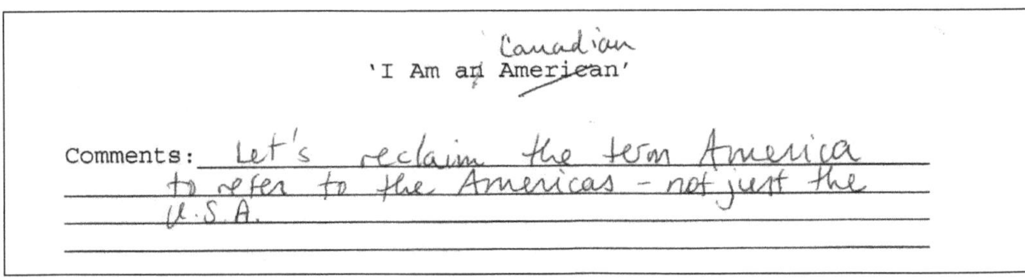

'I Am ~~an~~ ~~American~~ Canadian'

Comments: Let's reclaim the term America to refer to the Americas - not just the U.S.A.

Figure 61: Anonymous comment.

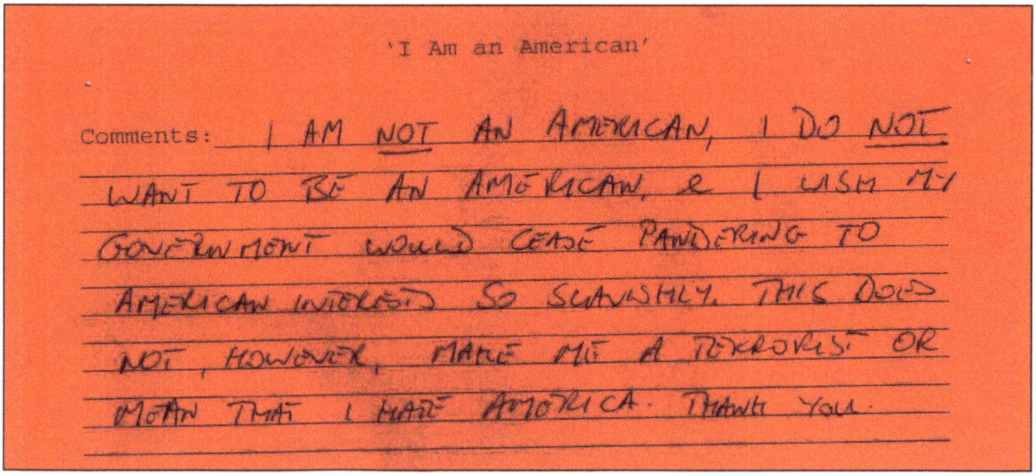
'I Am an American'

Comments: I AM NOT AN AMERICAN, I DO NOT WANT TO BE AN AMERICAN, & I WISH MY GOVERNMENT WOULD CEASE PANDERING TO AMERICAN INTERESTS SO SLAVISHLY. THIS DOES NOT, HOWEVER, MAKE ME A TERRORIST OR MEAN THAT I HATE AMERICA. THANK YOU.

Figure 62: Anonymous comment.

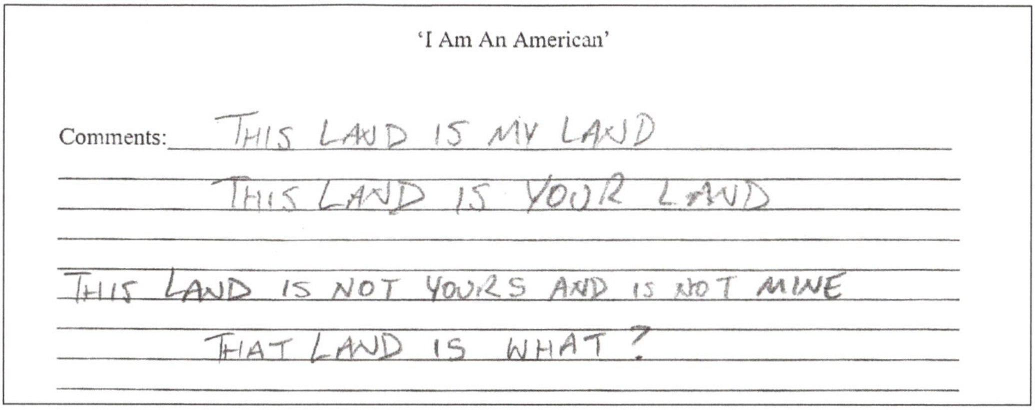
'I Am An American'

Comments: THIS LAND IS MY LAND
THIS LAND IS YOUR LAND
THIS LAND IS NOT YOURS AND IS NOT MINE
THAT LAND IS WHAT?

Figure 63: Anonymous comment.

The law

Scottsdale, Arizona: I'm in a recording studio taping Chris Simcox and Carmen Mercer, the President and Vice President of the Minutemen Civil Defense Corps, while they co-host their bi-weekly radio program. This is my second meeting with Simcox. Getting a follow-up interview has proved to be difficult, as Simcox and I are very much oil and water both politically and personally, and we both know as much. So this two hour radio program will have to take the place of a second interview.

The material is helpful. Simcox reviews the organization's mission statement, fields phone calls, and engages in a bit of banter with his co-host about topics of concern to Minutemen.

Figure 64: Chris Simcox on the air.

At every opportunity, Simcox reiterates that the Minutemen are all about upholding the law of the land. They have nothing against legal immigrants. They are not racist. They just firmly believe that everyone must be held accountable to the law. Period. And they are doing what they can to ensure this happens.

The discussion turns to the up-coming US Presidential elections and who the Minutemen will endorse. Most of the chatter is about potential Republican candidates, but then Simcox mentions Senator Barak Obama, referring to him distastefully as 'that Muslim Obama'.

This is a live radio program. I am there on the condition of my silence. I stare intently at my camera as I register Simcox's gleeful dissemination of not just misinformation but strongly implied religious prejudice.

The conversation turns to Arizona State Representative Kyrsten Sinema. It is Representative Sinema who introduced a bill that would outlaw the sorts of armed civilian border patrols that the Minutemen engage in and would re-label these activities 'domestic terrorism'. Needless to say, there is a lot of animosity between the two camps. Simcox makes

Figure 65: Bumper sticker on Minuteman car addressed to Mexican President Vicente Fox.

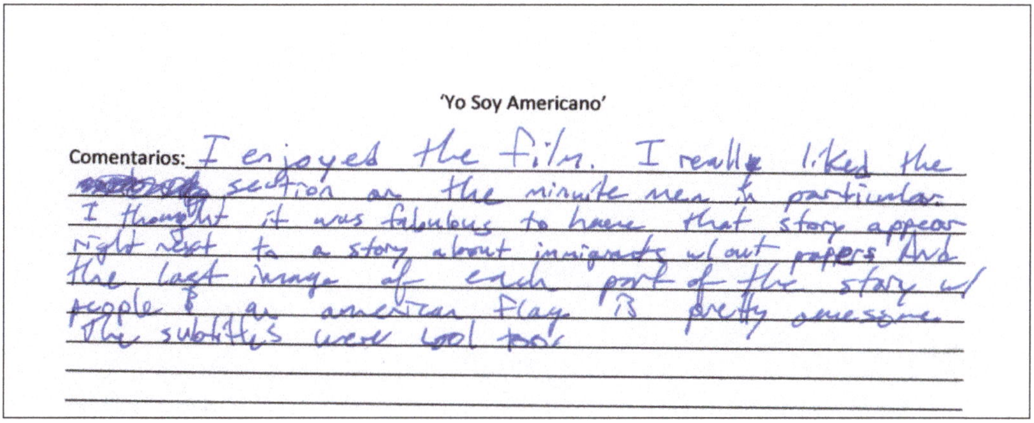

'Yo Soy Americano'

Comentarios: I enjoyed the film. I really liked the section on the minute men in particular. I thought it was fabulous to have that story appear right next to a story about immigrants w/out papers. And the last image of each part of the story w/ people & an american flag is pretty awesome. The subtitles were cool too.

Figure 66: Anonymous comment.

this personal when he refers to Sinema's 'alternative lifestyle' in such a way that listeners can almost hear Simcox's eyebrows rise and his eyes smile with mischief.

Simcox' expressions of Islamaphobia and homophobia in the wider context of his claims that the Minutemen are upholding the law remind me of just how prejudicial the law can be. For in the US right now, it is perfectly legal to discriminate against Muslims and homosexuals so long as the specific discriminatory practice stays within the limits of social acceptability. This is because the law in the US – as in any country – does not just unbiasedly exist. It gets made and remade every day to reflect the values and biases of society. So when society labels Muslims 'terrorists', the law makes it possible to suspend their legal rights indefinitely (think Gitmo, where *every* detainee is Muslim). And when society calls homosexuals 'perverts', the law makes it possible to limit their rights (think legal skirmishes over 'gay marriage' or adoption). These are acceptable forms of bigotry because they are enshrined in the law and because they do not (necessarily) fit conventional US understandings of intolerable intolerance.

Simcox returns to his recitation of Minutemen values. 'We welcome people from around the world. You come through the gate, you have the right documents and we will welcome you with open arms. But you will assimilate, you will learn to speak English, and you will leave behind unsavory cultural practices that don't fit in'. Carmen rushes to add, 'And it has nothing to do with racism'. Simcox agrees, 'No, that's right'.

The show breaks for a commercial. I suggest to Simcox that we run his 'I am an American' lines now, for safety sake, to have a take in the bag. This is not the shot I want. The shot I want, and the one Simcox and I have agreed to, is of Simcox putting a flag on the section of US-Mexico border fence that the Minutemen financed and built on private land. But I can't see myself ever getting this shot, as it seems clear that Simcox and I are unlikely to meet again. And so Simcox runs his lines in the recording studio. 'I am the Founder of the Minutemen Civil Defense Corps, and I am an American'. This is the end of the agreed line. But Simcox continues anyway, 'and proud of it. Proud to serve my country as an American'.

Over the next few months, I occasionally phone Simcox to arrange a flag shot at the fence. My calls always go to voicemail. None is ever returned.

'Saul Arellano: Boy Hero'

Aldaberto United Methodist Church, Chicago, Illinois: Eight-year-old Saulito comes home from school with his entourage – a Pastor from the church and various members of Sin Fronteras. Saul goes directly to his mother, then to his Knock Your Block Off boxing toy. Elvira is cooking dinner in the kitchen. Saul comes in for a snack. He decides on a bowl of cereal. Elvira and Saul review Saul's day – classes, friends, art project – and then move on to setting Saul's evening schedule – TV during snack time, homework, filming.

Saul is not happy to see me. He tolerates my presence only because his mother insists he does. I want to grant Saulito his wish, that I would disappear. I want to give him back a private life. But I also want to capture on film the strong bond I have witnessed between this boy and his mother.

Figure 67: Elvira and Saul Arellano.

Flor assuages my guilt somewhat. She tells me that children of undocumented immigrants have to grow up quickly, whether because they have been left back home by parents working abroad or because, as in Saul's case, their parent's status as a public figure draws them into the spotlight. Because Elvira has couched her defiance of her deportation order in terms of Saul's right as a US citizen to stay in the US where he can have a better life, there is unfortunately no escape for Saulito from the constant stream of reporters, film-makers, dignitaries, and well-wishers who make their way to this small Chicago church. And because Elvira cannot leave her sanctuary without an almost absolute guarantee of arrest and deportation, it is Saulito who performs symbolic public duties for her, like meeting with lawmakers in Washington, DC, and addressing the Mexican Congress. For all this, 'NobelSavage 1' posted a documentary about him on YouTube under the title 'Saul Arellano: Boy Hero'.[2]

Elvira and I have agreed that I will film her and Saul through the evening, getting candid 'at home in sanctuary' shots. Elvira has explained this to Saul. Yet whenever Elvira leaves the room, Saul takes the opportunity to tell me, 'I don't like to be filmed when I'm doing this stuff,' no matter what stuff he's doing. I lower my camera.

When Elvira returns, I film mother assisting son with homework. Saul learns his school lessons quickly. And even more quickly, he figures out how to get rid of me. When he protests again about the filming, his mother explains to him that I will leave after he goes to bed. And so Saul decides a full two hours before bedtime that he is tired. I briefly film Elvira taking Saul through his reading as she tucks him in. And then I turn off my camera for the night, relieved this is over. And so is Saul, who triumphantly pops out of bed, has another snack, and settles down in front of the TV.

Humanitarian assistance

A Ranch South of Three Points, Arizona: It feels like I imagine a drug deal feels. The Minuteman and I assemble at the back of my rental car where I open the trunk and pull out the goods – a laptop loaded with a rough cut of my Minutemen film. I've offered to show it to this rookie Minuteman to reassure him that I'm trying to accurately represent the Minutemen. If he is so reassured, then he will take me up in his airplane for a tour of the Arizona Desert he and his fellow Minutemen are patrolling during their Muster.

The rough cut begins to play. We both watch it without comment. But inside, I can't stop talking to myself. 'This is the first Minuteman to see my film,' I say to myself. 'Yes, the film is narrated by Chris Simcox, but there are so many provocative cuts and juxtapositions. Like there – where the camera lingers on the row of holstered pistols while Simcox speaks of 'the biggest threat to our national security'. Will this new recruit focus only on Simcox's words, or will he see how the cut raises questions about just who is threatening US national security? Oh, and there – where Simcox embraces what many people – including me – would regard as racist views about immigrants and then protests too much that his views have nothing to do with racism. Oh, well,' I think to myself. 'Even though I really want these aerial shots, at least I won't have to fly around in a small plane'.

The film ends. I brace myself for disappointment as the final credits roll. Before they finish, the Minuteman exclaims, 'That's great! I could *totally* be a part of *that*!'

I experience a slight shock, but I also get it. I have always thought of this Minutemen film as my *Jesus Camp*. *Jesus Camp* is a documentary about evangelical Christians who send their children to camp where they do things like speak in tongues and pray for George W. Bush by laying hands on his cardboard cut-out. For those critical of evangelicals, *Jesus Camp* is a testimony to the extremism of extreme evangelicalism. But the evangelicals themselves love the film, for they see it as an accurate representation of themselves, about which they are uncritical.

The rookie Minuteman is now jubilant. He doesn't wait until I turn my camera on before he starts telling me his own story about why he became a Minuteman. It was to do humanitarian work, he tells me. To make sure that IAs (illegal aliens) making the dangerous journey through the Arizona desert wouldn't die. And so Minutemen seek out IAs and turn them over to Border Patrol as a form of humanitarian rescue.

Figure 68: Minuteman tracking migrants from airplane.

Figure 69: Apprehended migrants being readied for deportation.

This explanation doesn't surprise me. Changes in Minutemen rhetoric justifying their actions are older than the Minutemen organization itself. Before they were Minutemen, they called themselves vigilantes. When they became Minutemen, they claimed to be patriots defending the state, and now they claim to be humanitarians. Or, really, now they claim to be humanitarian patriots.

Our aerial tour commences. I'm in the backseat filming desert-scapes, mountains, and migrant assembly points. About 40 minutes into the tour, my Minuteman pilot gets a call from Command Operations. IAs have been sighted crossing the desert in two vehicles. My pilot is instructed to fly circles over the vehicles so Border Patrol can locate them. He does this for about an hour.

With each circle, I feel sicker and sicker. It isn't just the motion of flying or the disorientation of trying to look through a camera lens while bumping around in the air that's making me sick. It's that after a few minutes, the migrants have figured out what is going on, abandoned their vehicles, and fled into the 100+ degree desert on foot. My pilot follows them, driving them deeper into the desert and farther away from food, water and shelter. He continues his pattern of searching and circling until he gets word from Command Operations that his plane has led Border Patrol to the IAs.

We land, I say my goodbyes quickly, and I foolishly pack away my camera, missing a shot of a Border Patrol truck parked outside of Minuteman Headquarters. But I am too shaken by this experience to care much about missed shots. I'm thinking about those migrants and how if Border Patrol has not found them, then their lives are in danger. And I'm thinking about this Minuteman's definition of humanitarian assistance, of rescue, and of how his activities made rescue necessary but not guaranteed.

On my drive back to Tucson, I stop at the gas station in Three Points which spectators of the Border Wars like me use to replenish exhausted supplies of liquids and which Border

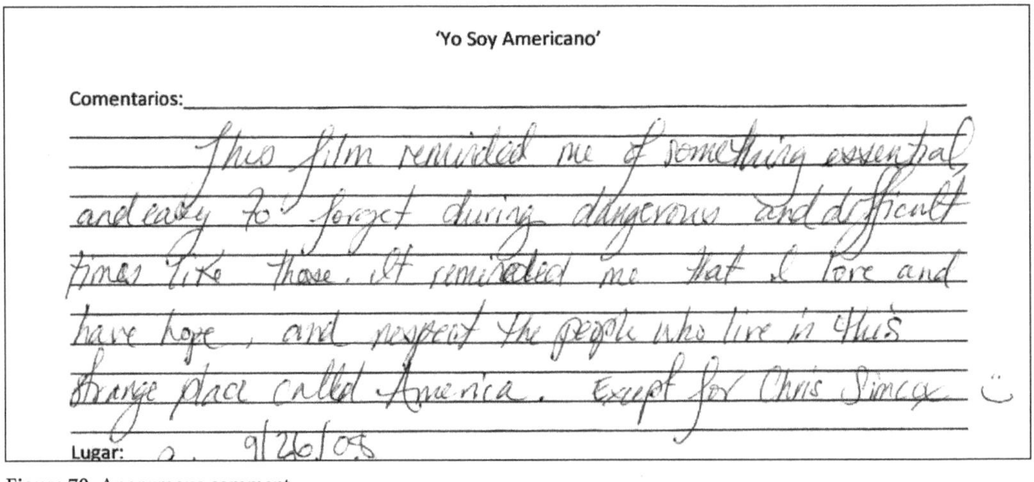
'Yo Soy Americano'

Comentarios: This film reminded me of something essential and easy to forget during dangerous and difficult times like these. It reminded me that I love and have hope, and respect the people who live in this strange place called America. Except for Chris Simcox :)

Lugar: 9/26/08

Figure 70: Anonymous comment.

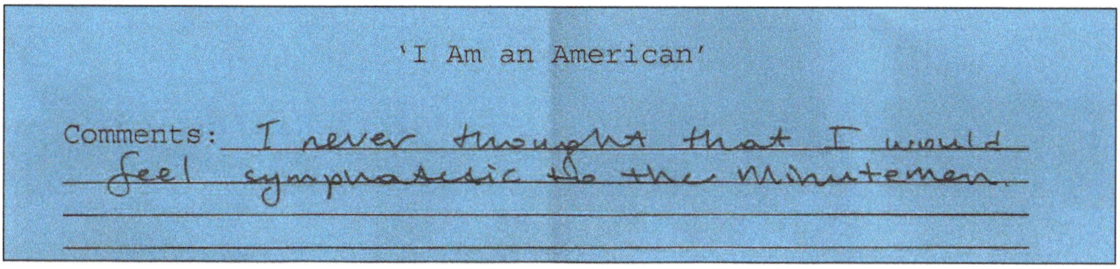
'I Am an American'

Comments: I never thought that I would feel sympathetic to the Minutemen.

Figure 71: Anonymous comment.

Patrol uses to transfer apprehended migrants onto buses bound for detention centers and deportation points. Here I spot a tow truck carrying one of the vehicles we were circling. Next to it is the other vehicle. And next to the bus are some three or four migrants. I have no way of knowing if these are some or all of the migrants who were in these vehicles. I tell myself this is them, this is all of them. But that sick feeling returns when I let myself know that I cannot know this for sure.

The other side

Sasabe, Mexico: I'm on a trip with the humanitarian aid group Humane Borders to meet with migrants preparing to enter the US from Mexico. We stop in Sasabe, one of the major 'base-camp' towns along the border where migrants gather. Here, rich migrants can arrange

Figure 72: Vans waiting to transport migrants to the Mexican-US border.

Figure 73: A migrant makes an offering to the Virgin asking for safe passage.

for fake US documents and car rides across the border. But we don't meet any rich migrants. Instead, we encounter only people whose poverty is leading them to the US in search of work so they can send money back to their families in Mexico or in other parts of Latin America.

I interview boys barely in their teens at a migrant hostel where they rest before walking to the border, men in the town square who will crowd into vans or truck for standing-room only rides to the border, and still other men making offerings to the Virgin of Guadalupe asking for safe passage for their walks across the desert.

All of them tell me exactly the same thing, that they would rather stay in Mexico or Guatemala or wherever home is than go to the US. But each of them feels they have no alternative but to go.

Desert realities

Tohono O'odham Nation, US-Mexico Border: Ofelia Rivas and I are filming her 'I am an American' lines. It is slow going. It is late June, and in this part of the Sonora Desert temperatures are hovering around 115 degrees. There is no shade. We both stop to drink every few minutes. We can only work in ten minute blocks. If we work longer, one or both of us gets heatstroke, which delays filming even longer.

I set up Ofelia's shot. To get the right angle and perspective, I need to go low. I rest one knee on the ground and use the other as a mount for my camera. When my flesh touches the desert floor, it burns so badly Ofelia spends precious energy returning to the house to bring me a towel to kneel on.

As I think about how difficult this shoot is, I can't get out of my mind how this very area has become a popular spot for migrants to cross over from Mexico into the US. This is because increased border surveillance to the East has driven migrants onto these much harsher Tohono O'odham lands. If they can, migrants avoid walking this part of the desert in the summer months, preferring to cross in April or October when desert days are cool enough for walking and resting and desert nights stay above freezing. But every year, thousands of people attempt to cross the desert in the summer, and every year hundreds die trying.

I imagine myself making such a crossing on a day like today. Unless someone found me, I would be incapacitated within hours and dead within days.

Everyday heroes

Tucson, Arizona: The humanitarian group No More Deaths is holding a press conference. Its purpose is to announce that Shanti Sellz and Daniel Strauss have been awarded the Oscar Romero Award for Human Rights, an award given to 'persons or organizations who

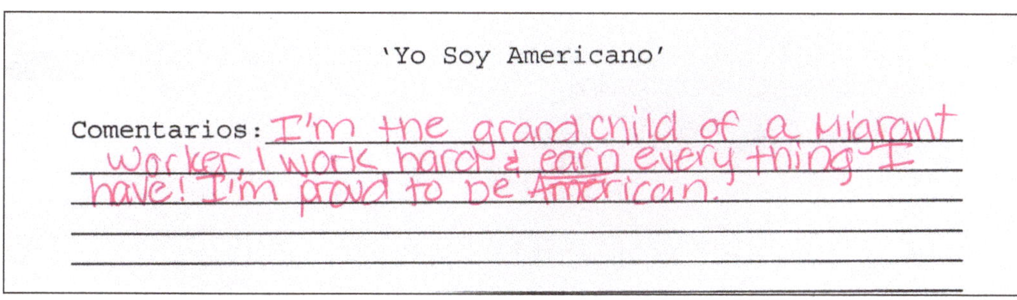

'Yo Soy Americano'

Comentarios: I'm the grand child of a Migrant worker, I work hard & earn every thing I have! I'm proud to be American.

Figure 74: Anonymous comment.

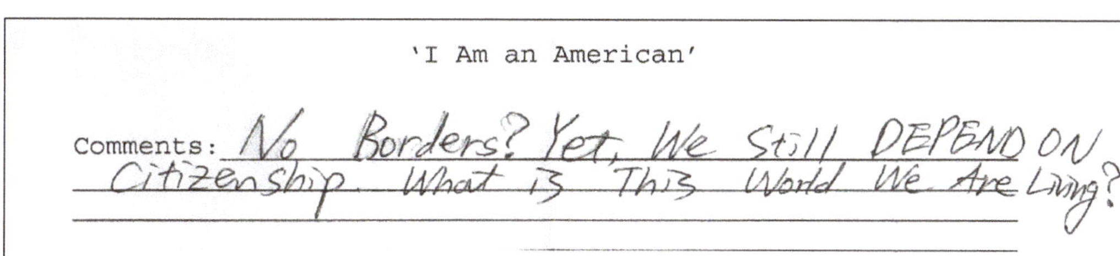

'I Am an American'

Comments: No Borders? Yet, We Still DEPEND ON Citizenship. What is This World We Are Living?

Figure 75: Anonymous comment.

distinguish themselves by their courage and integrity in defense of human rights and to honor those willing to risk their lives to honor human rights'. This is the first time in the history of the award that it has gone to anyone in the US.

But in typical No More Deaths style, the press conference has been turned around. Instead of honoring Shanti and Daniel as heroes, speaker after speaker gets up to note an individual migrant who is their hero – a corn farmer from Chiapas who risked his life journeying to the US so he wouldn't have to watch his children slowly die of starvation, a deported immigrant who made a new life giving aid and comfort to thousands of others returned to Mexico, and five anonymous migrants from Vera Cruz who upon finding an unconscious woman in the desert carried her to the highway, flagged down Border Patrol to assist her, and were of course themselves then deported.

Shanti explains that this is the organization's way of extending the Oscar Romero Award 'to the heroes and heroines of our time'. She displays a plaque made by a local artist that will be placed at the No More Deaths desert camp. It reads, 'How far would you walk to feed your family?'

Hey you, American!

The Lost Barrio, Tucson, Arizona: Shanti Sellz is troubling over her 'I am an American' line. We discussed my project at length before we began filming, and Shanti expressed her support of the project and of its framing devise, the 'I am an American' PSA. She has no

Figure 76: Shanti Sellz saying, 'I am an American'.

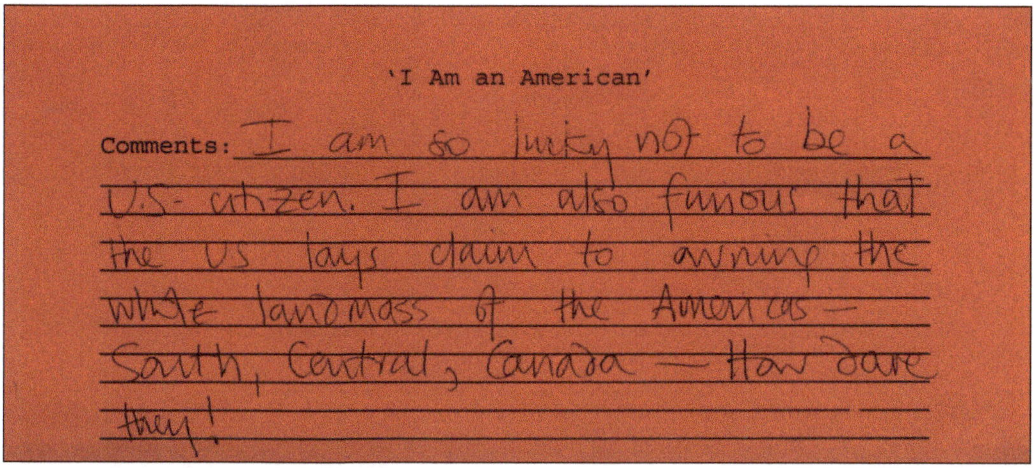
'I Am an American'

Comments: I am so lucky not to be a U.S. citizen. I am also furious that the US lays claim to owning the whole landmass of the Americas – South, Central, Canada – How dare they!

Figure 77: Anonymous comment.

trouble telling her story about her arrest. But when the time comes for Shanti to make her 'I am an American' declaration, she stumbles, then stops, and we discuss it all again.

'This is difficult for me to say,' she tells me.

'I am an American' is an articulation that has hemispheric reach, but it is used by US citizens as if it referred only to them. It is a phrase that has been co-opted by patriotic US discourses. What sways Shanti is not nationalism but humanism. The hail to identify as American is not one Shanti responds to.

I reassure Shanti that her film will convey this lack of fit between citizen and human, between legal status and social status, between Shanti herself and any flatfooted claim to 'American' identity. But our challenge in my one-minute re-mixed PSA is to *show* these ideas in how Shanti says her single line.

Shanti gives it a try, but her heart is not in it. In take after take, she says her line with less and less conviction. Her face assumes a 'you've got to be kidding me' expression. As she rolls her eyes, Shanti says, 'I am an American'. We have our shot.

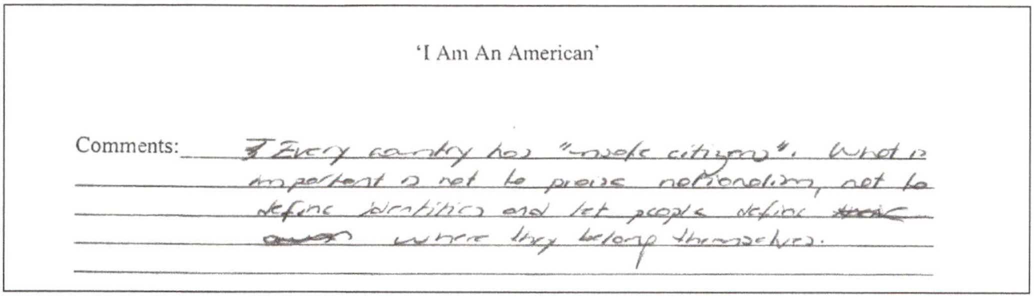
'I Am An American'

Comments: Every country has "model citizens". What is important is not to praise nationalism, not to define identities and let people define where they belong themselves.

Figure 78: Anonymous comment.

'I am a human rights activist, and I am an American.'

– Shanti Sellz, No More Deaths activist arrested for transporting dehydrated migrants to hospital.

Video Portraits of Post-9/11 US Citizens Series I by Cynthia Weber © Pato Productions 2008.

Previous Page – Figure 81: Shanti Sellz' flag shot.

A year later I get an email from Shanti congratulating me on the project's success and telling me she is honored to be a part of it. The subject line of her email reads, 'Hello from an American in Arizona'. I laugh out loud.

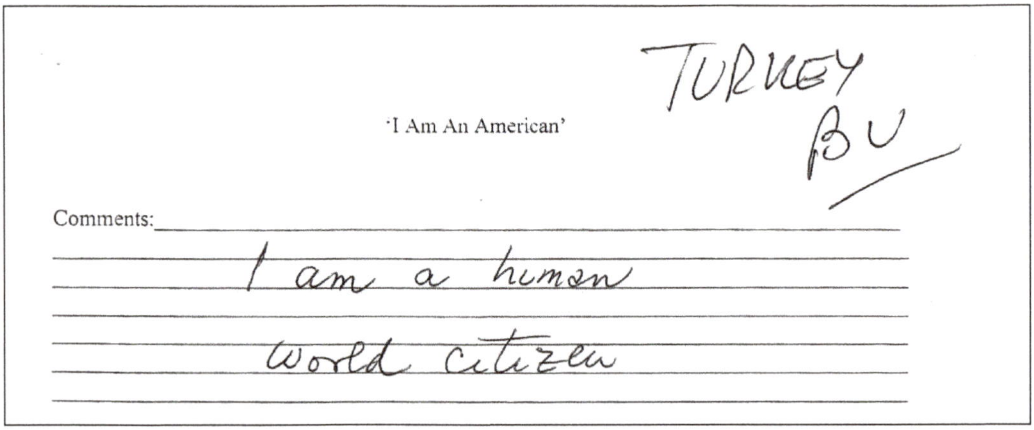
'I Am An American'

TURKEY
BU

Comments:

I am a human
World citizen

Figure 79: Anonymous comment.

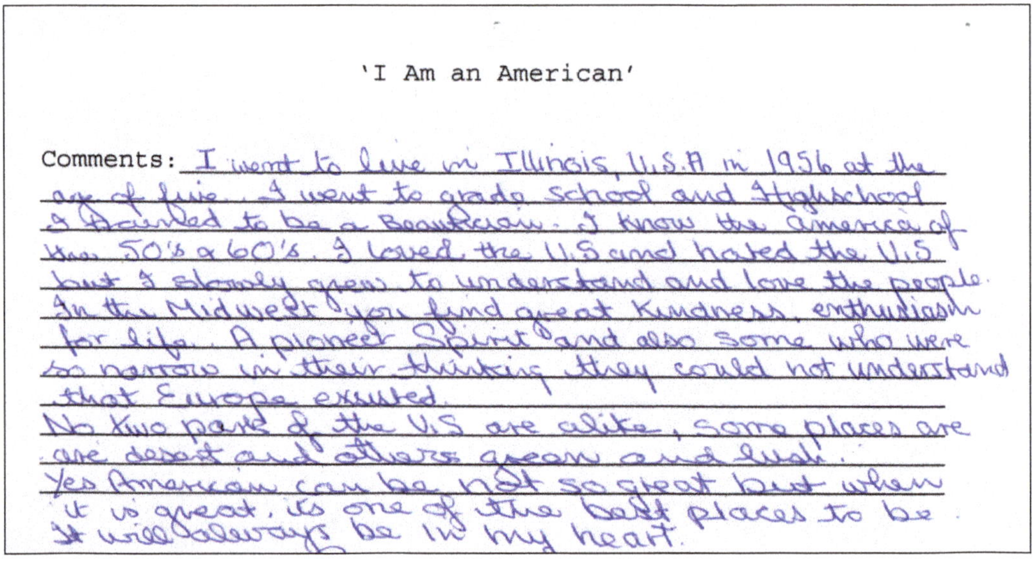
'I Am an American'

Comments: I went to live in Illinois, U.S.A in 1956 at the age of five. I went to grade school and Highschool I trained to be a Beautician. I know the America of the 50's & 60's. I loved the U.S and hated the U.S but I slowly grew to understand and love the people. In the Midwest you find great Kindness, enthusiasm for life. A pioneer Spirit and also some who were so narrow in their thinking they could not understand that Europe existed.
No two parts of the U.S are alike, some places are are desert and others green and lush.
Yes American can be not so great but when it is great, its one of the best places to be. It will always be in my heart.

Figure 80: Anonymous comment.

Distress signal

Tucson, Arizona: Shanti Sellz and I are filming her flag shot. Like her 'I am an American' line, this is another part of her film that makes her uncomfortable. And so we have a discussion about how she might again show her discomfort, this time using the US flag.

This is what Shanti does. She turns the US flag upside down, tilts her head inquisitively to one side, and looks directly into the camera while wearing an almost imperceptible smile. It is an interesting pose. One thing that makes it so interesting is that an upside-down flag is the international signal of distress. So Shanti seems to be signaling distress. But by holding the flag this way and holding her head as she does, Shanti is doing more than this. She isn't just straightforwardly signaling distress as she seems to be asking the question, 'Is the US nation now in distress?' And by asking this question, she is challenging all of us not only to think about whether the answer to this question is 'yes' or 'no'. She is challenging us to think about why the answer might be 'yes' or 'no'.

The vague smile on Shanti's face suggests she knows the answer.

O'odham Voice Against The Wall

Tohono O'odham Nation, US-Mexico Border: Like Ofelia Rivas' home that sits nearly on the US-Mexico border, Ofelia herself is someone who is crossed by national borders – not just US and Mexican but O'odham. And it is O'odham that Ofelia claims as her identity above any other. It is for this reason that Ofelia chose not to end her film by saying, 'I am an America'. Instead, she said, 'I am an O'odham American'.

It is also for this reason that Ofelia does not feel comfortable posing with the US flag in her final flag shot. For the US flag does not so much represent the transnational Tohono O'odham Nation as it asserts US nationalism over O'odham nationalism. This is not an assertion that Ofelia accepts. And so for her final flag shot, she substitutes the US flag with a banner that expresses both her O'odham nationalism and her individual identity within the O'odham nation.

This is what the banner looks like. At its center is the red and white symbol of the Tohono O'odham Nation. Encircling this circular symbol is the name of the organization Ofelia formed to protest the building of the border wall through O'odham territories – O'odham Voice Against The Wall. Above all this sits the title 'O'odham Rights'.

Standing next to this banner wearing a T-shirt bearing the same emblem and information, Ofelia poses for her flag shot.

Next Page – Figure 82: Ofelia Rivas' flag shot.

‘My nation is divided by an international border, and I am an O’odham American.’

– Ofelias Rivas, Indigenous Rights Activist protesting US-Mexico border wall dividing tribal communities.

Video Portraits of Post-9/11 US Citizens Series I by Cynthia Weber © Pato Productions 2008.

Rights
VOICE
the WALL

'We are not immigrants.'

– Jose Matus, Yaqui Ceremonial Leader and indigenous rights activist working to secure traditional mobility rights for indigenous people living on both sides of the US-Mexico border.

Video Portraits of Post-9/11 US Citizens Series I by Cynthia Weber © Pato Productions 2008.

Previous Page – Figure 83: José Matus 'We Are Not Immigrants'.

The border crossed us

Santa Rosa Learning Center, Tucson, Arizona: José Matus and I are discussing the mission of the organization he directs, Alianza Indigena Sin Fronteras/Indigenous Alliance Without Borders, a human/civil rights advocacy organization that promotes respect for indigenous rights, especially the indigenous right to mobility across borders.

As a Pascua Yaqui Nation member, José insists, 'We are not immigrants. We are not people who have come from other places [...] We have been here since time immemorial'. Yet when Yaqui Nation members cross the US-Mexico border, they are subjected to the same immigration requirements as any other foreign nationals crossing the border, requirements which are particularly difficult to meet for many indigenous peoples who lack passports yet who are subjected to increased document checks in the post-9/11 national security climate.

Alianza Indigena Sin Fronteras objects to these procedures on historical grounds, dating back to the 1884 US annexation of parts of Mexico that resulted in the disjunction of Yaqui lands. Since then, the Yaquis argue that when they travel from one part of the Yaqui Nation to another, they are not crossing an international border because, as José puts it, 'We believe that the border crossed us'.

Inside/outside

Lancaster, England: It's a rookie mistake and one that I never fail to make. It has to do with how inside light and outside light have different temperatures, which the camera picks up as different colors. On film, sunlight looks blue, and light bulbs look red. Every film student is taught to control their light so they can control their color. You do this either by making sure you shoot only under one kind of light (inside light or outside light), or you place corrective filters over spotlights or windows so that all the light looks the same color on film, no matter what its temperature.

I know all this, and I know how to do it. But I have neither the equipment nor the time nor the crew available to me to correct for mixed light during my shoots. Nor do I have the post-production skills to correct my images during my final edits. So if I'm relying on sunlight and indoor light on a single shoot, my subjects' faces look half blue and half red.

I know I'm supposed to hate this and consider it a major failing in my film-making technique. But I actually think it is the most fitting way to shoot my interview subjects for this project, and I wouldn't correct these images in post-production even if I could.

For isn't my point that all the 'different' US citizens I'm filming are both included in the laws and ethereal ideals of 'America' while at the same time are being placed outside of these very same laws and ideals by the War on Terror? And isn't the other thing that every film student is taught is that their images should convey their meaning not only through the content of their images but also through the aesthetic choices they make in the production of these images?

The effects of these mixed-lit shots are even more stark in the still 'video portraits' I produced of each of my interview subjects. That's because of how these images were created. Each image was shot twice – first as a live image with my video camera and then as a stilled screen grab playing off a DVD onto an analogue TV screen and reshot with a still photography camera. I choose this format for lots of reasons – because it references the American Ad Council's original 'I am an American' PSA which was first shown on television, because the TV screen pixelates and textures each image with data lines giving it an interesting aesthetic quality, and because the blue glow of the TV screen gives each image an eerie undertone, suggesting that the faces of these US Americans are ghosts haunting the original 'I am an American' PSA.

Nowhere is this more apparent than in the twice-shot face of Saul Arellano, which is illuminated more by outside light than by inside light. In this image, Saul looks less like the healthy little boy he is than a ghost whose haunted/haunting side is slowly overtaking his whole face. As I look at this image, I think to myself that sometimes getting it 'wrong' is actually getting it 'right'.

Figure 84: The mixed-lit face of Saul Arellano.

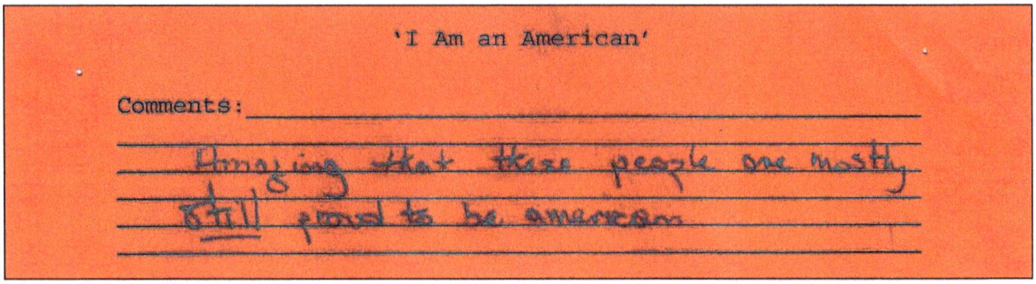
'I Am an American'

Comments: Amazing that these people are mostly still proud to be american

Figure 85: Anonymous comment.

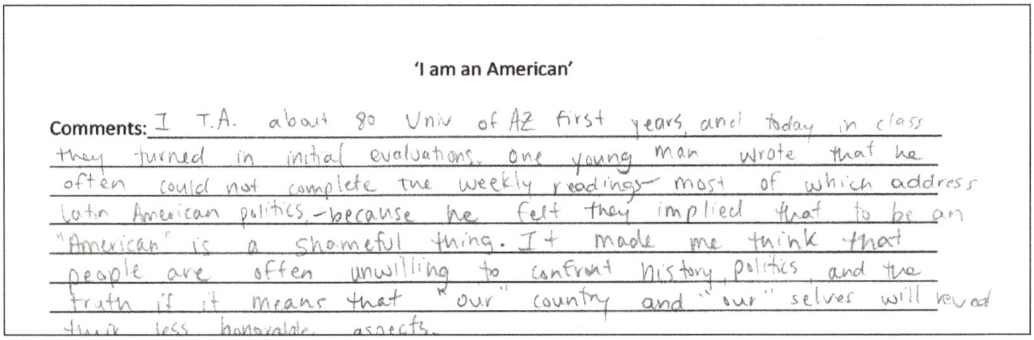
'I am an American'

Comments: I T.A. about 80 Univ of AZ first years, and today in class they turned in initial evaluations. One young man wrote that he often could not complete the weekly readings — most of which address Latin American politics, — because he felt they implied that to be an "American" is a shameful thing. It made me think that people are often unwilling to confront history, politics, and the truth if it means that "our" country and "our" selves will reveal their less honorable aspects.

Figure 86: Anonymous comment.

Notes

1. http://www.themuster.com/. Downloaded 3 January 2007.
2. http://www.youtube.com/watch?v=SBgDNlNLxzY. Downloaded 12 February 2006.

Chapter 4

Collateral Damage

Featuring Brandon Mayfield, Abe Dabdoub, Julia Shearson, Greg Avery, Glenda Avery, Will Potter, Steve Kurtz

I don't fit

Tucson, Arizona: I'm on the telephone with Brandon Mayfield, explaining my project and asking him to be a part of it. Brandon is the US citizen who the FBI suspected of being involved in the March 11, 2004 Madrid train bombings. Their evidence was a '100 per cent verified' exact match of Brandon's fingerprint with a print found on the bomb's trigger. On this evidence, Brandon was detained without charge for two weeks. When Brandon produced his passport that showed he was not in Spain but in the US during the bombings and indeed had not left the US for over a decade, the FBI considered charging him with falsifying documents because they did not/could not believe Brandon's alibi was genuine. It was only when the fingerprint led the Spanish police – who from the beginning had told the FBI that the print on the trigger did not match Brandon's – to an Algerian member of an al-Qaeda cell in Spain that the case against Brandon was dropped.

It is difficult to comprehend how Brandon – a white, middle class attorney living in Portland, Oregon – got positively identified by the FBI as the Madrid bomber until we learn two extraneous facts about his life. One is that in 2003, Brandon represented Jeffery Leon Battle when Battle was referred to Brandon through the Oregon State Bar Association's Modest Means Program that matches attorneys who are willing to work for reduced rates with low-income clients. As it happens, Battle was one of the 'Portland Seven', a group of people living in the US who were convicted for attempting to aid the Taliban. Brandon did not represent Battle in the government's case against him but in the civil matter of a child custody dispute. The other extraneous fact of Brandon's life is that after he met his Egyptian wife, Brandon converted to Islam. Apparently, these two harmless and legal acts were enough to convince the FBI that Brandon was capable of mass murder.

Brandon kindly agrees to look at the few films I've rough cut so far, about Lupe Denogean, Phil McDowell, Chris Simcox, and Elvira Arellano. Brandon is very complimentary about the project, to the point that he helps me to recruit James Yee as a participant. But regarding his own participation, Brandon's gut feeling is, as he puts it, 'I don't fit'.

I have to agree with him. Brandon is not a soldier who fought in a foreign war or a civilian who publicly declared a position in the border and immigration wars. Rather, Brandon is a private citizen who was minding his own business in an uncontested region of the US when he was hit by something that should have completely passed him by. The military term for people like Brandon is collateral damage.

After another round of discussions, Brandon wishes me well but graciously declines to tell his story on film. As I regroup to consider who to approach next, what strikes me is how long my list of suitable candidates is.

Hello. This is Abe.

US/Canadian Border: It seems like such an absurd ritual. Abe Dabdoub is preparing to return home from a visit with his family. They live in Canada. He lives in the US. And so returning home means crossing the Canadian border back into the US. As a divorced father of two small boys who live in Canada with their mother, Abe makes this journey at least twice a month. And every time he is about to do so, he calls ahead to the US Border Agents stationed there.

'Hello. This is Abe. I'll be crossing in a couple of hours'.

'Ok, we'll get the paperwork ready'.

The paperwork the agents prepare is for any person they must stop and search every time that person crosses into the US. Abe is such a person. Abe has been stopped and searched so many times by the same agents at the same crossing that Abe and the agents have developed a system to speed up the detention process. Abe calls ahead, the agents prepare the paperwork, they detain Abe at the border for a couple of hours while they run the required checks, and then they release Abe who continues his journey home.

Abe tells me this whole ordeal is relatively new for him. Indeed, Abe had been crossing this border without incident since he was five years old. That's when Abe and his family emigrated from Saudi Arabia to Canada and became Canadian citizens. In the twenty-odd years between then and when the detentions began, Abe routinely crossed back and forth from Windsor on the Canadian side to Detroit on the US side without ever thinking about it. When Abe settled on the US side with his young family, he decided to make his life in the US and become a US citizen. That was in 2006. And that, ironically, is when Abe's troubles began.

Abe's experience seems to be the opposite of what a new US citizen would expect when crossing into their new nation. If anything, a new US citizen would likely expect that their new citizenship would enable them to pass more quickly through US border checkpoints. In Abe's case, it has meant being detained every time is re-enters the US, amounting to some 50-odd consecutive detentions to date.

Abe won't say that his detentions are the result of US profiling practices – because he is a Muslim, because he was born in Saudi Arabia, because he is in some way 'different' to other US citizens he sees passing freely across the US-Canadian border. Instead, he tells me how much he loves the US, how he embraces the country and its freedom, how he tries to explain to his two small sons what a great country the US is, in spite of the ordeal their father goes through every time he crosses into the US.

Figure 87: Abe Dabdoub leafing through a catalogue of his detentions by US Customs and Border Protection.

As we are talking, Abe reflects back on the immediate post-9/11 atmosphere in the US, on how his heart sank when he saw the Twin Towers collapse, and on how his often wordless interactions with US citizens at that time made him ask himself questions like 'Did I do something wrong just because of who I am?' and 'Was there something about my heritage that wasn't wanted anymore?' Abe said those question went away over the next five years, as 'the American people just welcomed me in for who I was'. But after he became a US citizen and his border detentions began, 'it made me start wondering again', Abe tells me. 'Is my kind wanted here? Did I do something wrong? And why am I being stopped so many times?'

Relocation, relocation, relocation

New Orleans, Louisiana: All Greg and Glenda Avery wanted to do was stay put. Both were born and raised in Louisiana, so they were accustomed to riding out hurricanes, even those as menacing as Katrina. What made Katrina different, though, was that it broke the levy, the barrier between the city and the Gulf of Mexico that kept New Orleans from sinking under

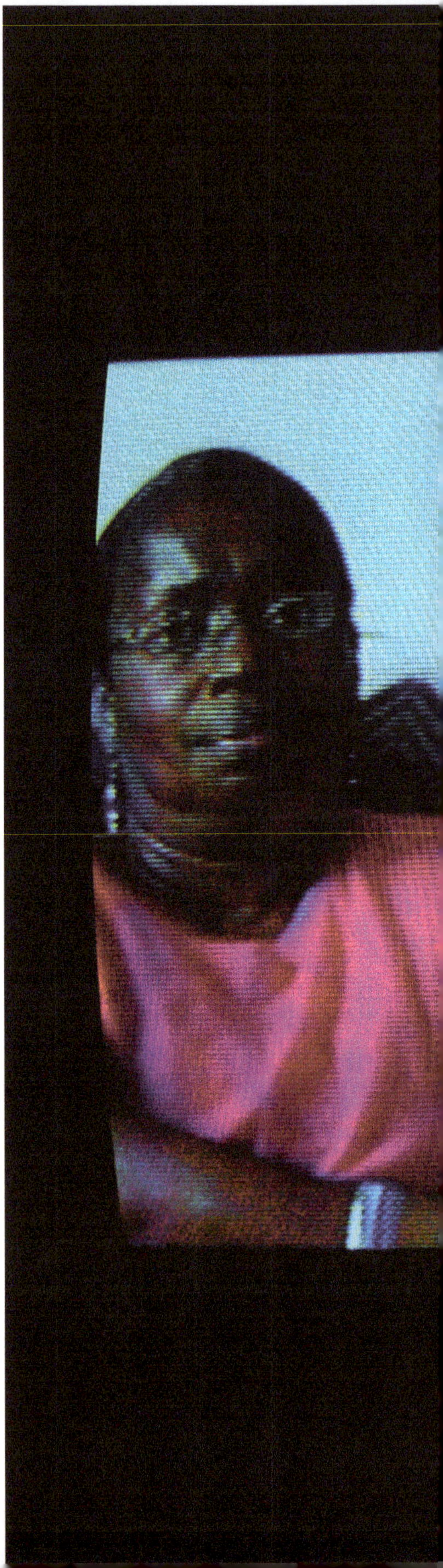

'We are Hurricane Katrina evacuees, and we are Americans.'

– Glenda and Greg Avery, New Orleans evacuees called 'refugees' by thir fellow US citizens.

Video Portraits of Post-9/11 US Citizens Series I by Cynthia Weber © Pato Productions 2008.

Previous Page – Figure 88: Greg and Glenda Avery.

water. The other thing that made Katrina different is that before and after the hurricane, rescue efforts for the city and its citizens did not seem to be a government priority. Whether this was because New Orleans voted Democrat and the Federal government of the day was Republican or because the city's population was largely African American and poor or because vital resources needed to secure the city in an emergency like National Guard troops were less available because so many had been redeployed to fight the War on Terror either in Afghanistan and Iraq or at the US border or for some other reason is unclear. What is clear is that these explanations and others circulated among US Americans who were trying to understand why so much went so wrong before, during, and after Hurricane Katrina.

When the levy broke, Greg and Glenda knew they had no other option than to evacuate. But because of a series of unforeseen circumstances, their evacuation plan fell through. So they moved themselves and their vulnerable neighbours into the top floors of a nearby schoolhouse, where they watched the floodwaters claim their streets and homes.

After several days, they were escorted by National Guard troops out of the building, thankfully not to the dreaded Superdome where overcrowding and disarray made for another

Figure 89: Little girl on ninth ward rooftop after Hurricane Katrina. Photo by Greg Avery.

kind of disaster but to the now nearly empty New Orleans Conference Center. From there, they waited for a flight out of the city. When they finally boarded a plane, they had no idea where they were bound for, as states and towns across the US were actively negotiating and renegotiating with the city and the federal government just how many Katrina evacuees they were willing to accept. In flight, the captain announced they were going to West Virginia. Upon arrival, Greg and Glenda spent about a month in a relocation camp before being permanently transferred to Morgantown, West Virginia.

While they rave about the kindness of the West Virginians who are still helping them settle in, Greg and Glenda are disillusioned with the government agencies that pledged to ease their transition. Promised loans either never materialized or came too late, promised housing assistance was cut to one third of what was publically announced, and new jobs in this new town just never materialized. And so, a few years after Katrina, Greg and Glenda are still unstable. Unable to return to their ninth ward neighbourhood where they were gainfully employed and enjoyed a comfortable life, they describe for me their new life in which they are chronically unemployed and constantly hounded by creditors.

Talking about Hurricane Katrina, Greg tells me, 'I don't know if any nation or community would have been prepared for it. But the problem is there are a lot of long-term effects that we're trying to deal with that are a result not just from the disaster but from the lack of response to the disaster in a timely manner'.

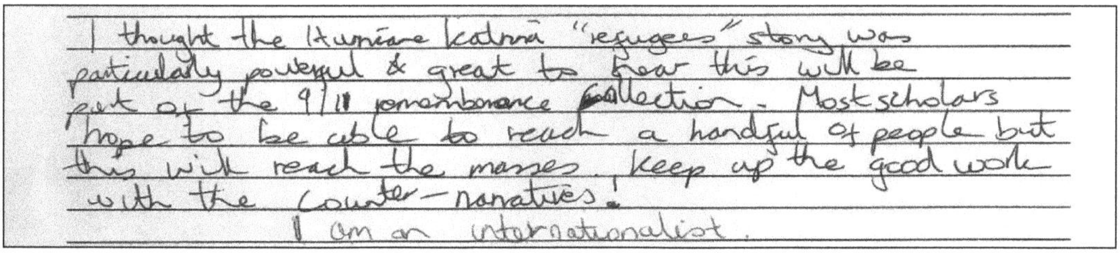
I thought the Hurricane Katrina "refugees" story was particularly powerful & great to hear this will be part of the 9/11 remembrance collection. Most scholars hope to be able to reach a handful of people but this will reach the masses. Keep up the good work with the counter-narratives! I am an internationalist.

Figure 90: Anonymous comment.

Armed and dangerous

Peace Bridge, US-Canadian Border: US citizen Julia Shearson and her four and a half-year-old daughter are returning from a weekend vacation to Canada. Julia passes without incident out of Canada across the Peace Bridge linking the two nations. But on the US side of the bridge, Julia experiences a most unexpected complication. When the US Immigration agent scans her passport, the agent's computer console displays the words 'armed and dangerous'. Alarms sound, the agent demands Julia's car keys, and Julia is led away in handcuffs and held for two and a half hours while checks are run, her car is searched, and she is interrogated.

Julia tells me that when the agents 'paraded me across twelve lanes of traffic, I just remember seeing these pickup trucks going through and thinking "Oh, yea. I used to be one of those ordinary white Americans that nobody paid any attention to, and now I'm something else"'. Indeed, Julia is a rather extraordinary white US American, whose ancestors sailed over on the Mayflower and fought in every major US war in US history and who herself graduated from both Harvard and Colombia Universities. And as an adult, Julia exercised one of the freedoms that the US nation was founded to preserve – the freedom of religion. She did this by converting from Catholicism to Islam. Julia's conversion had nothing to do with September 11 or the War on Terror but rather with the calling she felt to be a Muslim. But what it meant to be a US American Muslim changed for her on that day at the US border.

She tells me, 'When I saw another Muslim woman [who was also detained at the US-Canadian border] I thought, "You know they're doing this to me because I'm a Muslim"'.

As it turns out, Julia was neither armed nor dangerous, and so the US Immigration agents let her go. But this disturbing incident stuck with her. She wanted to know why it happened.

Figure 91: Julia Shearson with her Freedom of Information request documents.

When her Congressman could not help her, Julia filed a Freedom of Information Act request about her detention at the border. When months later she received the documents, 'they looked like Swiss cheese but only with black holes' as so much information was blacked out. But a phrase that wasn't blacked out said 'pertaining to terrorism' and was accompanied by sets of numbers that suggested Julia Shearson's name was on one or more Terrorist Watch List.

This could not have disturbed Julia more, for Julia's job as the Executive Director of the Cleveland, Ohio branch of the Council on American-Islamic Relations (CAIR) means she is 'helping to advocate for the Muslim American community, helping to defend the US constitution and a right to be free from illegal, unwarranted search and seizures and the right to practice our religious faith under the first amendment'.

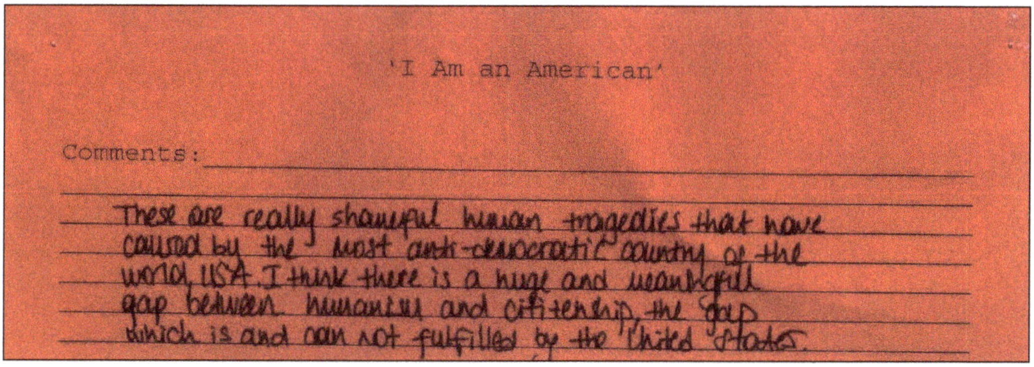

'I Am an American'

Comments: These are really shamefful human tragedies that have caused by the most anti-democratic country of the world, USA. I think there is a huge and meaningfull gap between humanity and citizenship, the gap which is and can not fulfilled by the United States.

Figure 92: Anonymous comment.

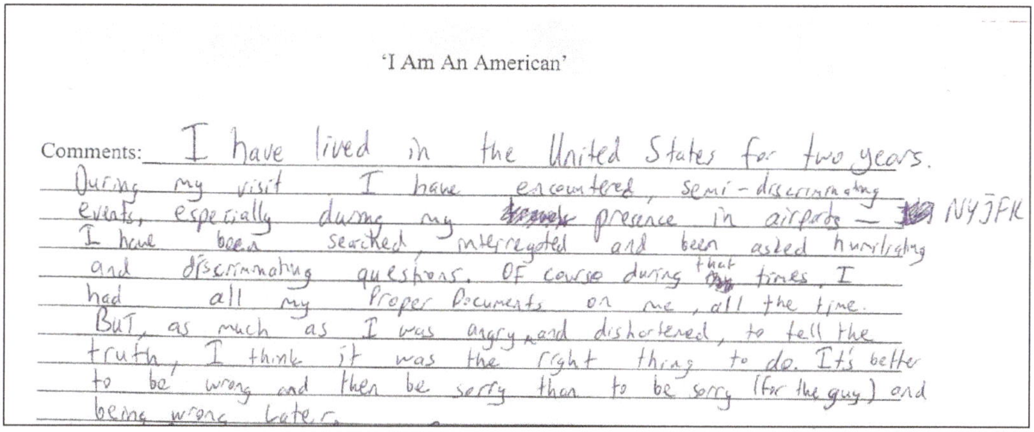

'I Am An American'

Comments: I have lived in the United States for two years. During my visit I have encountered, semi-discriminating events, especially during my presence in airports — NY JFK I have been searched, interregated and been asked humiliating and discriminating questions. Of course during that times, I had all my Proper Documents on me, all the time. BUT, as much as I was angry and dishortened, to tell the truth, I think it was the right thing to do. It's better to be wrong and then be sorry than to be sorry (for the guy) and being wrong later.

Figure 93: Anonymous comment.

'I understand people's fear post-9/11. I sympathize with that,' Julia tells me. 'We all have to be patient now. But patient I think doesn't mean being handcuffed as a law-bidding American citizen'.

'The government must be made to explain why this happened', Julia tells me. And this is why Julia is suing the government under the Freedom of Information Act and the Privacy Act to make them give her an account of what happened to her and her daughter on that day.

'I just want the government to give me back my good name. It does not belong on a watchlist because I'm not a threat to this country'.

Green is the New Red

Washington, DC: It's a blistery winter day in the nation's capital. So I'm pleased that today, unlike yesterday, independent journalist Will Potter and I will be shooting indoors. We meet up at his home and set up in the backroom that serves as his office. This is Will's journalistic base for his investigations of how environmental and animal rights activists are increasingly being labelled 'eco-terrorists' and 'domestic terrorists' by the US government.

Will explains that these groups have never harmed another human being. He tells me, 'They haven't flown planes into buildings. They haven't mailed anthrax through the mail. They haven't taken hostages or blown up an open air market. They haven't done anything most people think of as terrorism. At the most extreme, they set fire to empty buildings as economic sabotage. But these groups are being singled out as the number one domestic terrorism threat'.

I try to make sense of what Will is telling me, but it's difficult. Why go after environmentalists and animal rights activists who mostly take part in legal protests and who, when they do engage in illegal activities, are prosecuted for these crimes under existing US law? Surely, this can't be a US government priority during the War on Terror?

Will explains that one reason these groups have been singled out is because they target corporate property and profits, making them potentially destabilizing to the US economy. But Will believes the main reason these groups are being pursued isn't because of the actual damage they do but because of their political beliefs.

To make sense of this for me, Will explains that this isn't the first time in US history when groups have been targeted because of their political beliefs, even when they weren't doing much actual harm to the nation. His example is the 'red scare' of the McCarthy era, when suspected US communists were hauled before Congressional committees, blacklisted from work opportunities, and generally shunned in the US as internal enemies of the state.

McCarthy era tactics worked by 'relentlessly branding and demonizing people as communists, using that one word over and over again until it makes everyday people afraid to be associated with anyone labelled a communist. Now we've just changed words,' says Will. 'Instead of being a communist, they're labelling people as a terrorist, and they're making everyday people afraid of being associated with anyone being labelled a terrorist'.

But by calling people in the green movement 'terrorists', Will suggests that what is also happening is the government is 'making everyday people afraid that if they have controversial beliefs and they do non-violent civil disobedience, or if they are out leafleting or are out protesting, that they can be spied upon, that they can get an FBI visit, that there's new legislation that's gonna be passed to target them'.

Will sums it up like this, 'Green is the new red'.

This 'green scare' as Will calls it is something he insists should be of concern to all US Americans, regardless of their politics. As he explains, 'The reason every American needs to be very concerned is that when you give the government power to single out one group of people because of their political beliefs, they're not gonna stop with that one group. They've never stopped with one group in any government, in any era of history throughout the world. They always start with the most marginal, what is perceived as extreme, and go from one group to the next picking off dissenting viewpoints'.

For Will, this is 'really antithetical to everything this country is supposed to be about. Freedom is only worthwhile if you have the freedom to say something different, to say

Figure 94: Journalist Will Potter at work.

something controversial, to say something that really pisses people off and gets them upset and challenges the basic core assumptions of what it is to be a human being and what it is to live in this country. And I think that's what these activists are doing'.

'I Am An American'

Comments: After 9/11, Americans felt their security is under threat by Islamic fundamentalist terrorist attacks, but that film also shows that even US citizens are not safe from internal threats caused by their own gov't. That film was very useful for me to anticipate that nationalist aspirations that are produced by American decision-makers and foreign policy makers are only valid overseas, not at home. Why does a country forget its own citizens just to guarantee that they are secure a hundred percent, as a response to that question, the movie gives various explanations or reasons to get people to understand why US citizens face discriminations in their own country regardless of the original countries they came from or irrespective of their backgrounds, their occupations, social movements, religious orientations, etc. Lastly, i want to congratulate U for that great movie

Figure 95: Anonymous comment.

The death of Hope

Buffalo, New York: On May 11, 2004, Steve Kurtz woke up to a nightmare. Hope, his wife of more than 20 years, had died of congenital heart failure during the night. She was 45 years old. Steve called 911 to report Hope's death. When police arrived, they became concerned when they found a small biological laboratory and petri dishes containing harmless biological specimens in the house. Steve explained that he was an artist and a professor of visual studies who specialized in the intersection of art and science. The lab and the biological agents were part of his art practice, the results of which had been exhibited in internationally renowned museums for more than a decade.

Steve tells me that, given his work, he expected the police would understand how ordinary it was for him to have a science lab at home. But the police didn't see it that way. To put them at ease, Steve dipped his finger into one of the petri dishes, scooped up some of the biological agent, and ate it. But the police were not reassured. 'They were deeply, deeply suspicious, and I think were fairly convinced I had killed my wife somehow. And so it was a very long afternoon not just of being in shock but of being interrogated while being in a state of shock'. By the end of the interview, the police alerted the FBI.

The next day, as he was on his way to the funeral home to make arrangements for Hope's burial, Steve was detained by the FBI not only on suspicion of murdering Hope but also on the additional suspicion of bioterrorism.

'They confiscated my house, they confiscated my car, they confiscated all of my assets, they confiscated my lab – pretty much everything I had. I was left on the street with my cell phone and my wallet', Steve tells me.

While Steve was in custody, ATF and FBI agents in Hazardous Materials Suits raided his home as the whole thing was broadcast on network television. 'It was all political theater, and I suspect a training exercise', says Steve. 'It was all part of Bush's theater of fear – how you get the public pumped up and scared that there are people out there to get them'.

'I was sleeping on couches and rollaway beds [at friend's homes] while waiting for the FBI to decide on what the fate of my home would be, even on what the fate of my cat would be, which they also confiscated upon hearing that I was also putting germs in it and poisoning the neighbors with it'. At this point Steve finds the whole thing so bizarre, even he is laughing. 'The kind of paranoid scenarios they can come up with – no fantasy is too great'.

Even though FBI lab tests proved that the biological agents in Steve's home were harmless and even though the several autopsies performed on Hope's body – including those by the

Figure 96: Federal Agents search home of Steve Kurtz. Photo provided by Critical Art Ensemble.

FBI – concluded Hope died of natural causes, the government still pursued its case against Steve. In light of the autopsy evidence, there was no case for murder, but the government still went forward with its bioterrorism charge.

A Grand Jury refused to indict Steve on bioterrorism but did indict him on mail fraud and wire fraud. These charges pertained to how Steve had acquired the biological agents used in his art practice, which was by following the same standard procedure he and countless other scientists and academics have used for years – ordering the biological agents via mail order and confirming the reception of the transaction by email. As Steve explains, 'Mail fraud is one of the most broadly written laws on the books. Generally, it's used by the Department of Justice when they want to put someone away and they just don't have anything else'.

Although the details of Steve's case are complicated, two facts are clear and simple. One is that under the US Patriot Act, the maximum penalty for mail fraud rose from 5 years to 20 years, meaning that Steve was looking at some 'very serious hard time' if convicted. The other is that had the US government won its cases against Steve, the case would have eroded the distinction between civil law and criminal law. That would have allowed the government to prosecute civil cases (disputes between individuals over crimes that harm one of the parties in the case) as criminal cases (disputes between individuals and the government over crimes of such a serious nature that they harm the general public).

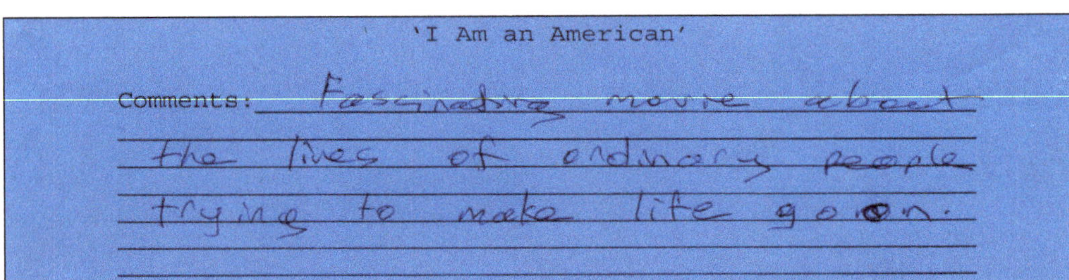
'I Am an American'

Comments: Fascinating movie about the lives of ordinary people trying to make life go on.

Figure 97: Anonymous comment.

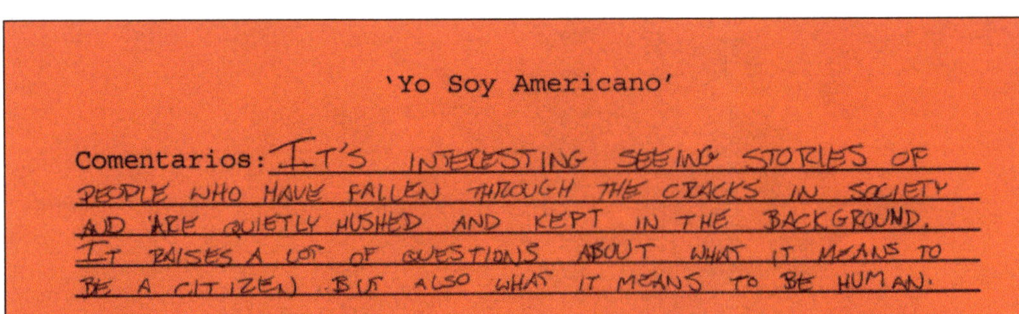
'Yo Soy Americano'

Comentarios: IT'S INTERESTING SEEING STORIES OF PEOPLE WHO HAVE FALLEN THROUGH THE CRACKS IN SOCIETY AND ARE QUIETLY HUSHED AND KEPT IN THE BACKGROUND. IT RAISES A LOT OF QUESTIONS ABOUT WHAT IT MEANS TO BE A CITIZEN BUT ALSO WHAT IT MEANS TO BE HUMAN.

Figure 98: Anonymous comment.

The government pursued its case against Steve for four years, until a federal judge finally ruled that the case had no merit.

'This all happily got thrown out,' Steve says. 'And when it did, it made for a very clear wall. The Justice Department does not get to pick and choose what is criminal and what is civil. If they had gotten to do that, God help us what may have followed from that!'

Asylum seekers

Morgantown, West Virginia: Glenda Avery is explaining to me the sort of subtle discrimination she and her husband Greg have been experiencing since they became Hurricane Katrina evacuees.

'I know we're African American, so we're used to prejudice,' Glenda tells me. 'But now we're being called refugees'. She pauses, clearly upset, then continues, 'To experience being called a refugee first hand was a bit much'.

Greg explains it was bad enough when they heard it through the media, 'but when we came face-to-face with that offense, it was a different story'.

'And the first time,' Glenda explains, 'I just smiled kindly and nodded my head because I just realized that it could have been ignorance of certain facts. But the second time was deliberate. It was like, "Didn't you hear me, *REF-U-GEE*?"'

Figure 99: 'Asylum Seekers' Greg and Glenda Avery.

Since these first experiences, Greg and Glenda have developed a response. They give a flyer to the offending party. On the flyer is the definition of the word 'refugee'.

'Refugee,' Glenda reads from one of these. 'It's a person who seeks shelter, especially in another country, from war, disaster, or persecution'. She continues, 'If the person is already in the United States, he or she may apply for the US asylum program'.

Glenda looks up at Greg, who is standing next to her. 'So, do we apply?'

'For asylum,' Greg asks smiling.

Glenda's now laughing. 'Are we eligible for asylum?'

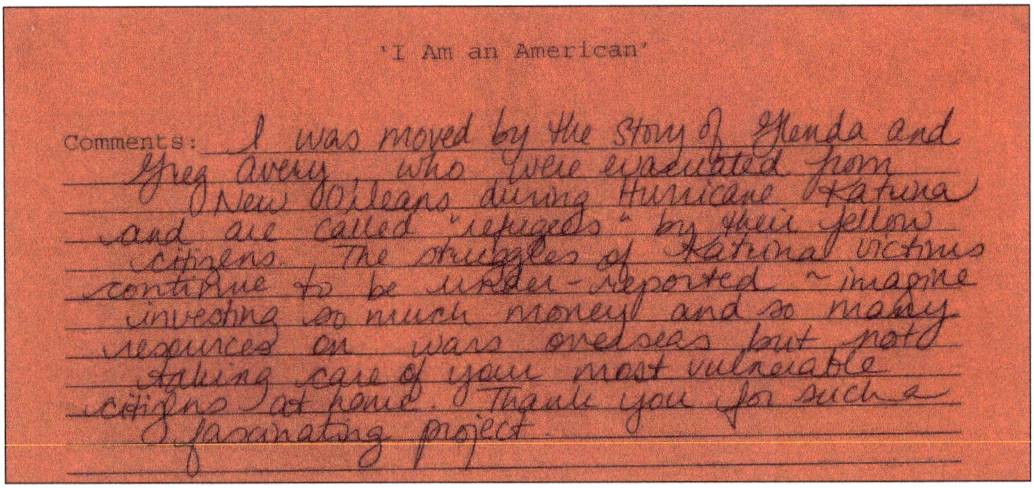

'I Am an American'

Comments: I was moved by the story of Glenda and Greg Avery, who were evacuated from New Orleans during Hurricane Katrina and are called "refugees" by their fellow citizens. The struggles of Katrina victims continue to be under-reported ~ imagine investing so much money and so many resources on wars overseas but not taking care of your most vulnerable citizens at home. Thank you for such a fascinating project.

Figure 100: Anonymous comment.

Mr Potter goes to Washington

Washington, DC: Will Potter is testifying before a Congressional Committee that is considering the passage of the Animal Enterprise Terrorism Act. This Act would grant US law enforcement officials greater powers in combating illegal activities by animal rights activists by expanding the realm of illegal activities 'to include protests, boycotts, undercover investigations, whistle blowing, and non-violent civil disobedience'.

Will explains that legislation already exists that guarantees the surveillance, arrest and conviction of those individuals and groups who are involved in illegal animal rights activities. But he cautions the Committee that the bill under consideration does something more. He tells them, 'The bill criminalizes any activity against an animal enterprise or any company tangential to an animal enterprise that causes damage, defined as including the loss of profits'.

'That's not terrorism,' Will insists. 'That's effective activism'.

Figure 101: Will Potter testifies before Congress. Still image from footage provided by Will Potter.

The secret lab

Buffalo, New York: Among the things that made US law enforcement officials suspicious of Steve Kurtz and his collection of harmless bacteria used in his professional art practice was the fact that Steve's house contains a 'secret lab'. This secret lab is not hidden away in a private part of Steve's house under lock and key. Rather, the secret lab is located in the hallway of the second story of Steve's house. It is the first thing you see when you climb the stairs.

Commenting on the absurdity of the FBI's description of his lab as secret, Steve tells me, 'This is not some secret lab. If it was, why would it be right in front of a big bay window?' I look out the window behind the secret lab. It looks right into the window of a house some 10 feet away, meaning that Steve's lab is and always has been on public display.

I ask Steve if he thinks I could get into the house next door to shoot Steve through the window working at his secret lab. Steve is sure this can be arranged, for he tells me, 'When I was detained, my neighbour put a sign on his lawn that said, "He's not a terrorist. He's my neighbor"'.

Figure 102: Steve Kurtz at work in his secret lab.

Electronic Manzanar

Cleveland, Ohio: Julia Shearson is rattling off the names of all of the US governmental electronic surveillance security lists she believes she is on.

'I'm on at least three watch lists. I'm on the Terrorist Screening Center watch list. I'm on the TIDE list, the Terrorist Identity Watch Data Mart Environment list. And I'm on the VGTOF list, the Violent Gang and Organization File list'.

She names so many more lists that she might also be on that my head is now spinning.

'The government post-9/11 has become addicted to lists', she tells me. 'Everyone wants security', she says, 'but keeping secret lists made by secret agents with secret information to which there appears to be no redress or no avenue to get off the list…' Julia is exasperated. 'It's so crazy. It's just so crazy'.

What else is crazy to Julia is that so many American Muslims are on these watch lists. 'I just think that there are better ways to keep our country safe than to put all of the Muslim community on the watch list. It's not right. It's not an effective national security practice, either'.

Julia tells me that how American Muslims are being treated in the post-9/11 US reminds her of how Japanese Americans were interned in camps during World War II because the US government feared these US citizens might have stronger allegiances to US enemies than to the US state. One of the most famous internment camps was in Manzanar, California.

Figure 103: Manzanar internment camp, US government photo.

Figure 104: Japanese Americans interned in Manzanar, California, US government photo.

As Julia speaks, I flash on those disturbing scenes in the film *The Siege* (Edward Zwick, 1998) which spectacularly imagine the transformation of parts of New York City into a 'Muslim Manzanar' where US Muslims are interned. I wonder if Julia is recalling these same images. But as she keeps speaking, I realize what Julia has in mind is even more sinister because it is invisible, untraceable, deniable.

She explains, 'The American Muslims have not been put in a physical camp, but we've been put in a kind of web of electronic surveillance that makes me feel like I'm in an "electronic Manzanar" – that's what I call it. And the thing about it is that you don't know you're in it because it's electronic'.

'Maybe it's better to put us in camps,' Julia wonders. 'It least we'd know we were in camps [because] this way we think everything's OK'.

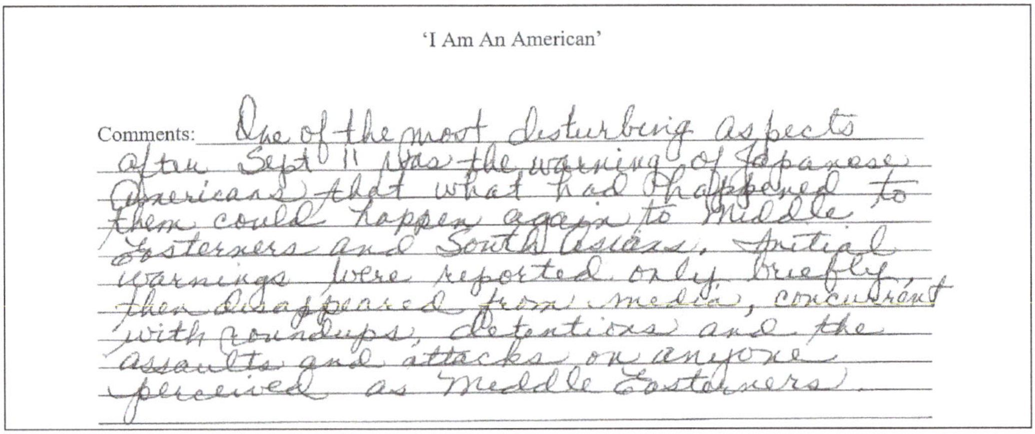
'I Am An American'

Comments: One of the most disturbing aspects after Sept 11 was the warning of Japanese Americans that what had happened to them could happen again to Middle Easterners and South Asians. Initial warnings were reported only briefly, then disappeared from media, concurrent with roundups, detentions and the assaults and attacks on anyone perceived as Middle Easterners.

Figure 105: Anonymous comment.

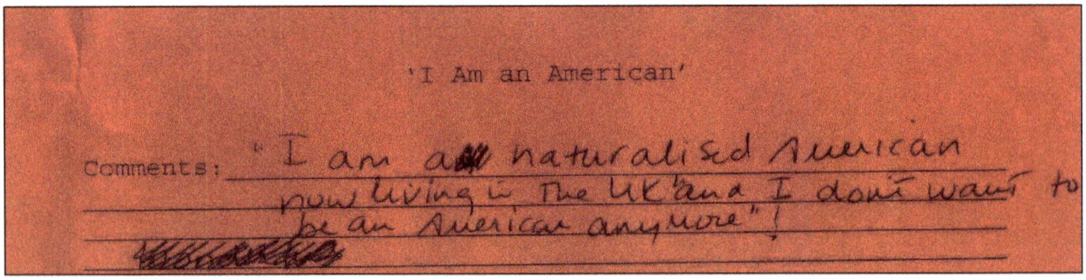
'I Am an American'

Comments: "I am an naturalised American now living in The UK and I don't want to be an American anymore"!

Figure 106: Anonymous comment.

Weighing up an image

Aurora, Ohio: Abe Dabdoub and I are choreographing his flag shot. Abe stands in his living room facing the camera. One of his hands is draped with a long US flag held at head height. The other is draped with an even longer spreadsheet that lists all of his detentions so far by US Border Officials since he became a US citizen. This list is held just above his waist.

What the image says depends upon how each viewer decides to read it. At least three readings are possible.

The first reading focuses on the objects in Abe's hands. It suggests that the promise of liberty, justice, and equality before the law (symbolized by the US flag) on the one hand and the realities of US power (symbolized by the list of Abe's detentions) on the other have been the twin facts of Abe's life since he became a US citizen.

The second reading focuses on how Abe holds each object. This reading suggests that because the US flag is respectfully held higher than the list, it and its promises of liberty, justice and equality before the law are more valued by and more valuable to Abe than the seemingly misplaced expressions of US power as they are applied to detain Abe for no apparent reason.

The final reading focuses on how Abe's body acts in relation to the objects it holds, not just as the individual Abe Dabdoub who became a US citizen and seemingly as a result has been detained by US Border Officials some fifty times in less than three years but as a third object in the picture. For by holding one object higher than the other, Abe's body itself can be read as a weighing scale determining the relative weight and value of the two objects it balances. And because Abe's body is weighing US promises against US power, his body is not just any scale but a version of the iconic scales of justice. A 'scales of justice' reading suggests that because Abe holds the US flag higher than the list of his detentions, US power is tipping the scales of US justice in the wrong direction, away from liberty, justice and equality for all.

The image does not direct its viewer as to which reading to select. Nor does it require the viewer to make a selection, as all three readings can be held by one viewer at the same time. Instead, all the image offers by way of direction is Abe's brief bio and his 'I am an American' line. This line reads, 'I am routinely detained, and I am a new and proud American'.

Next Page – Figure 107: Abe Dabdoub's flag shot.

'I am routinely detained, and I am a new and proud American.'

– Abe Dabdoub, detained more than 50 times since becoming a US citizen in 2006 as he returned to the US from visiting family in Canada, pictured holding a spreadsheet that documents his detentions.

Video Portraits of Post-9/11 US Citizens Series I by Cynthia Weber © Pato Productions 2009.

'I am not going to quietly watch history repeat itself, and I am an American.'

– Will Potter, independent journalist reporting on how McCarthy-era anti-communist 'Red Scare' tactics are deployed post-9/11 to create a 'Green Scare' by branding environmental activists 'eco-terrorists.'

Video Portraits of Post-9/11 US Citizens Series I by Cynthia Weber © Pato Productions 2009.

Previous Page – Figure 108: Will Potter's flag shot.

Reading a background through a foreground

Washington, DC: It's intimidating to try to stage a flag shot in Washington, DC, for everywhere I look I see displays of patriotism and nationalism and Americanism symbolized by the US flag. It's almost like DC is itself a big, bold flag, and everything that happens in this town is somehow overlaid upon this stately background. But of course, how we read this background depends very much on what lies on top of it. In DC, this could be either a purified ideal of Americanism expressed by the majestic monuments and government buildings lining Pennsylvania Avenue or a grittier image of Americanism expressed by the entrenched racial segregation and economic inequality found in this very same city.

It is this idea that is stirring somewhere around in my head as Will Potter and I work on his flag shot. After experimenting with several ideas, this is what we do. We hang a large US flag vertically, with its stars at the top, mimicking how I've seen the flag displayed on buildings throughout the city. Over this, we pin posters from Will's project 'Green is the New Red'. These show not only the logo from his website but also graphic, menacing images. One is of a face shrouded in a balaclava; another is two balaclavad figures placing their hands over the mouth of a woman who is struggling to speak. Jarring with their background both in content and in color, the effect of these overlaid images is to suggest that not all is well in America. This idea is reinforced by Will, who stands next to the flag with his arms folded in front of him, possibly suggesting he is fed-up with the usual ways that an ideal American background conceals a grittier American foreground.

He says his 'I am an American' line for the camera: 'I am not going to quietly watch history repeat itself, and I am an American'.

You can't be too careful these days

Buffalo, New York: Steve Kurtz is a late 40-something white male with long gray hair that sometimes hangs down around his shoulders and other times is neatly pulled back into a ponytail. He looks like an aging Arlo Guthrie. If you don't know what Arlo Guthrie looks like, think of the hippy scientist in the film *Independence Day* (Roland Emmerich, 1996) who works in the secret US military base Area 51 and whose classic line in the film is, 'They don't let us out much'.

Maybe it is because Steve's work as a public artist who re-enacts scientific experiments in internationally renowned art galleries gives him a flare for the dramatic or maybe it is because the spirits of his famous musical and filmic doppelgangers are somehow hovering in the ether as we film Steve's flag shot. But for whatever reason, Steve does not just give me a pose. He gives me a performance. And what a performance it is!

Seated in front of his 'secret lab' and in partial profile to the camera, Steve carefully pulls on a pair of latex gloves. On the table behind him are all sorts of lab equipment. In the middle of the table is a pipette rack, and among the objects it contains is a small US flag. Turning toward the flag, Steve wiggles his fingers like a B-movie scientist might before handling a dangerous yet exciting substance. With one gloved hand, Steve gingerly lifts the US flag by its wooden post. With his other gloved hand, he holds a corner of the cloth.

Turning around, Steve displays the flag in front of him saying, 'You can't be too careful these days. It's getting kinda toxic'.

Accidental citizens

Toronto, Canada: The benefits of citizenship are sometimes experienced in the most contradictory of ways. This is what Professor Peter Nyers is telling me, as we discuss the case of Yaser Hamdi. I would like to make a film about Hamdi, but I do not have access to him. And so I'm speaking to Professor Nyers to see if his narration of the Hamdi case might work as a substitute for Hamdi's narration itself.

Professor Nyers explains that Hamdi, a Saudi citizen, was in Afghanstan just after 9/11, where Hamdi claims he was doing humanitarian work but the US government claims Hamdi was supporting the Taliban. Hamdi was apprehended by the US military and taken to Guantanamo Bay, Cuba, as what the US government called 'an illegal enemy combatant' – someone who was fighting against the US but not as a conventional soldier. This new category of prisoner enabled the Bush administration to argue that Hamdi, like other illegal enemy combatants, was not a prisoner of war and therefore not entitled to the protections of the Geneva Convention.

Hamdi would likely have stayed at Guantanamo Bay indefinitely had a routine background check not revealed that Hamdi had been born in the US. According to US law, anyone born in the US automatically obtains birthright US citizenship. And so Yaser Hamdi was a dual US and Saudi citizen at the time of his detention, even though his US citizenship was accidental.

When the US government realized it had inadvertently detained one of its own citizens at Guantanamo Bay, it transferred Hamdi to a US military prison on US soil. As a result of this transfer, Hamdi's case became public, and a US lawyer volunteered to represent Hamdi to help him win his freedom.

Probably the most interesting thing about the case, Professor Nyers tells me, is that as Hamdi's case made its way through the US legal system, the US government offered Hamdi a deal. They would release him immediately if he agreed to several conditions. These included returning to Saudi Arabia, agreeing to restrictions on his international travel, and

Next Page – Figure 109: Steve Kurtz' flag shot.

'You can't be too careful these days. It's getting kinda toxic.'

– Steve Kurtz, artist detained on suspicion of bioterrorism and murder after he called 911 to report the death of his wife Hope and police found harmless biological materials used in his art practice in his home.

Video Portraits of Post-9/11 US Citizens Series I by Cynthia Weber © Pato Productions 2009.

renouncing his US citizenship. After several years in detention and an unknown outcome should he pursue his court case, Hamdi agreed to these conditions.

The irony of the case, Professor Nyers points out, is that it was only by renouncing his US citizenship that Hamdi received the full benefits of US citizenship.[1]

Citizenship

Morgantown, West Virginia: I have just asked my ultimate conversation stopper question – 'Has your experience made you reflect on your citizenship, on what it means to you to be a US citizen or on what US citizenship *should* mean?' I ask all of my interviewees this question. And while most of them have been interviewed countless times before, no one has ever asked them about their citizenship.

I've just put this question to Greg and Glenda Avery, two Hurricane Katrina evacuees from New Orleans. They don't answer it right away. Instead, we discuss the question literally for days. We consider the traditional definition of citizenship as being about rights and privileges given to us by our state and duties and obligations we owe our state in return. We reflect on how citizenship also affords us a sense of belonging, how it gives a sense of identity and identification to a state, a nation, a people – how US citizenship makes us feel 'American'. We run through as many types of citizenship as we can think of – legal, of course, but also cultural and consumer, social and sexual, racial and multicultural, birthright and accidental, cosmopolitan and metropolitan, safe and unsafe. Greg brings up democracy as the institutional context in which US citizenship is granted. I bring up citizenship as a practice – as less a neat definition that you'll read in a book than what nation-states and citizens do to define and redefine their relationship.

The citizenship question is the hardest question for my interviewees to answer because their citizenship is invisible to most of them. Citizenship is something most only think about when they apply for passports or travel abroad. It is not something they think about as they just go about their daily lives. It is only those people who do not have citizenship from the state they want it from (like 'unwanted immigrants') or those very rare people who do not have any citizenship (or, as in Ofelia's case, any proof of citizenship) who think about their citizenship regularly. For the rest of us, citizenship is just a stable fact of life we take for granted.

Greg and Glenda, though, are rooting through this concept, unpacking its intricacies and the contradictions that occur when citizenship is put into practice. It is as we consider how citizenship is meant to function within US society that Greg wonders if 'there is hypocrisy in our democracy'. He explains, 'You know, after 9/11 and Hurricane Katrina, you have groups of individuals who didn't get the American treatment that they were entitled to as a citizen of the United States. It was almost like individuals being treated like second-class citizens'. Greg is getting increasingly passionate about what he is saying. He continues, 'I just think we need to conduct our business differently, and it starts at home. We need to treat American citizens, no matter what race, creed or color, we all need to be treated fairly'.

Although he never claims it as one, I hear in Greg's remarks a definition of citizenship. Citizenship, according to Greg, is what is supposed to make our 'differences' invisible to our state and to our fellow citizens. What Greg is saying is what the US nation has been saying since its inception and what the American Ad Council has been reminding us of since 9/11, 'Out of Many, One'.

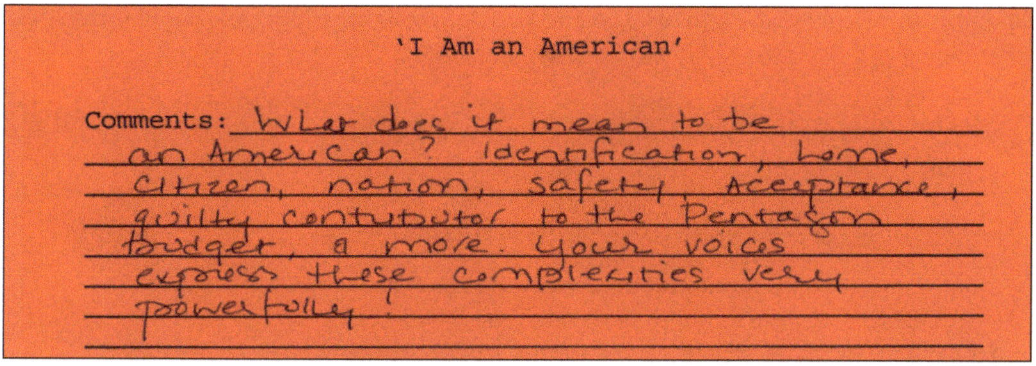
'I Am an American'

Comments: What does it mean to be an American? Identification, home, citizen, nation, safety, Acceptance, guilty contributor to the Pentagon budget, & more. Your voices express these complexities very powerfully!

Figure 110: Anonymous comment.

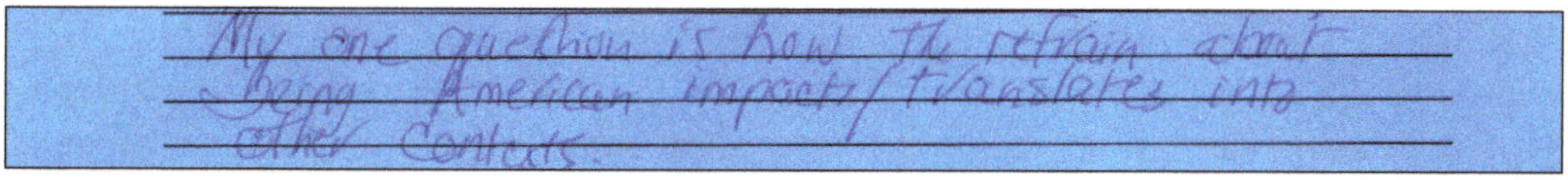
My one question is how the refrain about being American impacts/translates into other contexts.

Figure 111: Anonymous comment.

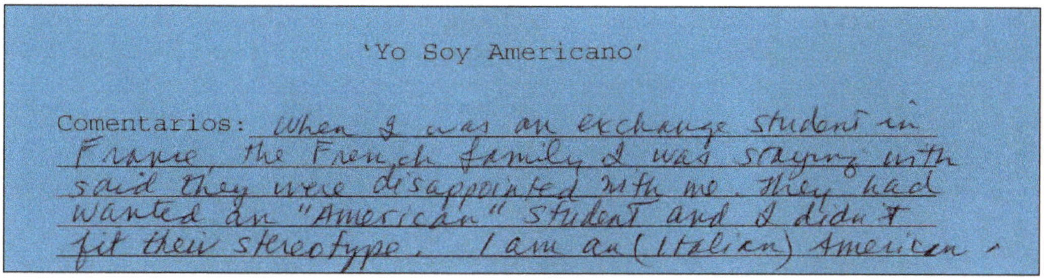
'Yo Soy Americano'

Comentarios: When I was an exchange student in France, the French family I was staying with said they were disappointed with me. They had wanted an "American" student and I didn't fit their stereotype. I am an (Italian) American.

Figure 112: Anonymous comment.

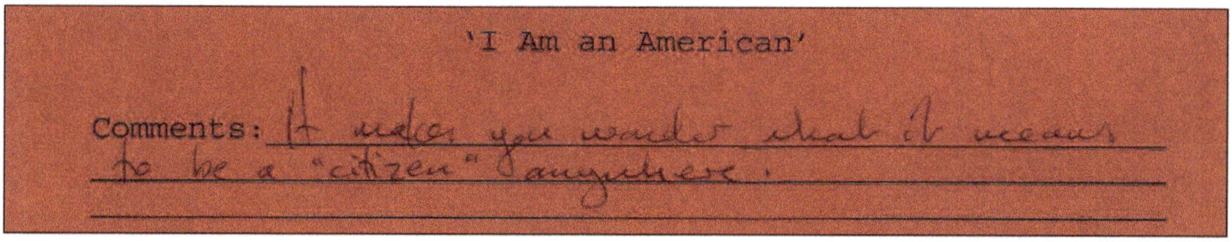
'I Am an American'

Comments: It makes you wonder what it means to be a "citizen" anywhere.

Figure 113: Anonymous comment.

From One, Many

http://www.youtube.com/watch?v=SPHSRniWdys: Even though I'm still filming, I've finished a few of my 'I am an American' films and published them on the Open Democracy website. Because I'm curious about how the films are being received, I check the comments page occasionally. There are all sorts of remarks there, from simply 'Good job' to 'God Bless America' to 'these films suck' to rants against the United States. One day, I find this exchange about how I end my films with a twist on the US Motto:

getalife768 (3 months ago) Reply 0

actually it is supposed to be "from many, one"

kathleeen1982 (3 months ago) Reply 0

actually, this is a response to the original Ad Council version,
where the line was 'out of many, one'. This version is
deliberately Ex unum, plurus, which means 'from one, many'.
If you think hard enough about it, you'll see why :)

This exchange makes me want to have a chat with kathleeen1982. I'm pleased she sees my reversal of the US motto from 'Out of Many, One' to 'Out of One, Many' as intentional, but I'm dying to know what she thinks my intentions are. Does she think I've reversed the motto because I believe that what the US motto has come to mean – that out of many different kinds of US Americans, we are one nation – is incorrect and that what was maybe always happening and definitely is happening in the post-9/11 US is that some particular kinds of different US Americans will not or cannot so easily melt into the ideal of the One? Does she think I'm going further than this with my reversal of the motto, to suggest that out of one US national ideal of The American Dream or of US citizenship, there are many unique experiences? Or does she think that the point of my reversal is not in the reversal of the motto itself as much as it is to show that the motto is reversible, the implications of which are to demonstrate that the US state, the US nation, and the US citizenry reserve for themselves the right to reverse their decisions about who is in the One and who is excluded

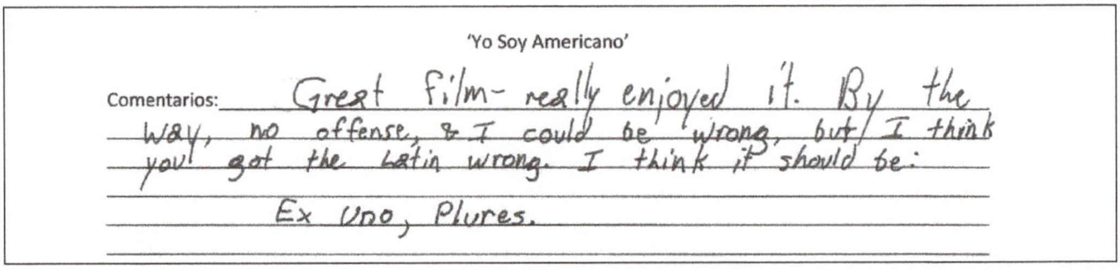
'Yo Soy Americano'

Comentarios: Great film- really enjoyed it. By the way, no offense, & I could be wrong, but I think you got the Latin wrong. I think it should be:
Ex Uno, Plures.

Figure 114: Anonymous comment.

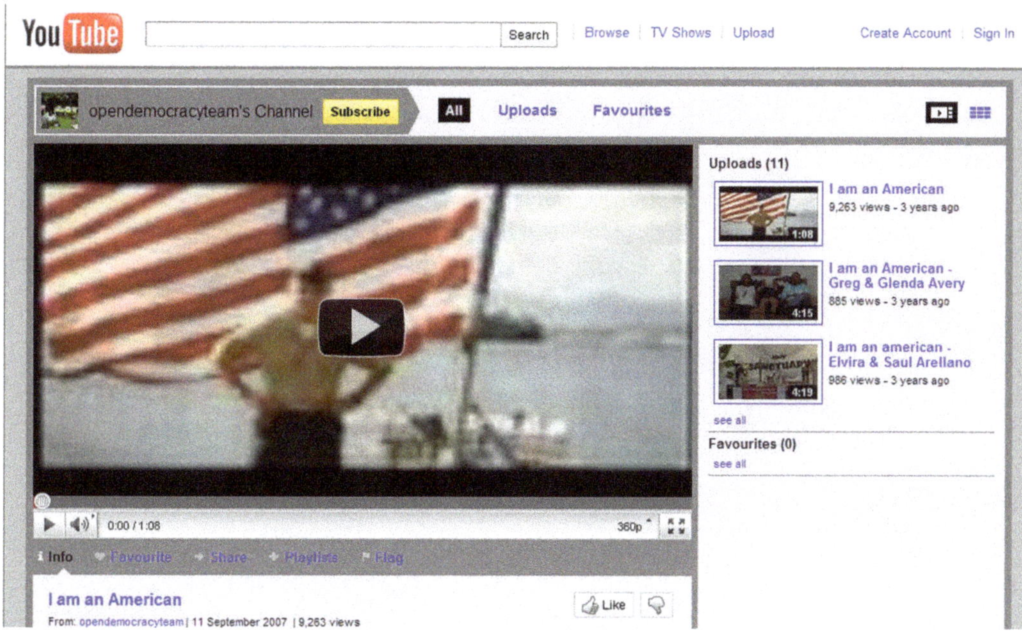

Figure 115: Films on OpenDemocracy.net.

from the One at any time in order to make The One seem to function as The One? Does she recognize how this kind of reversibility suggests that Liberalism and the Liberal promise of tolerance is itself reversible? I have no idea what katheeen1982 thinks about any of this. But I do appreciate her thoughtfulness in taking on what another viewer perceived as a mistake.

Sometime later, a different patron leaves a comment card after a screening that focuses on the very same line in the film. They have identified an unintended mistake in my Latin. The line shouldn't be 'Ex Unum, Plurus'; it should be 'Ex Uno, Plures'. I immediately make the necessary correction, appreciative of this help and also pleased that my bad Latin didn't keep earlier viewers from debating my point.

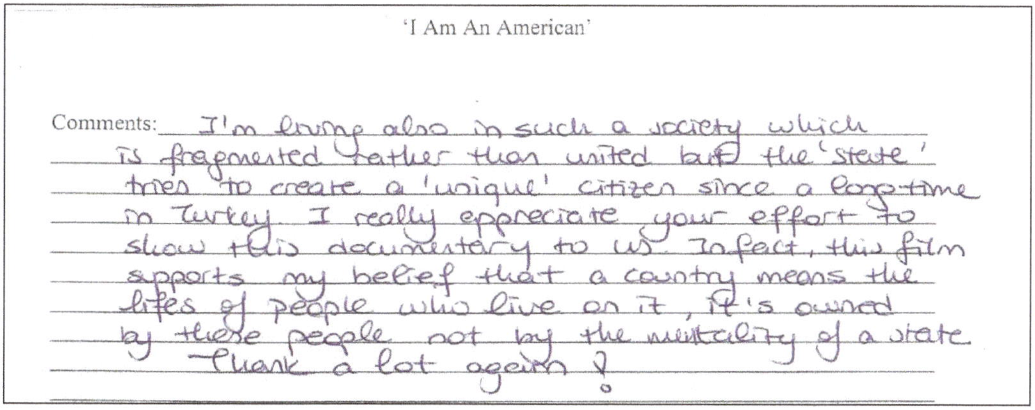
'I Am An American'

Comments: I'm living also in such a society which is fragmented rather than united but the 'state' tries to create a 'unique' citizen since a long-time in Turkey. I really appreciate your effort to show this documentary to us. In fact, this film supports my belief that a country means the lifes of people who live on it, it's owned by these people not by the mentality of a state. Thank a lot again!

Figure 116: Anonymous comment.

'I am number 384610 on the Terrorist Watch List, and I am an American.'

– Julia Shearson, Executive Director of the Cleveland, Ohio, office of the Council on American–Islamic Relations, who is suing the US government to be removed from the Terrorist Watch List.

Video Portraits of Post-9/11 US Citizens Series I by Cynthia Weber © Pato Productions 2009.

FOIA
CASE LAW

Previous Page - Figure 117: Julia Shearson's flag shot.

Number 384610

Cleveland, Ohio: It looks like she's building a fortress out of blue plastic crates. But what Julia Shearson is really doing is piling onto her desk the many boxes, folders and manuals she has amassed in her multi-year fight with the US government to get herself and her daughter removed from terrorist watchlists.

'This is Shearson vs The Department of Homeland Security,' she says indicating a box full of folders. 'This is case law. This is the media file. This is my civil litigation,' she explains as she lifts each pile into place. 'This one I can hardly pick up'.

Even though Julia has no formal training in the law, she is fighting this case herself. This means that all of her legal materials are right here in her office. And so box after box finds its way onto her desk until some of the stacks are taller than she is.

We decide to shoot Julia's flag shot with Julia standing behind this heap. What we soon realize is that if Julia continues to load her desk with litigation materials, this 5' 2" woman will be so barricaded by boxes that the camera will not be able to find her. And so Julia stops adding boxes, and I move a few out of the way. Julia stands behind her desk, but the boxes still obscure her. By this time, we are both too tired to rearrange these heavy materials again, so we transfer some documents to the floor, making an impromptu platform for Julia to stand on. Finally, Julia is in clear view.

Fortified by case law and case filings and litigation manuals, an exhausted Julia rests her elbow on the stack beside her and uses this arm to prop up her head. Nestled with her amongst the material evidence of her legal struggle is the symbolic evidence of what Julia is fighting for – a small US flag signifying to Julia the constitutional principles of freedom and privacy that she believes will one day get her and her daughter off the watchlists. But that day, should it ever arrive, is not today. And so this is what Julia chooses as her 'I am an American' line: 'I am number 384610 on the Terrorist Watch List, and I am an American'.

Necessary props

Ice House Gallery, Phoenix, Arizona: Deidra, a young white woman with a thick Arkansas accent, volunteers to do an on-camera 'I am an American' statement. This is an option open to all gallery patrons as a way of incorporating more US American voices, stories, and images into the project. I explain to Deidra that these short clips might become part of future films and shows. She gives her permission.

As I fuss with my camera and Deidra fumbles with the clip-on mic, I remember to tell her that she has the option of using the US flag in her shot. 'I'll take it,' she says as she reaches for the flag. Joking, she adds, 'If I don't take it, I'll be like Obama. I won't be American enough'.

Figure 118: Cynthia Weber films Deidra's flag shot. Photo by Christy Putz.

Deidra is referring to how some US citizens interpreted Barack Obama's decision to break with tradition and stop wearing a US flag pin on his lapel while he was a Senator because he claimed that after 9/11, such displays of the US flag 'became a substitute for [...] true patriotism, which is speaking out on issues that are of importance to our national security'. He continued, 'I decided I won't wear that pin on my chest; instead, I'm gonna try to tell the

Treated as a second-class citizen in Turkey because I wear a head scarf. I understand the need for these people to say that 'they' are american too and they don't have to 'fit in' to get their rights as citizens.

Figure 119: Anonymous comment.

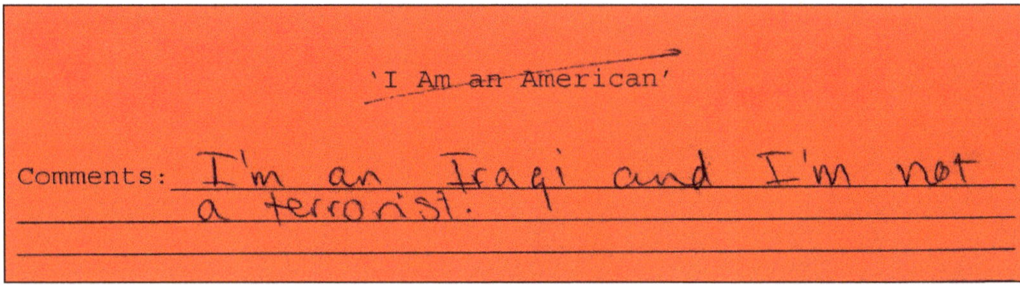
'I Am an American'

Comments: I'm an Iraqi and I'm not a terrorist.

Figure 120: Anonymous comment.

American people what I believe will make this country great, and hopefully that will be a testimony to my patriotism'.[2]

Whether it was because this explanation didn't convince them or because nearly a fifth of US citizens wrongly believe that Obama is a Muslim and some of them have difficulty equating US Muslims with patriotic US Americans, some US citizens began to question Obama's patriotism. Obama responded by wearing the flag pin again.

Dressed in traditional Islamic clothing, Deidra holds a US flag and says, 'I am a Muslim advocate in Arizona, and I am an American'.

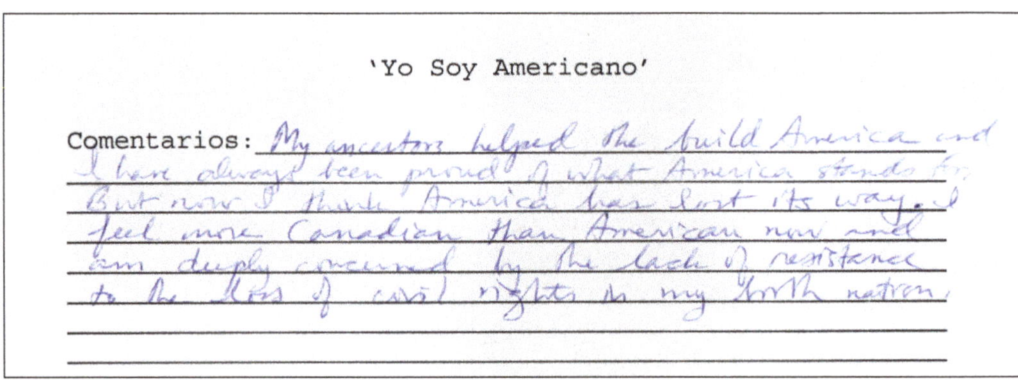
'Yo Soy Americano'

Comentarios: My ancestors helped the build America and I have always been proud of what America stands for. But now I think America has lost its way. I feel more Canadian than American now and am deeply concerned by the lack of resistance to the loss of civil rights in my birth nation.

Figure 121: Anonymous comment.

Future president

Cleveland, Ohio: Like many US school children, Julia Shearson's eight-year-old Arab-American daughter Dalal has decided that she wants to be President when she grows up.

But Julia tells me, 'Dalal isn't sure if you can be President of the United States and be on the watchlist. I've assured her that you can be President and be on the watchlist, but I think you have to get off of it first'.

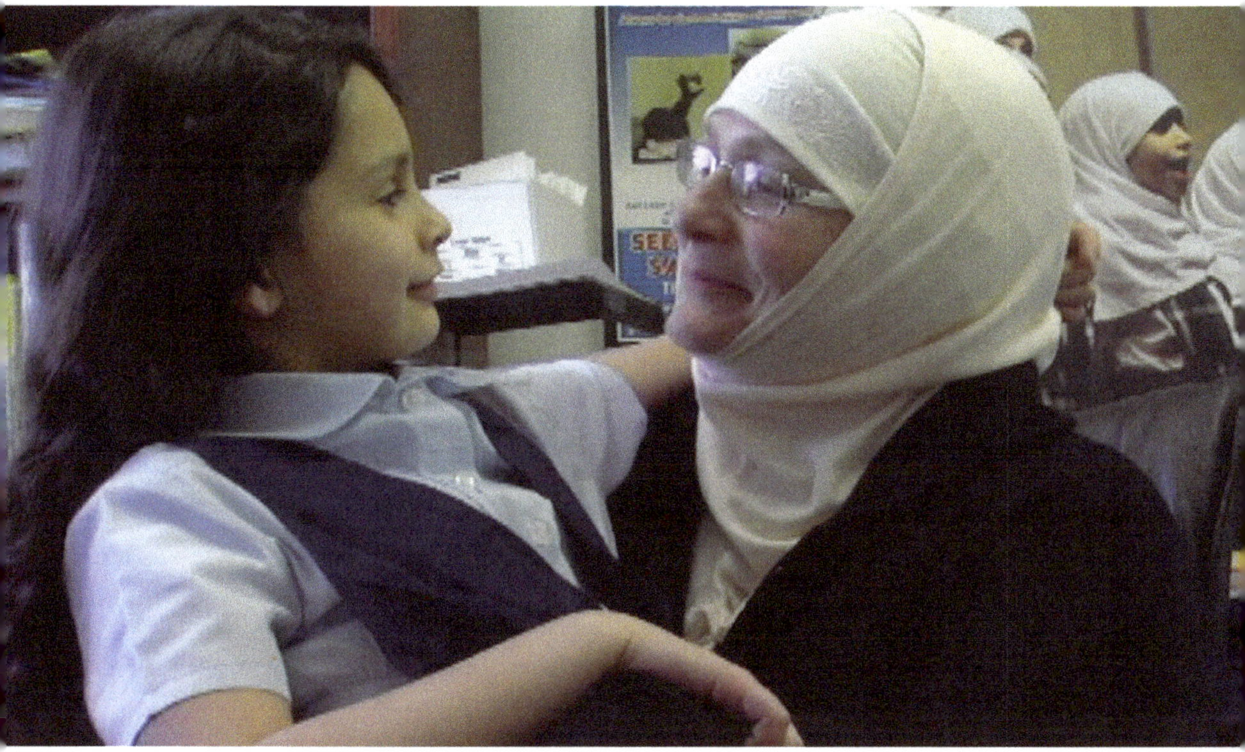

Figure 122: Julia Shearson with her daughter Dalal.

I am an American

Grosvenor Square, London, England: I have come to Grosvenor Square, the site of the US Embassy, to location scout for my film. I have never been to the US Embassy in London before, but I have seen an evocative series of pictures of the Embassy in Elizabeth Gill Lue's book *Building Diplomacy*.[3] Although the building itself is strikingly ugly, what I have come to see is the mesmerizing American eagle with a 35-foot wingspan that flies over the Embassy's entrance. It is a dramatic image and one that would nicely situate me as a US citizen living in England, should I decide to cut a version of the film with me in it.

I have no film equipment with me, just pen and paper. I follow all of the usual film reconnaissance procedures – analyze the size, lines, and shadows of the facade, note where the sun is and how it moves across the sky, consider foreground and background images as well as angles.

After no more than ten minutes gathering information and ideas, I sit in the adjoining park to jot down my notes. Moments later, two London metropolitan police officers on

METROPOLITAN POLICE *Working for a safer London* **Form 5090**

Stop/Search Form

Mission

Making London safe
for all the people we serve.
We make places safer.
We cut crime and the fear of crime.
We uphold the law.

Vision

To make London the safest
major city in the world.

Values

Treat everyone fairly.
Be open and honest.
Work in partnership.
Change to improve.

Figure 123: Cynthia Weber's stop and search documents.

METROPOLITAN POLICE SERVICE **Form 5090**

Reason Stop: J. | Reason Search: J. | Reason Arrest: —

Other info:

Ref. Source (CAD etc.): CAD 7897 / 2/6/2005.

Record requested, but not a recordable stop ☐

Stop ☑ Search ☐ Vehicle ☐

Driver ☐ Passenger ☐ Pedestrian ☑ Other ☐

Specify other:

Date of Stop: 2/6/05 Time Stopped (24 hrs): 18:07.

Family name: [illegible]ER.

Other name(s): CYNTHIA LYN

Address: [redacted]

Post Code: [redacted]

Gender: M / (F) SDE Code: W9. IC: 1.

DoB or A/Age: [redacted] Height: [redacted]

Stopped with: NONE.

Clothing *(including any branding)*

Headwear: BLUE "YANKEES" BASEBALL CAP.

Upper body: BLACK JUMPER.

Lower body: GREY TROUSERS.

Footwear: BLACK TRAINERS.

Hair: BROWN SHORT STRAIGHT.

Marks/scars: GLASSES.

Other details:

*Injury caused Y / (N) *Property found Y / (N) *Damaged caused Y / (N).

(*details:)

motorcycles – lights flashing, sirens wailing – cut through the foliage of the park, drive down the path toward me, and stop in front of my bench. They are clad in full-body leathers, heavily armed, anonymized behind mirrored sunglasses.

One officer functions as backup. The other hands me a flyer about the UK Terrorism Act. I am officially being stopped and searched because I showed 'an unusual interest in the building' that alarmed the Embassy Post Guard, the officer tells me.

I sit frozen to my bench, shaking uncontrollably.

'Do I have the right to look at the building?' I asked very hesitatingly and very politely.

'Yes,' he answers.

'Aren't images of the building shown on television all the time?'

'Yes,' he answers.

'I am a mainly self-funded film-maker,' I explain. 'I do not have the money to pay for rights to existing images so I need to produce my own. Is this something I am allowed to do?'

'Yes,' he answers. But also 'not necessarily'. The officer tells me that I am not allowed to collect information that might be useful to terrorists. Even though I make it absolutely clear to the officer that I have no such intention, this does not matter. Under the UK Official Secrets Act, simply obtaining information that could be useful to terrorists – information like the whereabouts of surveillance cameras on a secured building – is an offense, whether one shares this information or not. This is not the information I am collecting. My notes just show the way the eagle is positioned, the way the flag behind it waves, the way the light crosses the building. I explain all of this.

I also explain, 'I am an American', as if this might offer me some measure of protection. But at this particular time in the United Kingdom, the government is exercising the right to indefinitely detain any foreigner suspected of terrorism or of aiding terrorists. I take in the irony of how my US citizenship positions me not as a well-meaning tourist of US national landmarks abroad but as a suspicious foreigner.

I am interrogated. My notes are analyzed. My bag is searched. My name is exchanged over police radios. A report is filed. It is all surreal and goes on for an unbearable twenty-one minutes.

At some point, I notice the other people in the Square who are gripped by this event, by what is happening to me. For a moment, I see myself as they see me – as someone dangerous, as someone who could be a terrorist, as someone to be afraid of. In that moment, I feel in my guts all those things I have only half appreciated until then – about how categories of people are othered, marginalized, criminalized, because they fit the stereotype of someone who might do what 'normalized citizens' fear these 'others' might do.

I feel all the privilege of my white skin, my middle class profession, my Christian upbringing. I realize that this is going to be OK for me, not just because I have done nothing wrong but because I don't fit the War-on-Terror profile of someone who presumably might do something wrong.

The detention ends. The interrogating officer concludes that I have committed no offense and gives me a form that officially documents his conclusion.

'You scared the %(#& out of me,' I tell him.

He laughs in recognition, then adds, 'You'll dine out on this story for months'. As if dinner conversation were my number one priority. As if this experience could be reduced to something so glib, so trite.

A month or so later, a friend in the film industry tells me of a South Asian film crew who went through a similar experience. But their story ended differently. They were arrested and kept in custody until their white BBC producer got them released.

Hate is Hate

Washington, DC: I am browsing Will Potter's website GreenIsTheNewRed.com in preparation for our follow-up interview. Will's website not only chronicles how environmental activists are being targeted as new enemies of the US War on Terror but how additional categories of 'the suspect' are being invented all the time.

A recent post catches my eye. It is by Pat Boone, the clean-cut Christian singer who is an American icon, especially to those who remember him from his heyday in the 1950s. It was originally posted on Boone's blog, and Will has reposted it here.

Figure 124: Pat Boone calls Pro-Gay Rights Advocates 'sexual jihadists' on GreenIsTheNewRed.com. Reprinted with permission of Will Potter.

In the post, Boone labels Gay Rights Activists working to overturn California's ban on same-sex marriage as 'sexual jihadists'. Writing about these activities in the context of the November 2008 Mumbai terrorist attacks in which terrorists shot and bombed civilians at a Jewish center, a train station, and in various luxury hotels, Boone comments, 'What troubles me so deeply, and should trouble all thinking Americans, is that there is a real, unbroken line between the jihadist savagery in Mumbai and the hedonistic, irresponsible, blindly selfish goals and tactics of our homegrown sexual jihadists'.[4]

I find Boone's comments shocking and offensive, not only because they are baseless, illogical and extreme, but also because of how they might resonate with all those 'thinking Americans' who are his loyal fans.

Boone's blog entry continues, 'Hate is hate, no matter where it erupts. And by its very nature, if it's not held in check, it will escalate into acts vile, violent and destructive'.

My thoughts exactly.

Godhatesfags.com

Lancaster, England: Trolling the web, I come across another attempt to link violence in and on the US with homosexuality in the context of the War on Terror. This one is by the Westboro Baptist Church, whose website address is godhatesfags.com. This group has come to national attention for claiming that the death of US soldiers in the War on Terror is God's punishment for US public tolerance of homosexuality. Church members are famous for picketing military funerals where they trample upon US flags while holding up signs that say things like 'Thank God for Dead Soldiers'.[5]

The blatant intolerance of homosexuals by members of the Westboro Baptist Church not only illustrates the problems with intolerance. It also highlights some of the underlying problems with the idea of tolerance as well. For like intolerance, tolerance is premised on a couple of thoughts or feelings we have about another person. One of these is about whether or not this person is 'like us' or 'unlike us', for it is only people who are different to us that we would need to either tolerate or condemn. And how we usually determine if someone is 'like us' or 'unlike us' is by making a moral judgment about or having a gut feeling about that person's worth. Are they as good as us, or are they somehow morally deficient to us? If they are morally as good as us, then the question of whether or not we will tolerate them doesn't arise. It is only if we judge them to be morally inferior to us that we have to think about whether or not we will tolerate them. So whether we end up acting tolerantly or intolerantly toward someone 'unlike us', we have already determined that this person is morally inferior to us and different to us.

Tolerance then, like intolerance, allows us to hold prejudices against people who are not like us and to accentuate the differences between 'them' and 'us' as moral differences, with 'us' being morally superior to 'them'. This is the case even if we decide that 'we' should tolerate 'them'.

Figure 125: GodHatesFags.com website image. Reprinted with permission from the Westboro Baptist Church.

So even though intolerance allows us to see the hate – indeed, even celebrate the hate – we have for someone who we consider to be different to us, tolerance is not its absolute opposite. For tolerance is not about loving and accepting someone we think of as different to us as our moral equivalent; it is about making a determination in a particular moment to allow that person to be tolerated in spite of their moral inferiority to us. And that means that tolerance can be turned into intolerance whenever we feel morally justified in doing so.

Maybe the Westboro Baptist Church protests are so upsetting not only because of their gleeful celebration of intolerance but also because of how they expose the thin line between tolerance and intolerance.

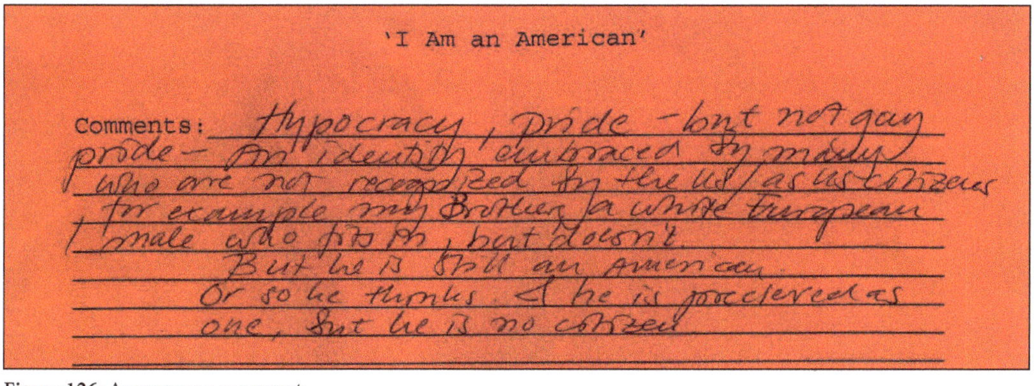
'I Am an American'

Comments: Hypocracy, pride – but not gay pride – an identity embraced by many who are not recognized by the US as US citizens for example my Brother a white European male who fits in, but doesn't.
But he is still an American.
Or so he thinks & he is percieved as one, but he is no citizen

Figure 126: Anonymous comment.

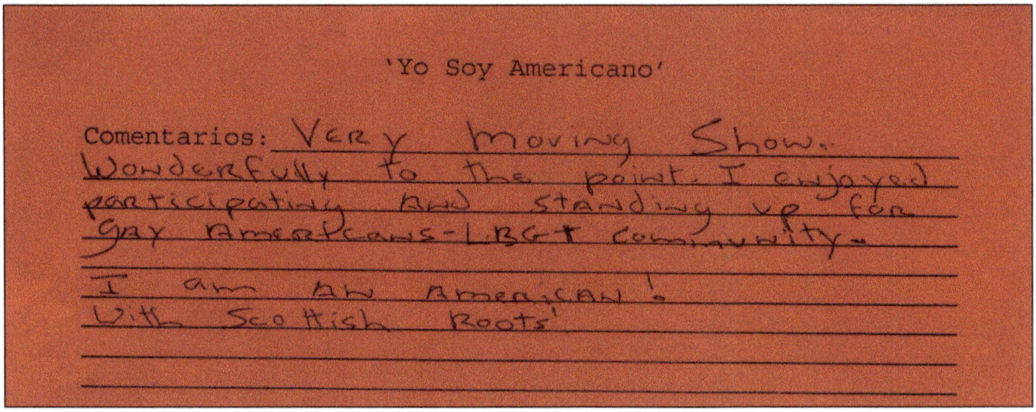

'Yo Soy Americano'

Comentarios: Very moving show. Wonderfully to the point. I enjoyed participating and standing up for gay Americans - LBGT community.

I am an American! With Scottish Roots'

Figure 127: Anonymous comment.

Pre-emptive justice

Buffalo, New York: It is a professional hazard for film-makers to constantly make film analogies. And so it isn't really surprising that in my discussions with Steve Kurtz, I compare his four year legal battle with the Bush administration to the film version of Franz Kafka's book *The Trial* (Orson Welles, 1962). 'It's like you are Anthony Perkins in *The Trial*, caught up in some bizarre legal entanglement with the government that has no rhyme or reason'.

Steve immediately refuses this analogy. 'I've always had a really ambivalent relationship to that description because on the one hand, [the case against me] is senseless. Why would this be happening? But there is a total logic to it. There's serious reasons why it happened'.

Steve explains these reasons. 'The Bush administration was very interested in the idea of thought crime, and that the thought crime would be indicative of real crime. So it had to be pre-empted'. He points to the case of the Lackawanna Six, the only successful post-9/11 US prosecution of thought crime. It involved six young US men of Middle Eastern decent who the Bush administration described as a 'sleeper cell'. Administration officials believed these men were thinking about committing a terrorist act against the US, even though there was no concrete evidence to support this belief, much less any evidence of terrorist activity.

I try out another film analogy. 'So you were in *Minority Report* (Steven Spielberg, 2002), the Steve Spielberg/Tom Cruise film about pre-emptive justice, where the government goes around arresting folks who are thinking about committing crimes to prevent them from actually carrying out the crimes'.

'Exactly,' Steve says. He then explains that the Bush administration had specific indicators of what constituted a thought crime, like asking if the suspect in question was 'thinking about anything radical or resistant or anti-Bush agenda or somehow counter ideology. They took that type of thinking as the equivalent of actually committing a crime. So they equated those two things and thereby could charge pretty much anyone they found [who] was not going along with the Bush idea of what America should look like'. The upshot, he explains, is that 'there's no longer innocent until proven guilty. Any type of ideological deviation from the Bush plan [was] considered a criminal offense. And I unfortunately fell into that, became one of those targets'.

'But why would the Bush administration target you,' I ask, 'especially given their incredibly weak case against you and your respectable public standing as an academic and as an artist?'

'Because it [was] intimidating to the artist community, the science community, the academic community, and the activist community. I had my feet in all of these territories, and all four of them generally speaking tend to be an anti-conservative force. This would be a great intimidation tactic for [the Bush administration], to show that we will come for you if you continue in activities like that'.

'What are they actually protecting us from?', Steve asks rhetorically of the Bush administration and its pursuit of pre-emptive justice. 'They're protecting us from things that are weird. And that's what we want. Creativity, invention, the novel, the new – when they first come out, they're weird because they're not rote. They're not something we know by habit or by expectation. And so because they are unfamiliar, they come out as weird. But weird is not criminal. In fact, often times and in the grand majority of cases, it's something very positive and helpful to society. And that's ultimately what they're stopping'.

Figure 128: Steve Kurtz holding FBI evidence of his 'thought crime', a Science Kit catalogue he used to purchase the sort of lab equipment found in any high school science lab.

Figure 129: Critical Art Ensemble poster 'Fear Power'. Provided by the Critical Art Ensemble.

I'm not there

Anonymous locations: My films feature some of the most recognizable post-9/11 figures in the US. What they fail to include are the many US citizens who were too afraid to speak to me on-camera or off – the US Muslim family who left the US because of the atmosphere of harassment, the parent who was threatened with job loss when their boss found out I was filming their story, the US resident who reluctantly became a US citizen after 9/11 to be 'safe' but who regrets this decision and does not feel safe speaking about it, the folks who have been to hell and back thanks to the War on Terror and who cannot risk making this journey again.

I offer every film-making option I can think of to find a way to let these people comfortably tell their stories. 'I will not show your face. I will not show you at all. I will shoot an empty chair in an anonymous location. I will disguise your voice. I will only use subtitles. I will subtitle your ideas but not your words'. Every one of them refuses, fearing what might happen if anyone linked their stories back to them through me.

I respect their decisions. I know too much about what they have been through or might have to go through to want any of them to risk speaking to me.

I have struggled to find ways to make their absence present. Here are my solutions. To speak about their absence. To write about their absence. To incorporate their absence into gallery exhibitions as blank slides projected onto the wall.

Figure 130: Blank slide as part of gallery exhibition.

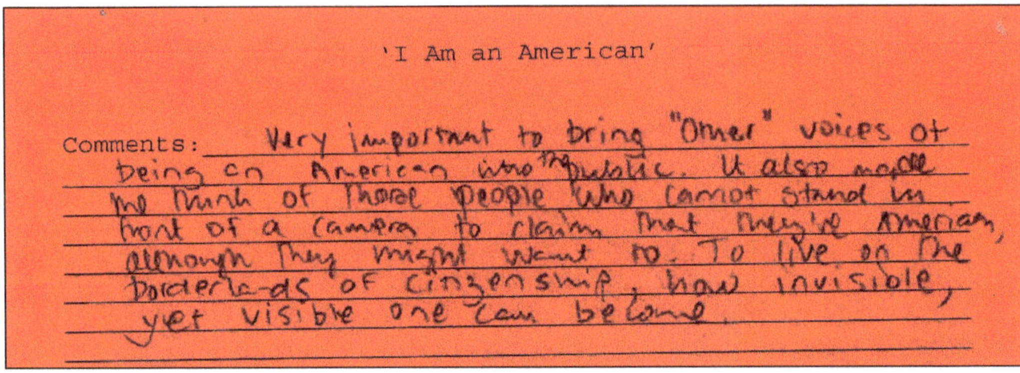

'I Am an American'

Comments: Very important to bring "Other" voices of being an American into the public. It also made me think of those people who cannot stand in front of a camera to claim that they're American, although they might want to. To live on the borderlands of citizenship, how invisible, yet visible one can become.

Figure 131: Anonymous comment.

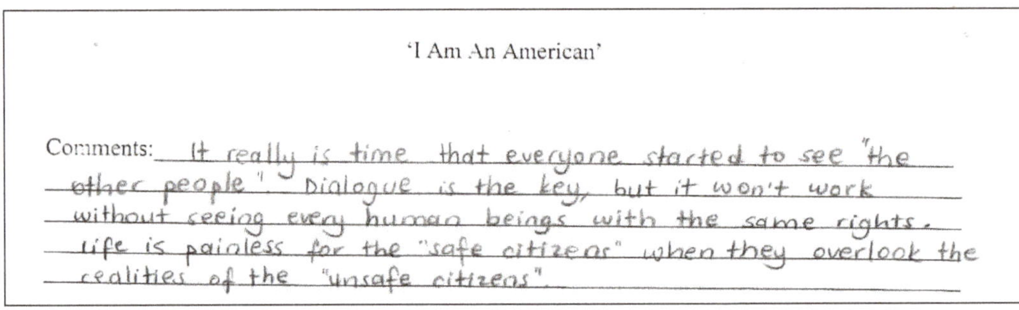

'I Am An American'

Comments: It really is time that everyone started to see "the other people". Dialogue is the key, but it won't work without seeing every human beings with the same rights. life is painless for the "safe citizens" when they overlook the realities of the "unsafe citizens".

Figure 132: Anonymous comment.

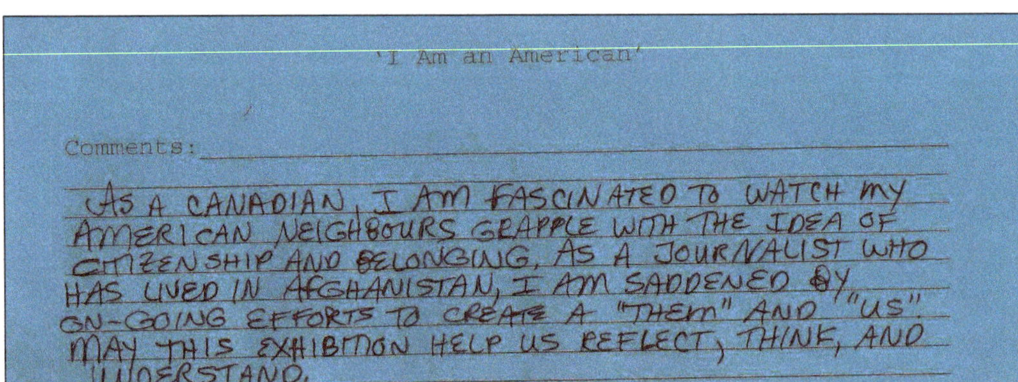

'I Am an American'

Comments: AS A CANADIAN, I AM FASCINATED TO WATCH MY AMERICAN NEIGHBOURS GRAPPLE WITH THE IDEA OF CITIZENSHIP AND BELONGING, AS A JOURNALIST WHO HAS LIVED IN AFGHANISTAN, I AM SADDENED BY ON-GOING EFFORTS TO CREATE A "THEM" AND "US". MAY THIS EXHIBITION HELP US REFLECT, THINK, AND UNDERSTAND.

Figure 133: Anonymous comment.

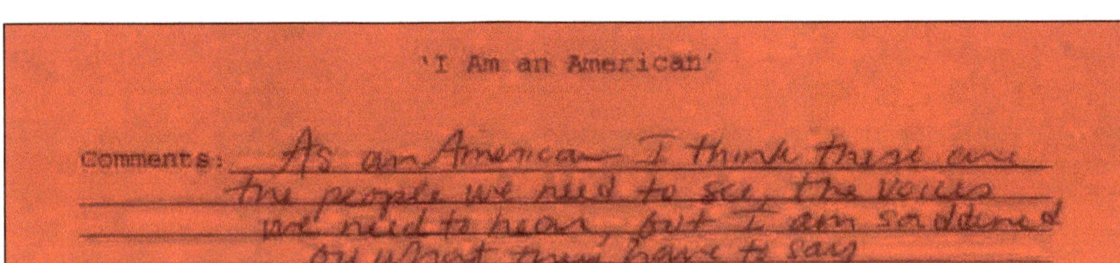

'I Am an American'

Comments: As an American I think these are the people we need to see, the voices we need to hear, but I am saddened by what they have to say

Figure 134: Anonymous comment.

Notes

1. Professor Nyers' understanding of 'accidental citizenship' is more detailed than I have presented it here, as it theoretically engages with Paul Virilio's understanding of how accidents are built into all technologies, even 'technologies' of citizenship. See Peter Nyers (2006), 'The accidental citizen: acts of sovereignty and (un)making citizenship', *Economy and Society*, 35:1, pp. 22–41.
2. Stanley Renshon (2007) 'The Political Mind: Obama denounces flag-pin patriotism', October 23, http://www.politico.com/news/stories/1007/6502.html. Downloaded 14 September 2009. For more on this controversy, see Media Matters (2008) 'Caplis Criticized Obama Over Flag Pin, But Omitted Obama's Explanation For Not Wearing One', April 18, http://colorado.mediamatters.org/items/200804190002. Downloaded 14 September 2009.
3. Elizabeth Gill Lue (2004), *Building Diplomacy*, Ithica, NY: Cornell University Press.
4. Pat Boone (2008) 'Hate is Hate, in India or America', http://www.greenisthenewred.com/blog/?s=pat+boone. Downloaded 14 September 2009, and http://www.wnd.com/index.php?fa=PAGE.view&pageId=82830, December 6. Downloaded 14 September 2009.
5. In a similar spirit, the Reverend Jerry Falwell commented shortly after September 11, 2001, that God may have allowed the terrorist attacks to punish the US for its moral decay evidenced by things like the ACLU, abortionists, feminists, gays, and the People for the American Way. He later retracted these comments – CNN.com (2002) 'Falwell apologizes to gays, feminists, lesbians', September 14, http://archives.cnn.com/2001/US/09/14/Falwell.apology/. Downloaded 7 September 2010.

Chapter 5

Transitions

Becoming one of us, reprise

Lancaster, England: I'm listening to a speech by President Barak Obama about immigration[1]. In it, he mentions a woman named Perla Ramos. Perla was born and raised in Mexico. But after 9/11, Perla immigrated to the US and ended up joining the US Navy. At the time of President Obama's speech, Perla was in the process of becoming a US citizen.

Perla's life echoes many of the experiences of fast-tracked US citizen Guadalupe Denogean. And so as I listen to President Obama speak, I can't help but think about Lupe and the many references President Bush used to make to him in immigration speeches. Like President Obama's speech, President Bush's speeches stressed the ways that immigrants are not a threat to the US but instead are an economic and military asset to the nation, even though US policy in practice doesn't always treat (all) immigrants this way. But how each President articulated this idea is quite different.

President Bush spoke of America's 'genius for making us all Americans', as if the United States of America were some static ideal that magically transformed immigrants into US Americans and as if what it means to be a US American were itself static. In contrast, President Obama is speaking about how immigrants themselves transform the US for the better. As he puts it,

> These women [like Perla] [...] remind us [...] that being an American is not a matter of blood or birth. It's a matter of faith. It's a matter of fidelity to the shared values that we all hold so dear. That's what makes us unique. That's what makes us strong. Anybody can help us write the next great chapter in our history.

As I listen to President Obama speak, two images flash before my eyes simultaneously. One is of Presidential Candidate Obama saying, 'Yes we can'. The other is of a severely injured Lupe Denogean who thinks of himself as the embodiment of the American Dream. As I turn off the radio, I'm fending off a third image – of Perla going off to war.

Dying to be American

San Isidro, California: Fernando Suarez del Solar is meeting with a group of Hispanic High School students at a community center. Some of them are US citizens; some of them are

Figure 135: Guerrero Azteca Por La Paz meeting.

Mexican citizens. All of them are considering a career in the US military. Each has a different reason – to get a better job or a better education or a better chance at US citizenship. But all these reasons are more or less the same – to get closer to achieving the American Dream.

These students have come to listen to Fernando because his son Jesus received US citizenship thanks to his military service. Jesus joined the US Marines as a Mexican citizen upon graduating from High School. After 9/11 he was deployed to Iraq. In the first few days

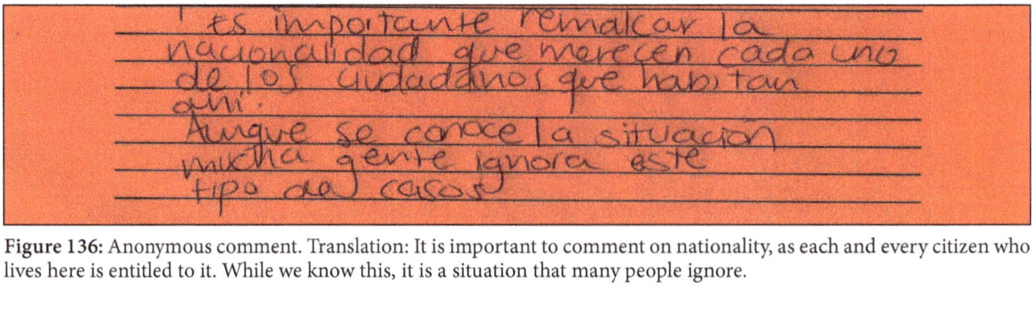

Figure 136: Anonymous comment. Translation: It is important to comment on nationality, as each and every citizen who lives here is entitled to it. While we know this, it is a situation that many people ignore.

of the war, Jesus was killed. It was after his death that the US government awarded Jesus US citizenship.

In Jesus' memory, Fernando formed an organization called Guerrero Azteca Por La Paz/ Aztec Warrior Peace Project to discourage other Hispanic youth from joining the military. What motivated Fernando was not just Jesus' death but the discrimination Jesus suffered in the US military as an Hispanic.

'It is not necessary to die to feel American or get an education or serve your country', Fernando tells the students. 'The military is only for war'.

Talking about Jesus' injuries and death, Fernando explains, 'This is the reality of war. Don't enter the military. Don't enter, under any pretext'.

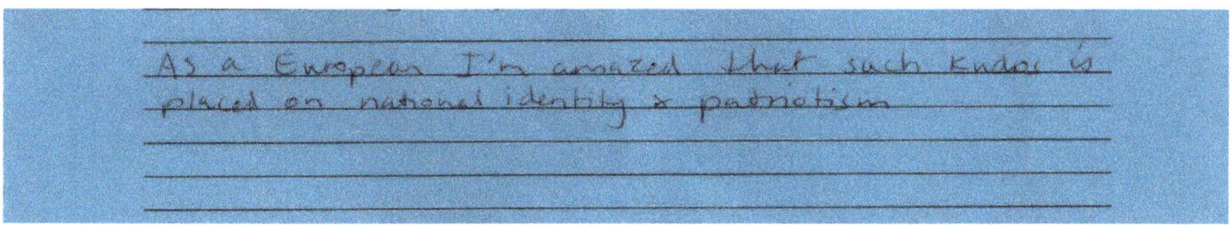

Figure 137: Anonymous comment.

Let them stay

Ottawa, Canada: The last time I saw Phil McDowell and Jamine Aponte in person, they were standing before a crowd of thousands on the steps of the Canadian Parliament building. Behind them, a handful of Iraq War Resisters held up a banner that read, 'BUSH OUT, RESISTERS IN'. The crowd had assembled to rally before marching in protest of President George W. Bush's then-upcoming visit to Canada.

Phil briefly told his story and explained the War Resisters' view that the war in Iraq is illegal and unjust. He also led the crowd in an anti-Bush, pro-Resisters chant. But Phil's comments to that Canadian audience were intended to do more than just protest President Bush's pending visit. They were to remind the Canadian public that, under current Canadian law, there is nothing preventing the deportation of War Resisters back to the US, where they could face felony charges and prison time. This is in stark contrast to how thousands of Vietnam War draft dodgers from the US were treated when they fled to Canada in the 1960s and 70s. And so Phil was there to rally Canadian support for changes in Canadian law that would guarantee these former soldiers the right to stay in Canada.

It's been a difficult case to make because, unlike in the Vietnam War, no US soldiers were formally drafted into service in the Afghanistan or Iraq Wars. Yet the War Resisters caution US Americans against drawing the conclusion that the US military is now a purely volunteer corps. They point out that, on the one hand, you have US soldiers like Phil who were 'effectively drafted' through stop-loss policies.

Figure 138: Phil McDowell speaks at rally in Ottawa, Canada.

On the other hand, you have what Campaign Organizer Lee Zaslofski calls 'the poverty draft'. As Lee puts it, 'If you can't afford to go to college, if not having been to college you don't have the skills to get a decent job in the United States, there are several options for you. One of them is Walmart, another is McDonalds, and both of them are crap jobs that lead nowhere, particular in small-town America. Or you can join the military and, as you're promised [by your recruiter], resolve those problems and get out of the small town you feel confined in. We regard that – and I think many Americans regard that – as a poverty draft'.

Since this rally, the Canadian Parliament has been considering legislation that would allow the Resisters to remain in Canada indefinitely. So far, this process has taken years. And, as Lee tells me, it is likely to take years more, during which time Phil and Jamine could be deported.

'The best hope for Phil and Jamine – the best hope for every one of the Resisters – is for a change in the Canadian government', Lee tells me. This, Lee explains, is for two reasons. One is that it is the main opposition party that – right now at least – is among those who are supporting the War Resisters' legal right to stay in Canada. The other is that the Obama Administration has shown no signs of changing US policies on the treatment of War Resisters.

I call up Phil, who has now spent several years as a War Resister in Canada. I ask him, 'If there were no charges against you – no threat of a custodial sentence or a dishonorable discharge (which amounts to a felony conviction) – would you and Jamine want to go back and live in the US now?'

Without hesitation, Phil says, 'No, for a couple of reasons. I still feel that I was betrayed by being forced to go to Iraq in the first place and then by the US military's attempting to send me back again. I feel resentment for that'. But there is another reason Phil and Jamine would rather stay in Canada. As Phil puts it, 'The principles of tolerance that the US is supposed to stand for are getting harder to accomplish these days because the political parties and the political interests in the US are at war with one another. And that's hurting the society in general'.

Phil's point was borne out in the run-up to the US mid-term elections, when Tea Party candidates running as far-right Republicans rejected much of what Phil might understand as the principles of tolerance and when left-leaning TV comedians Jon Steward and Steven Cobert responded by holding a 'Rally to Restore Sanity' in Washington, DC. It remains to be seen which position will win out in the everyday practice of US politics in the years to come and how much US society will benefit or be hurt by these terms of political engagement.

Making the dream a reality

Lancaster, England: I'm filming US Army Muslim Chaplin James Yee give a public lecture at Lancaster University. As I do this, I'm thinking about how for a good year or two, James was the only Muslim US citizen who would speak to me on camera, out of the many I approached. I've often wondered why that was. Maybe it was because his distinguished record of military service to the US afforded him some degree of safety. Maybe it was because James' experience of being sent to hell and back so strengthened his faith that he knew he could handle whatever anyone might throw at him. Or maybe it was because his heart-felt message that religious freedom and patriotism are compatible is, like the American Ad Council's circulation of the melting pot myth after 9/11, an ideal about the US that James is helping to make real.

This comes through when James tells this crowd of his belief in the American way of life and the values embodied in the US constitution – 'diversity, religious freedom, equality, justice, the humane treatment of prisoners'. It is these values, he believes, that will hold the US together and see us through this difficult time.

James mentioned these very same values to me some time ago when I first filmed him. Now, as then, I am struck by his inclusion of 'diversity' in this list. James has explained to me that diversity is an Islamic value, but I am less sure it is a US constitutional value. This is because throughout US history the constitution has been used as an instrument to deny 'diverse' US citizens their rights as often as it has been used to grant them rights.

After his lecture, James signs copies of his book *For God and Country* (New York: Public Affairs, 2005), for an appreciative crowd who are still asking him questions.

'Do you really believe America is the land of the free?' someone asks.

Figure 139: James Yee at book signing.

'Not for everyone', James replies. 'But I'm hoping that my efforts will work towards that'.

To further his efforts to make all US Americans embrace freedom, patriotism, and diversity as compatible US American core values, James accepted a post as the Executive Director of the Council on American-Islamic Relations in New Jersey. 'I have my work cut out for me battling the new wave of Islamophobia in America stemming from the Lower Manhattan Mosque controversy', James tells me.

What James is referring to is the attempt to locate an Islamic mosque in New York City near the site of the former World Trade Center. Some US Americans have objected to this project on the grounds that because a small group of Muslims were responsible for the World Trade Center attacks on September 11, placing a mosque so close to Ground Zero would dishonor the memory of those who died in the terrorist attacks. Such a view forgets that the 9/11 terrorists' interpretation of Islam is rejected by the vast majority of Muslims living inside and outside of the United States, meaning that the equation of 'terrorism' and 'Islam' is at best inaccurate and at most Islamophobic. It also forgets that many Muslims were in the World Trade Center at the time of the attacks, making Muslims as well as people from other religions among the innocent victims on that day.

More generally, though, what this controversy highlights is how 'diversity' is not the universally celebrated US principle that James wants it to be.

Speaking truth to power

San Francisco, California: Since disbanding Camp Casey outside of President George W. Bush's Texas ranch, Cindy Sheehan has remained involved in politics. Undeterred by her unsuccessful bid to become a US Senator from California, Cindy now hosts a weekly radio program. I'm in the studio as Cindy tapes her show.

In addition to interviewing her guests and giving her views on the political topics of the day, Cindy tapes the lead-ins and lead-outs for the program in which she recaps the name of the show and adds her tagline, 'This is Cindy Sheehan's Soapbox. I'm Cindy Sheehan, speaking truth to power'.

This tagline of 'speaking truth to power' perfectly encapsulates Cindy's position. It expresses how, for Cindy, truth and power are opposed to one another, how power oppresses

Figure 140: Cindy's soapbox.

the truth, and how the best strategy for resisting and potentially even overthrowing power is to speak the truth back to power. That's precisely how Cindy sees what she has been doing since Casey's death led her to reconsider her views on the Iraq War and to challenge the Bush administration's policies. As I reflect on it, I realize that not just Cindy but all of the soldiers and their loved ones I've been interviewing are attempting to speak truth to power, with the exception of Lupe Denogean who is just grateful that the US state benevolently exercised its power toward him by finally granting him US citizenship.

While there are merits to 'speaking truth to power', there are also difficulties with it. Such as, because everyone claims to be speaking the truth, how do we know who really speaks the truth? And how can we be sure that truth is pure and opposed to power rather than saturated through and through with power, as someone like the philosopher Michel Foucault has argued? And even if we were to accept that some pure truth were opposed to power and that we could replace power with that pure truth, doesn't that new truth just become the new power? And then don't we have to speak a new, better truth to it?

But probably the biggest difficult of trying to speak truth to power during the War on Terror was revealed in a famous comment made by a senior adviser to the Bush Administration to *New York Times* reporter Ron Suskind. The exchange is worth quoting at length. Suskind writes,

> The aide said that guys like me were 'in what we call the reality-based community,' which he defined as people who 'believe that solutions emerge from your judicious study of discernible reality.' I nodded and murmured something about enlightenment principles and empiricism. He cut me off. 'That's not the way the world really works anymore,' he continued. 'We're an empire now, and when we act, we create our own reality. And while you're studying that reality – judiciously, as you will – we'll act again, creating other new realities, which you can study too, and that's how things will sort out. We're history's actors [...] and you, all of you, will be left to just study what we do.'[2]

What this aide's comments suggest is that speaking truth to power is not a sufficient strategy for redirecting US power, whether that power is wielded by a specific administration during the War on Terror or by a specific media organization like the American Ad Council.

Hurricane Katrina, The Opera

Lancaster, England: I'm catching up with Hurricane Katrina evacuees Greg and Glenda Avery over the phone. These two incredibly industrious individuals are filling me in on the work they've been doing since I initially filmed them. They tell me about numerous trips they've made back to New Orleans to help friends, family and their 9th District community. They explain how they've set up the West Virginia New Orleans network that 'gives voice to the concerns of willing evacuees through art projects'. And they tell me about Greg's photographs of the tragedy being exhibited in various shows. But what really catches my attention is when they tell me they are writing an opera. Indeed, they are writing *Hurricane Katrina, The Opera*.

'Why an opera?', I ask them.

I'm expecting them to tell me that this is an attention-grabbing gesture that puts unlike things together in the vein of the only opera I have so far seen in my life, *Jerry Springer, The Opera*. But I'm completely mistaken.

Greg explains that growing up in New Orleans, he was exposed to many types of music, from jazz to funk to rhythm and blues to opera. For Greg and Glenda, opera is the form of music that for them 'captures the essence of the city and its people' because it 'puts the magic back into the musical'. *Hurricane Katrina, The Opera* will not only draw upon Greg and Glenda's experiences of living through the hurricane; it will offer stories from many other evacuees as well. Its message, Glenda tells me, is to serve 'as a friendly reminder that we could all walk in those shoes. That no matter what background we come from, no one is exempt from tragedy'.

Beyond using the arts to remind people of the plight of Hurricane Katrina evacuees, this opera has another purpose. Greg tells me that if any revenue is generated from the project,

Figure 141: Glenda Avery at work in the recording studio. Photo by Gregory Avery.

it will be used to establish a debt reduction program for evacuees, to help the more than 100,000 evacuees still living outside of New Orleans recover financially from the massive debts they have incurred in relocating and to help some of them return to New Orleans if they wish.

'I see it just like what President Obama did for the banks and the car industry', Greg tells me.

And there is another thing that Greg and Glenda say they have in common with President Obama, 'an insatiable optimism and belief in America'. As Greg puts it, 'We know it's not a perfect America, but we really want to put positive energy out there. We need to show our children that they can have liberty and happiness in their lifetimes'.

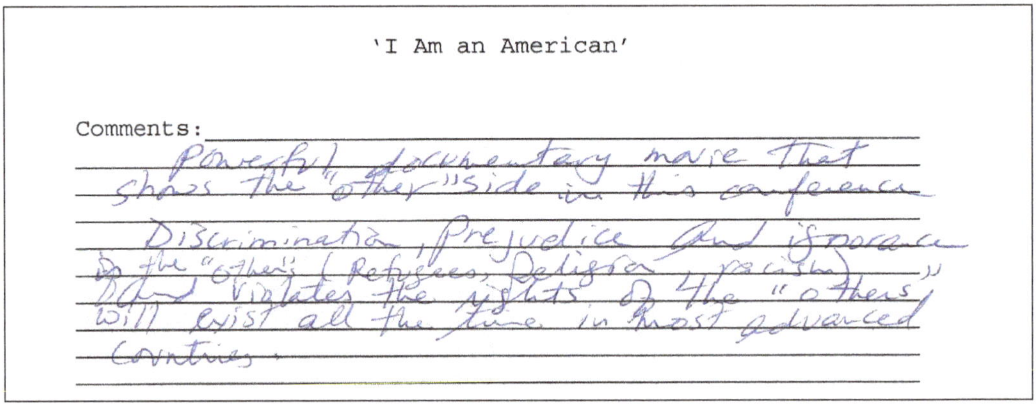
'I Am an American'

Comments: Powerful documentary movie That shows the "other" side in this conference Discrimination, Prejudice and ignorance to the "others" (Refugees, Religion, racism) and violates the rights of the "others" will exist all the time in most advanced countries.

Figure 142: Anonymous comment.

Right of passage

Tohono O'odham Nation, US-Mexico Border: Ofelia Rivas is explaining to me why she has founded the organization O'odham Voice Against the Wall, her protest organization against the building of the US-Mexico border fence through O'odham lands.

It was a 'directive from the elders' of the Nation, she tells me, who are concerned about how the vehicle barrier being constructed at the US-Mexico border is cutting off traditional routes across the Nation and disrupting the traditional O'odham way of life.

'I volunteer to transport the elders [around the Nation], and every time that I'm travelling I do have very elderly people that I take to their communities in Mexico and back across, maybe to the health facility or visit their family or to a funeral or to a birth ceremony'.

'It's very discouraging to a lot of our people that our Tribal Government is not actively and aggressively protecting our people'. And the most discouraged are the elders who follow traditional ceremonial practices. Ofelia explains, 'The elders are very upset, and they're

Figure 143: Ofelia Rivas near the US-Mexico Border.

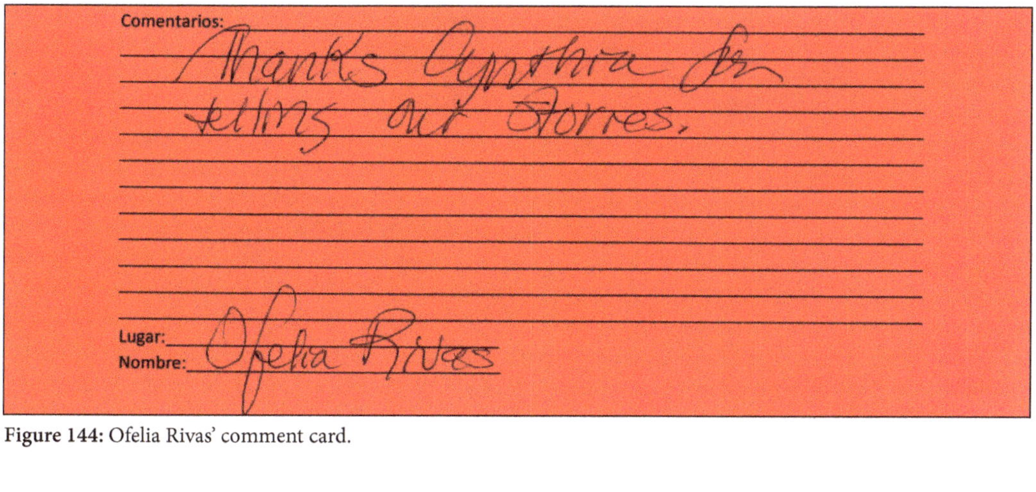

Comentarios: Thanks Cynthia for telling out Storres.

Lugar:

Nombre: Ofelia Rivas

Figure 144: Ofelia Rivas' comment card.

confused. And they're wondering how are we going to go to ceremonies this year' because 'our road is closed and they [Border Patrol] are forcing us to come up with documents that we cannot produce', like passports that prove citizenship which few O'odham tribal members possess because they cannot prove which side of the Nation they were born on since 'all midwives that birthed us at home have passed on'.

The journey across O'odham lands is becoming more dangerous. 'There have been times when we have been forced off the road in our vehicle by US Border Patrols, thinking that we are human traffickers or drug traffickers. They claim that we do not stop, and yet they tailgate us to a point that it's so scary that they do run us off the road'.

'All we want', Ofelia explains, 'is someone to hear that we do live on both sides of the border, and we do continue to cross that border'.

Melting

Santa Rosa Learning Center, Tucson, Arizona: José Matus is explaining to me what is at stake in keeping the indigenous peoples on Yaqui lands connected. José tells me what is at stake is 'our cultural survival' because 'US policy for the past 500 years based on Manifest Destiny wants to do away with indigenous people – to make them all [Europeanized] Americans'. The legacy of these policies is that 'most of our people have been displaced or removed from reservations and put into the White Man's society. A lot of them have lost their language. A lot of them have lost their Indian ways. A lot of them have been ashamed to admit, "I am Indian"'.

Alianza Indigena Sin Fronteras believes 'our resistance is our native language and our native cultural traditions'. To keep these alive, José tells me, 'we need to involve our relatives from Mexico so we can maintain and continue our fight. If we don't do that, then we become nothing. We become part of the melting pot'.

The prospect of becoming part of the American melting pot saddens José. He tells me it would mean that Yaqui's would be reduced to 'doing plays in community centers and urban centers around the nation saying, "This is what the Yaqui's used to do 100 or 20 years ago" [...] That's all we're gonna have'.

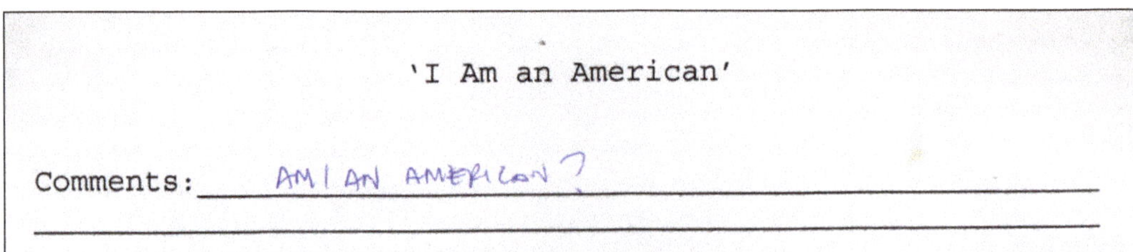

'I Am an American'

Comments: AM I AN AMERICAN?

Figure 145: Anonymous comment.

Déjà vu all over again

Tucson, Arizona: A year or so after I completed my initial filming, I've returned to Tucson to do follow-up interviews and publically screen my films. While I'm here, the humanitarian aid organization that Shanti Sellz works for, No More Deaths, holds a press conference. One of their volunteers has been convicted of a crime. The volunteer is Dan Millis. The crime is littering. The sentence is no sentence.

Dan received the citation for littering from a Fish and Wildlife enforcement officer when he and two other volunteers were putting sealed jugs of water on a desert trail used by migrants to provide them with clean, safe water that might save their lives as they cross the desert. Dan says that the officers removed the jugs of water, but did not take the trash Dan and the other volunteers had picked up off the trail. Instead of paying the $175 fine, Dan went to trial. He received his guilty verdict the day I arrived in town.

'I feel like this is a passive-aggressive message from the government', Dan said. 'It says that what we are doing – in essence saving lives – is illegal, but that there's no punishment for it. We want to hear something clear that says humanitarian aid is not a crime'.

Figure 146: 'Humanitarian Aid Is Never A Crime'.

At the screening of my films, another No More Deaths volunteer tells me, shaking his head in disbelief, 'The tradeoff is bodies for bottles'. Dan knows this all too well. Two days before he received the citation for littering, he found the body of 14-year-old Hernandez Quinteros from El Salvador in the desert. 'Had we found her sooner, or had she found our water, she would have been celebrating her Quincenera [her sweet 15 party] just last week', said Dan.

Since Dan's conviction, another 17 humanitarian aid workers were cited for the same offense, with one going to trial.

Dan appealed his conviction. On September 2, 2010, the US 9th Circuit Court of Appeals overturned Dan's conviction. In a 2-1 decision, they ruled that 'clean bottles of drinking water placed on known migrant trails could not be considered "garbage" due to their intended purpose of preventing death-by-exposure'.[3]

Upon hearing the ruling, Dan said, 'I continue to be saddened by the ongoing tragedy along the border; but I am pleased and relieved that the Court has finally made clear that humanitarian aid is never a crime'.[4]

Simcox for senate

Lancaster, England: It is a day like any other. I do some work, check my email, and then visit my bookmarked web pages. Among these is the YouTube page that hosts a sample of the 'I am an American' films I've published on OpenDemocracy. As I look over this page, I notice something unusual. My film about Chris Simcox has had 7000 hits in the past 24 hours. That's more than four times the number of hits it has had in the past year. I have no idea why the film is suddenly being viewed so heavily. I decide to google 'Chris Simcox – I am an American'. When I do, a link directs me to the 'Simcox for Senate' homepage which launched the day before. Shockingly, I find my film embedded in the header of this webpage. Next to my film – also in the header – are the words, 'DONATE NOW', with instructions on where to send your checks.

I go absolutely numb. What bothers me most is not that the campaign's use of my film is a flagrant violation of copyright laws; it is that its use of my film is a flagrant violation of my politics. For I have not and never would give my consent to Simcox or his campaign committee to use my work to sell Simcox to his constituency or to solicit contributions to his campaign. Not only would I not allow the film to be shown in such an extreme context. I already never allow the film to be shown out of the context of the wider project. Indeed, I insist that any screening or exhibition of the Simcox film always happens in conjunction with the films about Elvira and Saul, Shanti, and Ofelia, if not with all of the films in the collection, to prevent anyone who misses my critical cuts in the Simcox film from taking away a one-sided view of the Immigration Wars.

I find the whole episode politically offensive, but also weird. On the one hand, it confirms my suspicion that the Minutemen are oblivious to how my film criticizes their project. On the other hand, I am just stunned that of all the films made about Chris Simcox and the

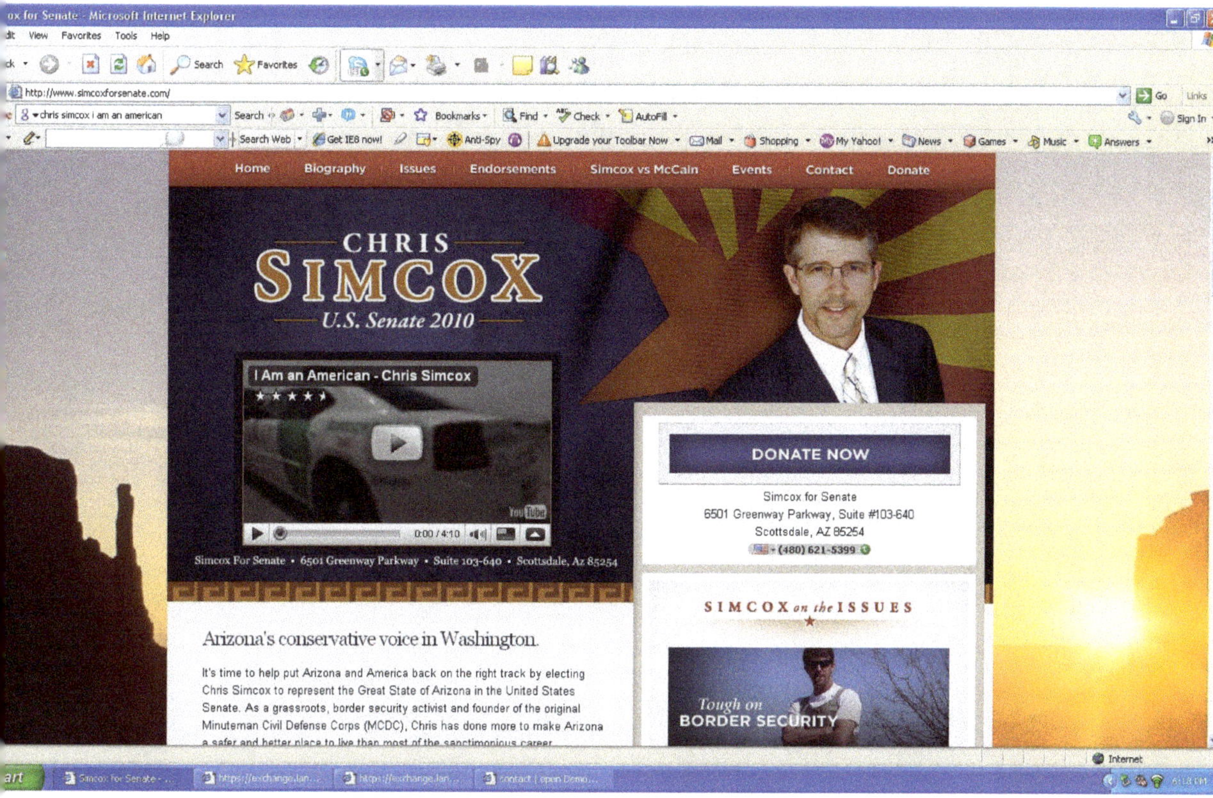

Figure 147: Photo of 'Simcox For Senate' web page.

Minutemen since 2001, it is my film that has been hijacked for his campaign. What makes this all the more ironic is that in my first conversation with Simcox, he told me that his wife is a documentary film-maker.

I immediately instruct OpenDemocracy to remove my film from the web and to inform Simcox and his campaign that they are not authorized to use my film at any time for any reason in any form whatsoever.

Saulito's will

Gatineau, Canada: My initial stay in North America is winding down. I'm spending my last week in a basement, editing the films. Occasionally, I emerge long enough to check my email and read the online news. I find a headline – 'Elvira Arellano Deported'.

I had been bracing myself for this. About a week earlier, Elvira held a press conference to announce that she would be leaving sanctuary to speak at a rally in Los Angeles and, more generally, to lobby US lawmakers for changes in immigration laws. Since then, all I've been thinking about is Saul. It's been difficult enough for him to deal with his mother in sanctuary, but it will be infinitely more difficult for him to deal with her deportation, even a deportation that Elvira effectively orchestrated.

I read the press accounts. Elvira had Saul with her when their vehicle was stopped and surrounded by immigration police. Sirens, lights, megaphones, and a terrified little boy sobbing in the back seat. All accounts write him up as traumatized.

Elvira was arrested and hours later deported to Tijuana. Saul stayed in the US and was paraded in front of the press at a news conference the next day. Tearfully, he hid behind his godmother. He did not speak or even look at the cameras.

A week or two later, Saul left the US to join his mother in Mexico. And so Elvira's prophesy was fulfilled – 'If the government deports me,' she foretold, 'they will effectively be deporting Saulito against his will'.

'Saulito's will'. What an odd construction. And how hypocritical. For none of us – neither me, nor Elvira, nor those giving Elvira sanctuary – have ever put Saulito's will above our own. Was it Saulito's will to be in my film? Was it Saulito's will for his mother to leave sanctuary? Was it Saulito's will for him to be with his mother when she knew she would be arrested?

Intellectually, I get the dilemmas about personal happiness vs self-sacrifice for the greater good. But is it ever justified to ask an 8-year-old boy to sacrifice his personal happiness for other people's politics?

Figure 148: Saul Arellano waves a US flag.

Permission

Armory Park, Tucson, Arizona: 'Do you make films about children?', a 12-year-old boy asks me.

He is the relative of one of the people I made a film about last year. He and his family have just watched a compilation of my films for the first time. So he knows the answer to this question, as Saul Arellano is one of the key figures in the film.

'I make films with children in them only if I have the permission of their parents', I tell him.

'I want you to make a film about me', he says.

This has to be my new criteria for filming children – that I have their parents' permission and that I have their permission.

An expensive mistake

Lancaster, England: As I do my early morning web browsing, I read that Brandon Mayfield settled part of his case against the US government for his wrongful detention in relation to the Madrid bombings. Brandon won a formal apology and $2 million in damages from the government. What is probably more important, though, is that in Brandon's legal challenge to the US Patriot Act, a judge initially ruled that those provisions of the Act that made Brandon's detention possible were unconstitutional.

But that decision did not hold up during the appeals process. While the damages and apology stood, the appeal – filed by the Bush administration and successfully argued by the Obama administration – restored the constitutionality of those provisions in the Patriot Act that were initially declared unconstitutional.

Are You a Terrorist?

Lancaster, England: I'm searching the web to see how the Animal Enterprise Terrorism Act (ACTA) – the legislation that independent journalist Will Potter testified again which has since become US law – is being implemented.

I start by checking out Will's website Greenisthenewred.com. On the website, Will recounts case after case where 'right wing activities' like those of Oklahoma City Bomber Timothy McVeigh are not labelled terrorist activities by some US government officials while 'left wing activities' like protests by environmental and animal rights groups are labelled terrorist activities. He sums up his position with this flow chart.

Figure 149: 'Are You a Terrorist?' Provided by Will Potter.

But Will's site also chronicles some of the obstacles the government is confronting in implementing AETA. Two cases in particular bear mention. One case pertains to a group that used the internet to post news of both legal and illegal protest actions, and another case pertains to a group that 'allegedly chalked slogans on the sidewalk, distributed fliers and attended protests'.[5] In both cases, these groups were indicted under AETA, and in both cases their indictments were thrown out, either on the grounds that the government had failed to explain what it was about these activities that amounted to 'terrorism' and/or because in the views of the presiding judges the government might be treating protected politics protests as criminal crimes.[6]

Will writes that 'this is a victory worth celebrating'[7] but cautions that these activists could be re-indicted for these same activities if the indictments are rewritten to taken into account the judges' concerns.

Back from the brink

Buffalo, New York: I've asked Steve Kurtz how his experience of being suspected by the US government of being a bioterrorist who murdered his wife and how his long legal battle to clear his name have affected his view of citizenship.

'I don't think my relationship to citizenship has changed much because of this experience. I still feel as motivated as ever, and I think that the tide is turning. I think America is taking some steps backward from the brink of Neo-Fascism that Bush lead us to'.

Not only does Steve believe the tide is turning. He believes that because US Americans are tiring of the War in Iraq and because the country is mired in a deep economic crisis, 'this is potentially another time much like 9/11'. While the crisis of 9/11 led President Bush down the path of Neo-Conservatism, Steve believes that the economic crisis and its long-term fallout might lead President Obama down a more progressive path that could include 'peace in Iraq, universal healthcare, a ground-up distribution of the wealth instead of giving it all to the wealthy and letting it all trickle down'.

Steve says of President Obama, 'He's talking the talk I want to hear, and maybe in this crisis moment with the right amount of pressure and enough people motivated by the desperation of this economic crisis, we will be able to make Obama keep these promises'.

'This is citizenship again', Steve explains, because 'we're gonna have to make him do these things'.

Figure 150: Steve Kurtz performing a biomedical art project. Image provided by the Critical Art Ensemble.

This is our time

Cleveland, Ohio: I am at the Council on American-Islamic Relations Ohio offices interviewing Julia Shearson about her case against the US government to get herself removed from the Terrorist Watch List. At the time of our interview, Barack Obama has recently replaced George W. Bush as President of the United States. Julia and I reflect on the hope the new President promises for the nation, and I remind Julia how President Obama evoked the US motto, 'Out of Many, One' in his election-night victory speech. This is what the President said:

> This is our time – to put our people back to work and open doors of opportunity for our kids; to restore prosperity and promote the cause of peace; to reclaim the American dream and reaffirm that fundamental truth – that out of many, we are one; that while we breathe, we hope, and where we are met with cynicism and doubt, and those who tell us that we can't, we will respond with that timeless creed that sums up the spirit of a people: yes, we can.[8]

I ask Julia what difference the Obama presidency has made to her case.

Julia knows that President Obama and his administration have abandoned the Bush administration phrase 'War on Terror'. In the spirit of putting Bush's tactics for fighting terrorism behind him, President Obama signed an executive order making it illegal for any officer of the US government to engage in torture, and he has promised to close the Guantanamo Bay prisoner detention centers and withdraw US forces from Iraq as soon as possible.

In light of these developments, Julia clearly wants to embrace the President's hope. But in her role as an advocate for the rights of US Muslims, Julia is well aware of how promises and good intentions do not always translate into realities.

'Obama is President, and I'm still on the watch list', she tells me.

About a year later, I call Julia up to ask her if anything has changed with her case. Julia explains that nothing material has changed. But as Julia keeps on speaking, it is clear to me that something immaterial has changed for her.

She puts it like this.

'One thing that has really jelled for me through this experience is that the struggle to preserve the Republic and a constitutional form of government where the executive does not have the authority to violate the law is not an easy endeavor. It's like holding back the wilderness. It takes tremendous sacrifice. And I just hope in the end it's worth it'.

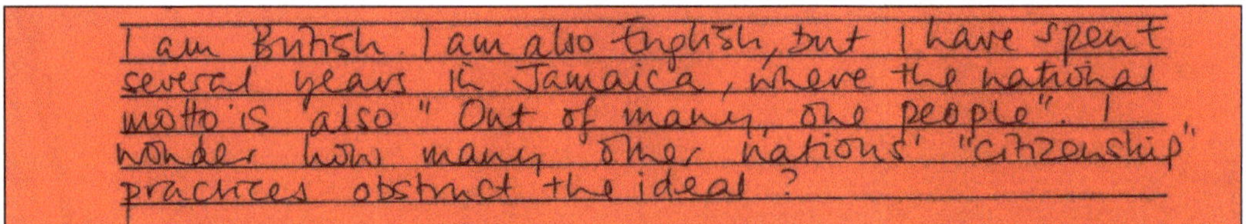
I am British. I am also English, but I have spent several years in Jamaica, where the national motto is also "Out of many, one people". I wonder how many 'other nations' "citizenship" practices obstruct the ideal?

Figure 151: Anonymous comment.

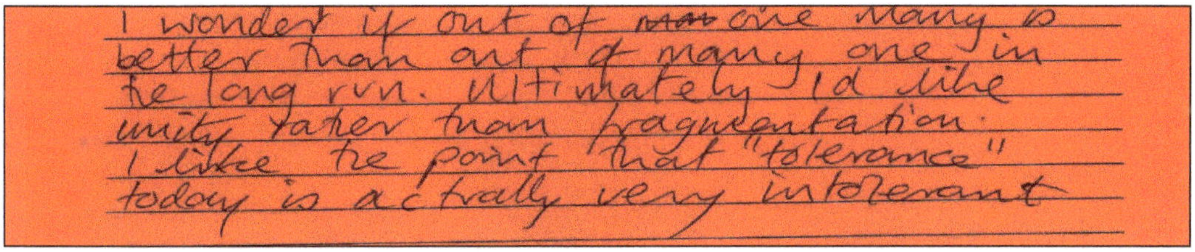
I wonder if out of one many is better than out of many one in the long run. Ultimately I'd like unity rather than fragmentation. I like the point that "tolerance" today is actually very intolerant

Figure 152: Anonymous comment.

Out of touch

Lancaster, England: For almost two years now, I have failed to renew my contacts with Abe Dabdoub, the Canadian of Saudi descent who became a US citizen and who had since been stopped and searched some fifty consecutive times when crossing the Canadian-US border. I had no idea if Abe was still being detained when he tried to re-enter the US from Canada. I had no idea if he was still living in the US or if he had returned to Canada, where he also holds citizenship. And I had no idea how he felt any longer about being a US American.

Then, after countless attempts to re-establish contact, I get an email from Abe. He tells me he has moved to California to take up a new job. He also tells me that he has not been detained crossing the US-Canadian border for two years now. He writes, 'I think when I was

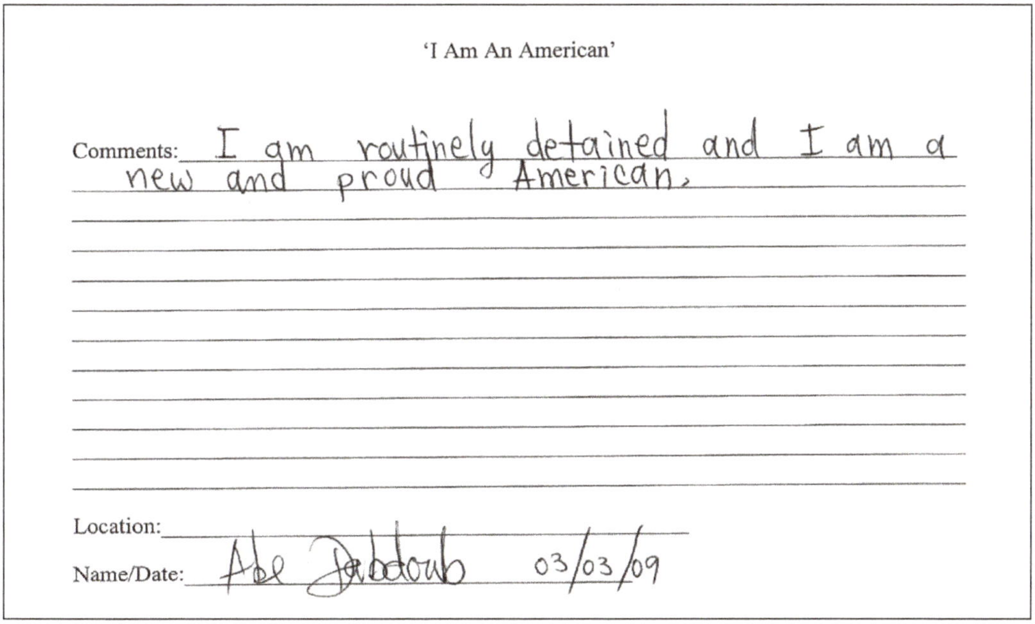
'I Am An American'

Comments: I am routinely detained and I am a new and proud American.

Location:

Name/Date: Abe Dabdoub 03/03/09

Figure 153: Abe Dabdoub's comment card.

part of the ACLU [American Civil Liberties Union] suit against the government, it helped me'. That lawsuit challenged the US detention of people like Abe on the grounds that the US government was involved in racial profiling. The lawsuit has since been dropped, but it seems even as a potential challenge to US border detention practices, it had a positive effect on Abe's life.

When I ask Abe if he has any further reflections on what it means to him to be a US citizen in light of his case, this is what he writes: 'I am happy to be a dual citizen of the United States and Canada'.

Filming the Fear of Difference

Goldsmiths College, London, England: My academic colleague Kate Nash invites me to screen my films at her university. She asks me to suggest a title. All I can come up with is 'I am an American'. She suggests a longer title: '"I am an American": Filming the Fear of Difference'.

I consider my project through this new title. I like how it suggests a neat opposition between the claim to be an identity – to be a US American – and the fearful difference that makes this claim exclusive. 'I am an American' is a nationalist articulation. Identity/'Americanness'/US Americans are supposed to be located within this national space, within the United States. Fear of the other usually refers to the fear of those others who are citizens of other states. During the Cold War, we called these fearful others 'communists'. During the War on Terror, we call them 'terrorists'.

But the identity/difference opposition that runs through my project doesn't work like that. It is not referring to the identity of the US state as opposed to the presumed difference of other states (a very loaded claim in and of itself). Instead, it examines how difference functions *within* the US, *within* categories like citizenship and patriotism and tolerance and justice where we US Americans want to believe there is no consequential difference. It does so by examining a moment in US history when some US citizens labeled other US citizens 'terrorist' or 'refugees' or 'undeserving immigrants' as a way to deny them their citizenship rights, even though these US citizens were not guilty of any crimes.

I think about Barbara Johnson's idea of 'critical difference' – the idea that difference always exists within the One, that difference keeps an identity from corresponding to its image of itself as One, as whole, as united, as complete.[9] Taking Johnson's observation seriously, this means that the United States of America as a lived reality will never correspond to our ideals about it, and US citizens in their everyday lives will never correspond to our ideals about them, us.

I think about the US Americans I interviewed. Every one of them is either fearful of this 'critical difference' or personifies this 'critical difference' either in body or belief. Those who are most fearful of difference are the very ones who most fervently claim to be American, as if 'American' were an unchanging, completed category. Their fear is very simple – that 'different' US Americans will change what it means to be a US American and change what

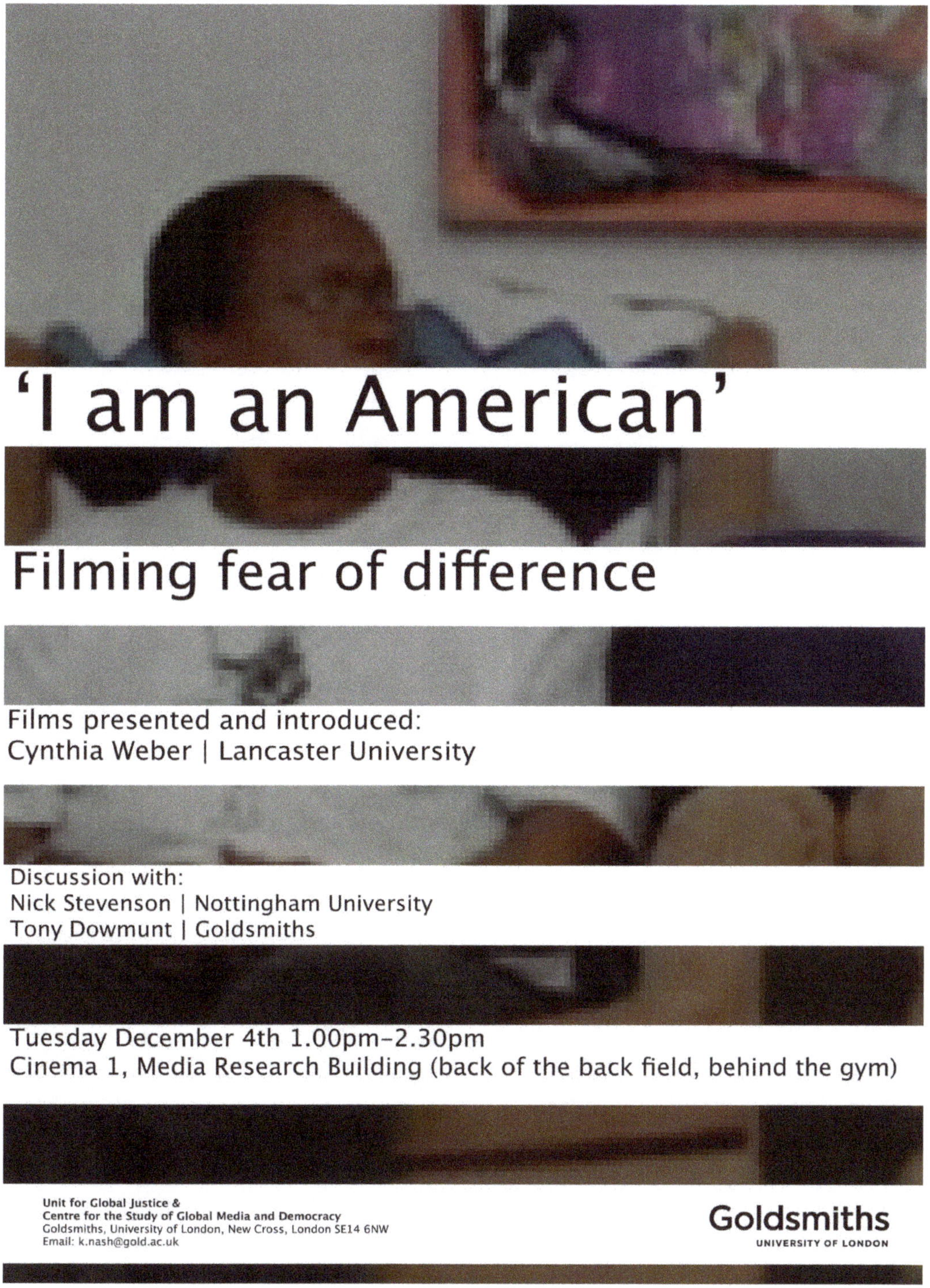

Figure 154: 'Filming the Fear of Difference' poster. Provided by Kate Nash.

the United States of America is. They forget that this is what has been happening since the moment the US became the US. They fail to grasp how they themselves are changing the US, whether they are modern-day Minutemen or other types of American Dreamers.

This is why, as I was filming this project, it was so important to me that 'different' US Americans proclaimed their difference *and at the same time* made their claims to be US Americans, saying things like 'I am a political refugee from America, and I am an American' or 'I am a wrongly accused terrorist spy, and I am a patriotic American'. For by doing this, they begin to erode this identity/difference dichotomy, this 'American'/'fearful difference' opposition. And as some of them make this claim – like Phil McDowell and James Yee and Ofelia Rivas – they begin to erode another dichotomy as well, this time between the citizen and the human in ways that remind us that one's citizenship or relationship to citizenship should never be taken as an excuse to treat people inhumanely.

People like Phil and James and Ofelia and everyone else I interviewed live their lives as 'critical difference' – as that lack of correspondence between being US citizens and being 'ideal US Americans'. We all do. Most of the people I interviewed just happen to be more aware of their lack of fit into a fixed notion of 'America' because 'America' claims that these people are or were 'unfit citizens', for they expose the gap between the reality and the ideal of being a US American.

My thoughts return to where I started, to the American Ad Council's 'I am an American' PSA. For the first time, I grasp that the makers of that PSA were, like me, filming the fear of difference. For this fear of difference described the mood in the US immediately after 9/11, a fearfulness of 'others' out there in other countries who had infiltrated 'us' in our own country. What the PSA tried to put to rest was the creeping concern that some of 'us' might actually be some of 'them'. Its strategy for avoiding a backlash was to erase (most) difference at the same time that it celebrated (some) difference, by showing how the Many were already part of the One. In so doing, the Ad Council denied the existence of 'critical difference' and therefore denied US Americans the opportunity to critically reflect on what it means and should mean to be a US American in the aftermath of 9/11.

I chose a different strategy: to acknowledge the gap between the One and the Many, to chronicle the 'critical difference' that – every bit as much as its melting pot myth – makes

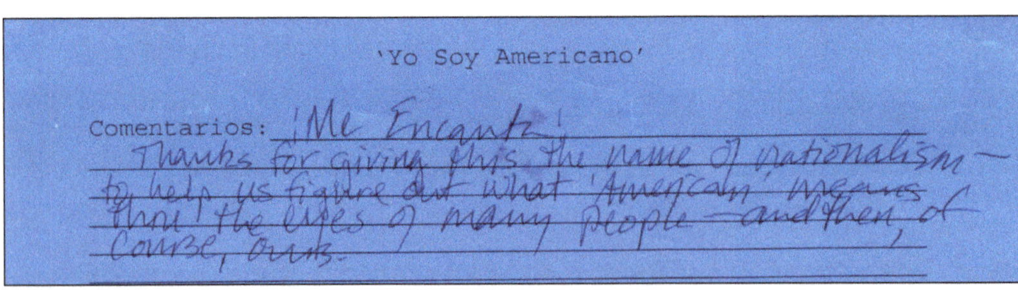
'Yo Soy Americano'

Comentarios: ¡Me Encanta! Thanks for giving this the name of nationalism – to help us figure out what 'American' means thru the eyes of many people – and then, of course, ours.

Figure 155: Anonymous comment.

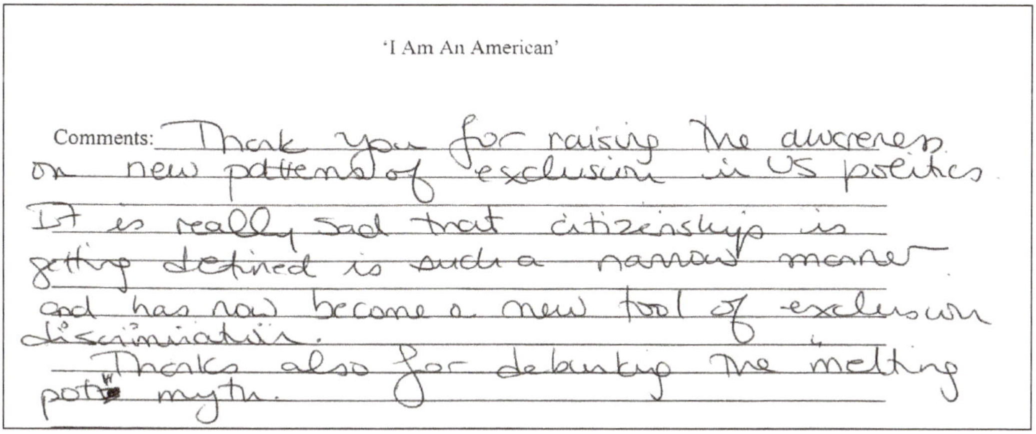
'I Am An American'

Comments: Thank you for raising the awareness on new patterns of exclusion in US politics. It is really sad that citizenship is getting defined in such a narrow manner and has now become a new tool of exclusion discrimination. Thanks also for debunking the melting pot myth.

Figure 156: Anonymous comment.

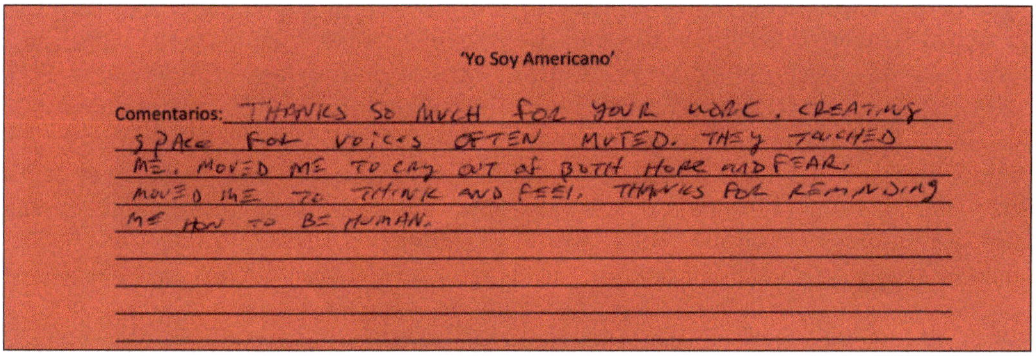
'Yo Soy Americano'

Comentarios: THANKS SO MUCH FOR YOUR WORK. CREATING SPACE FOR VOICES OFTEN MUTED. THEY TOUCHED ME. MOVED ME TO CRY OUT OF BOTH HOPE AND FEAR. MOVED ME TO THINK AND FEEL. THANKS FOR REMINDING ME HOW TO BE HUMAN.

Figure 157: Anonymous comment.

the US what it is, and to valorize those exercises of US citizenship that mobilize this critical difference in ways that might make us not just better citizens but better human beings.

I write to my colleague. 'Great title. Don't change a word'.

Forget September 11

Copenhagen, Denmark: I am fielding questions about my project after a public screening. Among those in the audience are several students and scholars of international relations. After a few initial questions, a graduate student raises his hand to ask a question critical of the project. 'Even though it doesn't mean to, doesn't your project memorialize September 11, 2001? And wouldn't we be better served to "forget September 11"?'

This student certainly has a point. For when we consider how the memory of September 11 has been mobilized by the US government and the US media to justify foreign wars, suspend civil liberties, and increase security measures that effectively make many people and states less secure, forgetting September 11 seems like a pretty good idea. When you add to that that the Obama Administration has – with mixed success – been trying to reverse some Bush Administration policies (like the indefinite detention of 'enemy combatants' at Guantanamo Bay, Cuba), contain others (by withdrawing US combat troops from Iraq), and forgot others altogether (by dropping the phrase 'the War on Terror' from its lexicon), it might well be time for the rest of us to move beyond September 11 and the War on Terror it spawned as well.

The student also has a point about how my project works in relation to the memorialization of September 11, not only as it functions at small public screenings like this one but because I have agreed to donate the project to the permanent collection of the September 11 Memorial Museum which will stand at the former site of the World Trade Center in New York. Surely, no gesture on my part could be more complicit in the memorialization of September 11 than this one.

But things aren't quite that simple, either in terms of US history or in terms of the politics of memory. Thinking about US history first, on the one hand, the Obama administration has continued far more Bush administration security policies than it has discontinued. Gitmo is still open, US troops and/or 'military advisors' are still in Iraq and Afghanistan, and US civil liberties are still seriously curtailed under the renewed Patriot Act. On the other hand, September 11, 2001, has always been about much more than the specific policies of the Bush or Obama administrations. In more general terms and maybe even more importantly, September 11 is about how it became possible for a majority of the US citizenry to consent to its government's mobilization of a crisis to generate an indefinite war, designate a new brand of enemy beyond its borders, and divide the US citizenry itself among those whose differences can be tolerated and those whose differences are intolerable.

So here's the problem. Even if we were to agree that the War on Terror was President George W. Bush's war, September 11, 2001, was not the only time in US history when a US president mobilized a crisis to generate an indefinite war and designate new enemies foreign and domestic with the consent of the US public. President Harry Truman did it when he declared the Cold War against the Soviet Union, which among other things perpetuated an economically expensive nuclear arms race and a civilly expensive witch hunt for US communists during (and sometimes after) the McCarthy era . President Richard Nixon did it when he declared the War on Drugs, which among other things justified the US-backed militarization of some Latin American states where this war was fought and created legal and illegal Drug War refugees from these states who fled to the US as often resented immigrants. And I can guarantee you that future US presidents will use future crises to declare future indefinite wars against future enemies. And part of how these future presidents will determine who is a friend and who is an enemy will be by deciding what it means to be unquestionably American, tolerably American, and intolerably American. So the historical situation is complicated.

It's also complicated when we think about the relationship of September 11 to memory. If by forgetting September 11, US citizens could leave behind the more distasteful policies

Figure 159: I am an American.

of the War on Terror and the particular mobilizations of US memory that made and make these policies possible, then there is good reason to forget September 11. But if by forgetting September 11, US citizens forget to pay attention to the techniques and strategies employed by not just the Bush administration and the contemporary US media but by many past and I expect future administrations and media organizations, to mobilize memory in times of crisis for questionable political ends, then we would be forgetting September 11 at our peril.

What this means is that the issue isn't whether or not we remember or forget September 11. The issue is *how* we remember or forget September 11 and what that remembering or forgetting makes possible.

As Maja Zehfuss has persuasively argued, the memory of those US citizens who died on September 11 was mobilized by the Bush administration not only to justify a specific set of US domestic and international policies but to preclude 'the contemplation of alternative responses to the events [of September 11]'.[10] This was made possible as much by government and media interpretations of the events of September 11 as it was by the incessant replaying of dramatic images of those events on television and the internet. Our memory of September 11, then, is not only emotional or intellectual; it is visual. As Zehfuss puts it, 'We remember the picture'.[11]

By producing an alternative set of pictures about some US citizens living in the wake of September 11, my project does not forget those who died on September 11. But it does insist that US Americans also remember those living, often 'intolerably different' US citizens who bear the consequences of the US foreign and domestic policies of the War on Terror because they live in the shadow of the promise of what it means to be an American.

Maybe my unofficial image-based accounts of the living can function differently than the official image-based accounts of the dead. Maybe they can interrupt official memorializations of September 11, even – or indeed especially – when housed in the most sacred US memorial to that day. Maybe they can encourage US citizens to rethink the positions to which they have been assigned[12] – whether by the US state or by the US media – regarding citizenship, identity, tolerance, nationalism, patriotism, justice and indeed memory itself. Maybe in the first instance US citizens

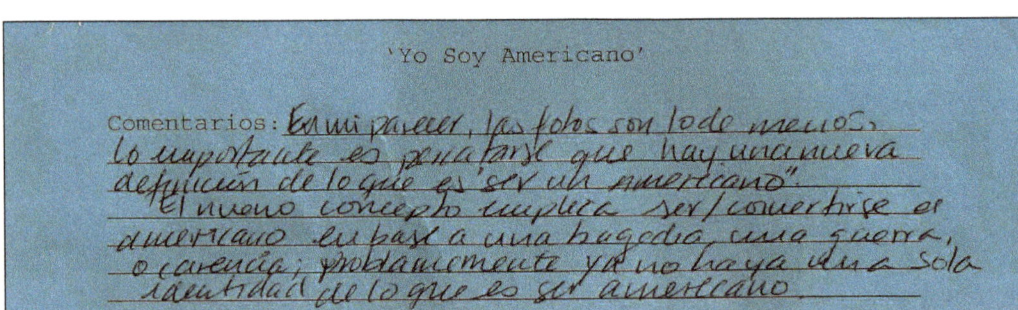
'Yo Soy Americano'

Comentarios: En mi parecer, las fotos son lo de menos, lo importante es pensarse que hay una nueva definición de lo que es 'ser un americano'. El nuevo concepto implica ser/convertirse en americano en base a una tragedia, una guerra, o carencia; probablemente ya no haya una sola identidad de lo que es ser americano.

Figure 160: Anonymous comment. Translation: From my perspective, the photos are the least of it; what's important is to think about the new ways 'to be an American' is being defined. One way suggests that to be/become an American is to embrace a tragedy, a war, a lack; this probably isn't the only way to be American.

might rethink these positions in relation to the War on Terror. And maybe as US history goes on, they can rethink them again beyond this context and beyond its nationalist parameters.

Of course, I have no idea how this project will be received, how it will be used, and what it might do. All I know for sure – and this is what I tell the student who asked me his question – is that I will forget September 11 when the US government and media do.

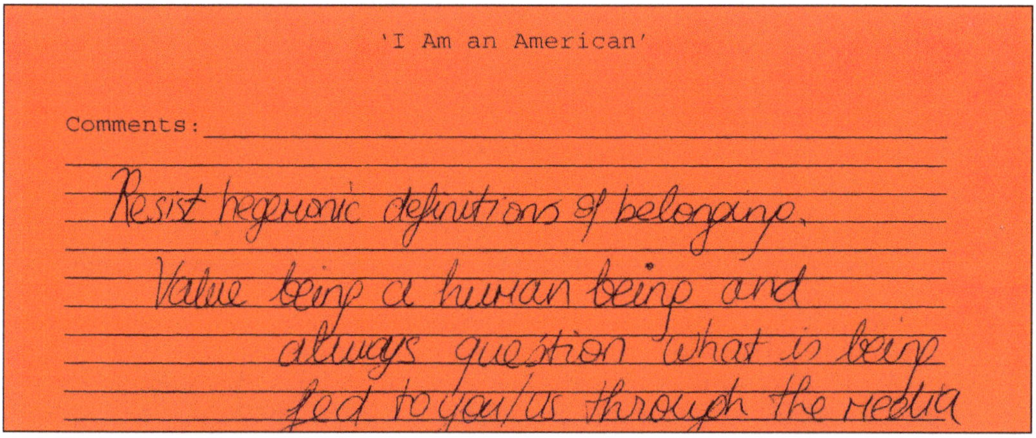

Figure 161: Anonymous comment.

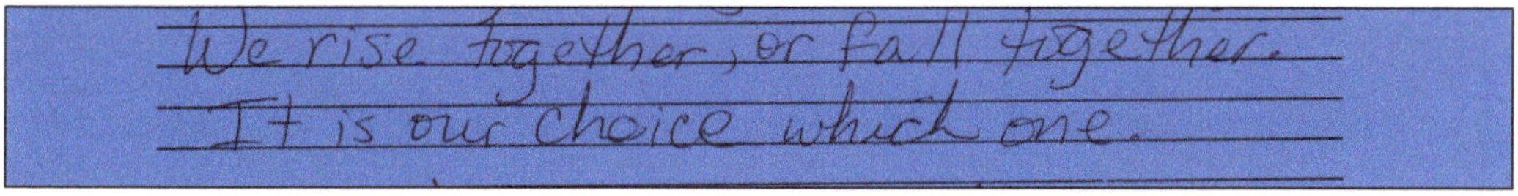

Figure 162: Anonymous comment.

Figure 163: Anonymous comment.

Notes

1. For a transcript of President Obama's speech, see: http://blogs.wsj.com/washwire/2010/07/01/transcript-of-obamas-immigration-speech/. Downloaded October 27 2010.
2. Ron Suskind (2004), 'Without a Doubt', *The New York Times Magazine*, October 17, http://www.ronsuskind.com/articles/000106.html. Downloaded 12 September 2009.
3. 'Huge Victory! "Littering" Conviction Overturned', No More Deaths Press Release, September 2, 2010, http://www.nomoredeaths.org/Press-Releases/littering-conviction-of-border-volunteer-overturned-by-appeals-court.html. Downloaded 3 September 2010.
4. 'Huge Victory! "Littering" Conviction Overturned', No More Deaths Press Release, September 2, 2010, http://www.nomoredeaths.org/Press-Releases/littering-conviction-of-border-volunteer-overturned-by-appeals-court.html. Downloaded 3 September 2010.
5. 'BREAKING: aeta 4 Case Dismissed, But re-Indictment Possible', http://www.greenisthenewred.com/blog/aeta-4-case-thrown-out-dismissed/3015/. Downloaded 25 September 2010.
6. For more details on the specifics of these cases, see 'BREAKING: aeta 4 Case Dismissed, But re-Indictment Possible', http://www.greenisthenewred.com/blog/aeta-4-case-thrown-out-dismissed/3015/. Downloaded 25 September 2010.
7. 'BREAKING: aeta 4 Case Dismissed, But re-Indictment Possible', http://www.greenisthenewred.com/blog/aeta-4-case-thrown-out-dismissed/3015/. Downloaded 25 September 2010.
8. Barack Obama (2008), 'Change Has Come To America', November 4, http://www.america.gov/st/usg-english/2009/January/20090113162144jmnamdeirf0.2681696.html. Downloaded 25 September 2010.
9. Barbara Johnson (1985), *The Critical Difference: Essays in the Contemporary Rhetoric of Reading*, Baltimore: The Johns Hopkins University Press. Johnson is here working with Jacques Derrida's idea of *différance*. As Derrida explains, a culture is able to 'take the form of the subject only in the non-identity to itself, or if you prefer, only in the difference with itself. There is no culture or cultural identity without this difference *with itself*. What interests me is the differences or *différance* within US national culture that the statement 'I am an American' evokes, erases, and defers every time US citizens utter it. See Jacques Derrida (1992), *The Other Heading: Reflections on Today's Europe* (trans. Pascale-Anne Brault and Michael B Naas), Bloomington, IN: University of Indiana Press, pp. 9–10.
10. Maja Zehfuss (2003), 'Forget September 11', *Third World Quarterly*, 24:3, p. 513.
11. Maja Zehfuss (2003), 'Forget September 11', *Third World Quarterly*, 24: 3, p. 513.
12. Here I am paraphrasing a comment made by Judith Butler in response to the question she was asked of why she mobilizes a US identity – a 'US we' – in her comments about September 11. Butler's response was that she does this deliberately in order to offer 'a way of working one's way out of the position to which one has been assigned'. Judith Butler (2009), 'Frames of War', public lecture for the Research Institute for Cosmopolitan Cultures, Manchester University, February 5.

Part II

Academic Responses

International Political Sociology Forum on Cynthia Weber's Multi-media Project 'I am an American'

Introduction by Jef Huysmans

As a response to the American Ad Council's advertising campaign 'I am an American', Cynthia Weber developed a multi-media project 'I am an American': Video Portraits of Unsafe US Citizens. It raises questions about the form of presenting and developing knowledge and the place of aesthetics and modern video techniques in engaging politically and intellectually with national identity construction, the constitution of citizenship and insecurity, and negotiating the relation between being a citizen and being a human in contemporary world politics.

Since the project intertwines questions about aesthetic forms of politics with substantive interrogations of contemporary political being, the journal invited five authors to comment on the medium of presentation, citizenship and political being, and implications for international studies.

From 'Am I an American?' to 'I am an American!' Cynthia Weber on citizenship, identity and security

by Timothy W. Luke

Cynthia Weber's 'I am an American' multimedia video art installations (Weber 2007) are remarkable achievements. These works capture the conflicted tensions of the Bush (43) era during which many citizens asked themselves in the shadows of Abu Ghraib, Guantanamo, or post-Katrina New Orleans, 'Am I an American?' While her focus is upon the contestable character of American nationality, Weber's narrative depicts how civic identity is expressed diversely during severe crises by its multicultural citizenry. At least since the first World Trade Center bombing in 1993, many pundits have set 'Americanism' against 'Terrorism' in the United States to discover 'threatening others', but Weber's innovative interventions artistically re-examine the moral nuances that complicated such searches for, or defenses against, 'unsafe citizens' (Weber 2008).

Her artwork – whether as digital prints or video installations – is aimed at the world as well as US audiences, but her portraits are decisive. They re-examine the limits of America: the borderlands where 'Americans' per se rapidly can fade or even disappear under pressures from nation-states pushing against 'the outside' along the many invisible dividing lines that conventional maps fail to trace. In the American Southwest or along the Canadian-American border, the barriers can be physically obvious; but liminal zones of inside/outside are in any space. Consequently, Weber ranges far and wide, probing many sites with her art and unsettling the comfortable zones that give national identity such intensity.

There always are deeper dynamics of national soulcraft and citizenship training in play with the many divergent ways that raw force and harsh law can be reconstructed in art exhibitions (Luke 1992). Indeed, museums have served for decades as mechanisms for 'imagining community' and 'inventing tradition' (Anderson 1991), especially in the diverse, multicultural society of the United States of America. As these tendencies crystallize in Weber's project, she deftly leverages the new media ecologies of web-based content, public social science, cinemagraphic critique, and video art to reveal the power of a unique intertextual aesthetic. In her interventions, it is clear Weber explores those

> manifold relations of power which permeate, characterize and constitute the social body, and these relations of power cannot themselves be established, consolidated nor implemented without the production, accumulation, circulation and functioning of a discourse. There can be no possible exercise of power without a certain economy of discourses of truth which operates through and on the basis of this association. (Foucault 1980: 95)

Within the traditional economies of discourse usually associated with safety and citizenship in many conventional civic art works, one can witness how those discourses of truth cash in and out of the manifold relations of power from the renowned 2001 Ad Council campaign, 'I am an American'. Each of Weber's video portraits, on the other hand, expertly rethinks the truth discourse of contemporary citizenship as this public service announcement (PSA) produces, accumulates, and circulates its ideological functions in the relations of national identity that underpin American power.

Started first in 1942 with its famous World War II-era 'Loose Lips Sink Ships' and 'Buy War Bonds', these American Ad Council campaigns are unique ideological artifacts. The group's own accounts of its civic contribution to US society are 'to improve the lives of Americans' and 'effect positive change' (http://www.adcouncil.org/). From the initial mobilization ten days after 9/11 in today's on-going GWOT (Global War on Terror), the 'I am an American' campaign arguably is designed to meet worthy goals. That is, it means to short-circuit a 'possible backlash against Arab Americans and other ethnic groups after the attacks', so the 'I am an American' PSA rapidly runs through multiple images featuring 'people of many ages, races and religions' proudly stating 'I am an American' (Ad Council of America 2001).

The rush of this collage draws deeply from image and idea stocks that public multiculturalism has generated since the 1960s. With an intense swirl of signs, it signals diversity of age, race, gender, occupation, region and class; but, at the same time, the Ad Council also observes that its 30-second and 60-second spot 'ends with the words, *E Pluribus Unum*, which means out of many, one'. That phrase communicates that 'out of many faces, religions, geographical backgrounds, and ethnicities, we are one nation' (Ad Council of America 2001).

Cynthia Weber's aesthetic project reworks the images and ideologies in this campaign through the same medium: video portraits. She contests the purpose of such PSAs, questioning how big business, professional expertise, and the state in this Ad Council configuration actually are 'addressing critical social issues for generations of Americans' (http://www.adcouncil.org/default.aspx?id=15). Weber takes the Ad Council's campaign title, which is filmed with its fast cuts of images and slick sound splices to hang that tag line together in a constant positive riff, but she turns the whole PSA on its head. In turn, its stock image rushes become her video palette. Recast, retaped and reshot, Weber's video portraits then carefully retrace how nationally enforced, or even just endorsed, these citizenship identities can run afoul of coercive reality when public safety is in question. Yet, from such obstacles and occlusions, she discovers a more robust pluralistic quality in the United States, namely, an obverse, parallel, or shared actuality. In each film, it gels as one of *Ex Uno, Plures*, or 'out of one, many'.

Culture warriors from the right, like Lynne V. Cheney, fret ruefully;

> Museums used to be places that invited visitors to learn about great works of art, to understand their society, and to know more about the course of history. Today, like so many other cultural institutions, they appear instead to be in the business of debunking greatness, Western society, and even history itself. (Cheney 1995: 144)

Cynthia Weber's art should be seen as working both sides of the ideological fences that Cheney runs over the ranges of American cultural identity, and this open-ended outcome is very constructive. While debunking one narrow sense of national greatness, Western civilization of historical development, Weber is, in fact, using powerful video art to move viewers and visitors to reconsider what Cheney sees as 'the course of history' as well as how greatly ordinary individuals struggle to make good on the real promise of America's ethical, legal, and political ideals that Cheney believes should be denied to many Americans in her moral panic over traditional national identity.

From the perspective of museum studies, today's networked computing environments coupled with the global culture industry's reoccupation of many urban built environments in American cities large and small create entirely new sites of exhibition for the edgy work of innovative critics like Cynthia Weber. Likewise, the 'museum politics' (Luke 2002) of such flexible spaces are evolving in important new ways. Not unlike the imperial dominions in which America now commands 'an empire of bases' (Johnson 2004), and on which the sun never sets, Weber's artistic project is a 24 × 7 act of intervention whose resistance does not fade at dusk. Thanks to OpenDemocracy, YouTube, and many other websites, from urban weekly newspapers online to art gallery hosts, Cynthia Weber's work is always out on display for visitation, contemplation and recognition. Of course, this unique work also has a gallery life. For some people, Weber's work is appreciated while circulating through small display spaces and looking at glossy still-prints and continuous film loops. Moreover, this exhibit's openings at several venues in cities large and small across America's empire of bases have been well-received. As an intertextual aesthetic project with its own shows of force (Luke 1992), Weber's production paradoxically parallels the 24 × 7 surveillance state with its wonderful critical interrogation of the United States as well as a spirited defense of individual difference across America during Washington's Global War on Terrorism. Museums, art galleries and video servers are carriers for cultural texts, political memories, and national identities. In turn, art displays and historical exhibits are among society's most accessible relays of moral expectations and behavioral education. Hence, this work helps us re-evaluate how galleries and museums – whether brick-and-mortar or online – serve as 'sites of finely structured normative argument and artfully staged cultural normalization' (Luke 2002: xxiv).

Ever since their rapid proliferation in the Victorian era, museums have come to be regarded as secular cathedrals charged with the guardianship of this or that nation's shared history, cultural treasures, and moral identity. Weber's use of conventionalized public service announcement tropes in a subversive art work about America after 9/11 is an excellent conceptual maneuver to get her viewers to reflect more critically about how shared America's history is, who is an American cultural treasure, and what moral identity American citizens should aspire to acquire. By organizing exhibition spaces or coordinating art displays, curators act as significant normative authorities by organizing what museum visitors see, experience and perhaps come to accept, question or value. Indeed, this historical discretion has prompted the curators of the US September 11 Memorial Museum to invite Weber to include these stirring video artworks in their permanent collection.

As artist/film-maker, then, Weber brings a sharper personal focus to the abstract phenomena of sovereign power that she also explores as scholar/teacher. Together and alone, each of her subjects represent the actual 'manyness' of Americans as well as potential 'oneness' of the United States of America. Made by circumstance into refugees, dissenters, resisters or detainees, they speak about the emptiness as well as the fullness of the US as a nation. While believing everyday civic dreams in America, and reaffirming they are American, they also show the dark divides in everyday life between class, ethnicity, gender, and race. 'We are not all white, elite people', as one of the film's featured persons, Ofelia Rivas, a Tohono O'odham indigenous rights activist fighting the new US-Mexico border fence dividing her First Nation's lands, strongly underscores.

The sweep of American influence is pervasive, and it persistently hunts down the 'unsafe noncitizen' opposing its expansive empire of bases (Johnson 2004). Yet, as the life of Ofelia

Rivas indicates, many Americans always have had to endure being unsafe and bear doubts of their non-citizenship as familiar problems in their everyday life. With this art project, however, one can observe how passionately – in the face of bureaucratic disasters and state failures – that they, and arguably millions of others, still can answer their own nagging questions on camera for Cynthia Weber with clear answers by affirming 'I am an American'.

References

Ad Council of America (2001), 'I am an American', http://adcouncil.org/default.aspx?id=141.

Anderson, Benedict (1991), *Imagined Communities: Reflections on the Origin and Spread of Nationalism*, revised edition, London: Verso.

Cheney, Lynne V. (1995), *Telling the Truth: Why Our Culture and Our Country Have Stopped Making Sense – and What We Can Do About It*, New York: Simon and Schulster.

Foucault, Michel (1980), *Power/Knowledge: Selected Interviews and Other Writings, 1972–1977*, New York: Pantheon.

Johnson, Chalmers (2004), *The Sorrows of Empire*, New York: Metropolitan Books.

Luke, Timothy W. (2002), *Museum Politics: Power Plays at the Exhibition*, Minneapolis: University of Minnesota Press.

Luke, Timothy W. (1992), *Shows of Force: Power, Politics and Ideology in Art Exhibitions*, Durham: Duke University Press.

Weber, Cynthia (2007), 'Video Portraits of Post-9/11 Citizens Series', Lancaster: Pato Productions.

Weber, Cynthia (2008), 'Designing Safe Citizens', *Citizenship Studies*, 12: 2, pp. 125–142.

Flag code

by Alex Danchev

What kind of film is Cindy Weber's 'I am an American'?

Is it a war film – a war on terror film – or, more appropriately, an anti-war film? Embedded in it are some of the perennial themes of that perennial genre: honor, conscience, resistance, collaboration, death, glory, futility, interior emigration, posthumous commendation, and ritual commemoration.

Is it a documentary? The War on Terror raises in acute form the problems of show and tell (Danchev 2009). What images to show? Whose stories to tell? Which idiom to employ, feature film or documentary, the dramatic or the analytic? It is a moot point; and the distinction can blur. Errol Morris's *Standard Operating Procedure* (2008), on Abu Ghraib, may be the most important cinematic treatment of the War on Terror yet to appear (Danchev 2008). *Standard Operating Procedure* is a documentary that looks like a feature film. Morris calls it a non-fiction horror movie, a formulation which echoes Truman Capote's famous 'non-fiction novel', *In Cold Blood* (1966). Alex Gibney, director of *Taxi to the Dark Side* (2007), which won the Oscar for Best Documentary Feature in 2008, prefers to speak of 'authored non-fiction' rather than documentary film. Framed so, 'I am an American' is perhaps a non-fiction state-of-the-nation movie, a report on another country, a series of vignettes at once ordinary and unfamiliar – defamiliarized – a kind of *Let Us Now Praise Famous Men* (Agee and Evans 1988[1941]) by other means. 'Who are you who will read these words and study these photographs', wrote James Agee, apostrophically, in the preamble to that unforgettable collaboration with Walker Evans, 'and through what cause, and for what purpose, and by what right do you qualify to, and what will you do about it?' (Agee 1988[1941]: 9).

Is it art? If so, what kind of art is it? America's finest film critic, Manny Farber, drew a celebrated distinction between 'white elephant art' and 'termite art' that is apt to the purpose:

> Movies have always been suspiciously addicted to termite-art tendencies. Good work usually arises where the creators [...] seem to have no ambitions towards gilt culture but are involved in a kind of squandering-beaverish endeavor that isn't anywhere or for anything. A peculiar fact about termite-tapeworm-fungus-moss art is that it goes always forward eating its own boundaries, and, likely as not, leaves nothing in its path other than signs of eager, industrious, unkempt activity. [...]
>
> Masterpiece art, reminiscent of the enameled tobacco humidors and wooden lawn ponies bought at white elephant auctions decades ago, has come to dominate the over-populated arts of TV and movies. The three sins of white elephant art: (1) frame the action with an all-over pattern, (2) install every event, character, situation in a frieze of continuities, and (3) treat every inch of the screen and film as a potential area for prizeworthy creativity. (Farber 1998[1962]: 135, 137)

A classic example of masterpiece art in this domain is *In the Valley of Elah* (2007), written and directed by Paul Haggis, and 'inspired by actual events' – a Hollywood movie notable for its moral purpose and political courage. It centers on the disappearance of Mike Deerfield, a young infantry soldier recently returned from Iraq, and the investigation by his father Hank (Tommy Lee Jones), a former military policeman. Mike is to all intents and purposes a good soldier: a patriot with a conscience. Among his buddies in the section, his nickname is 'Doc'. This is a puzzle for his father, and remains a puzzle, until it is revealed that Mike had the trick of sticking his finger into the open wounds of Iraqi prisoners, and asking if it hurt. 'They shouldn't send heroes to places like Iraq', one of the section tells Hank. 'It's all fucked up'.

It transpires that Mike has been murdered by his buddies, after a night on the town, back home in New Mexico. They cut him into pieces, expertly, and set fire to them, before going for a chicken dinner.

In this morass, Hank Deerfield is the repository of integrity, the moral center of the film. His symbolic action has to do with the American flag. At the beginning of the film, at the start of his odyssey, he notices that the Stars and Stripes on the flagpole of the local high school is upside down. He stops and rectifies it, giving the Salvadorean school custodian a swift lesson in civics and citizenship and the rules of the game. Flying the flag upside down is an international signal of distress, he tells the man, a sign that you are in serious trouble. At the end of the film, when he returns home, he finds that his son had sent from Iraq a battle-worn Stars and Stripes, together with a group photograph of the section, smiling their souvenir smiles. Early the following morning he drives to the high school and hoists the tatterdemalion emblem, taping the rope to the pole for good measure. The camera pulls back. The flag is upside down.

For all its virtues, *In the Valley of Elah* is a textbook case of white elephant art, with its all-over pattern, its frieze of continuities, and its prizeworthy creativity. 'I am an American', by contrast, can be claimed for the termite tendency. 'My films are hauntologies', muses Weber, 'historical barbs that pierce through common sense about America and Americans and particularly about what has been occurring in the name of "America" and "Americans" in the wake of 9/11'.[1] These barbs seem to have no ambitions towards guilt culture; they are at the same time affecting and unaffected. The two films are utterly different, and yet they traffic in some of the same themes, and there is a striking affinity of image and message. The moral centre of 'I am an American' is more of an idea: the idea of the good American. In the ethics on display here, the quiet is the enemy of the good. There are many examples of moral courage in the film – almost as many as there are interviewees. What they tend to have in common is precisely that they are unquiet. The unquiet American has found her voice, and stance, and cause. I am haunted by the image of the human rights activist Shanti Sellz, vaguely self-conscious and slightly askew, holding the flag upside down as she struggles with her double-edged pledge (Figure 81, pages 106–107, Chapter 3).

The American flag is a potent symbol – and now, it appears, an essentially contested concept. The etiquette of the US Flag Code could not be clearer: 'It is flown upside down only as a distress signal' (US Flag Code). Cindy Weber's film is a disquisition on distress; a termite-tapeworm-fungus-moss approach to symbols and signals and codes. It is about what happens when we lose our way and abandon the rules of propriety. As the Chinese Book of Rites reminds us, 'the ruin of states, the destruction of families, and the perishing of individuals are always preceded by the abandonment of the rules of propriety' (Visser 1992: 23). It is about the codes we live by and the distress we feel when we slip anchor and part company with our country, or unsubscribe (as one might say) by caste or creed or conscience. 'I don't know how I feel about being an American anymore', says the Iraq war resister Jamine Aponte, more in sorrow than in anger. 'I used to think it was the greatest place in the world. I don't know if I believe that any more'. 'I am a soldier, a citizen, and a patriot', declares the former Army Chaplain James Yee, defiantly, at the conclusion of his memoir, *God and Country*. 'But in the eyes of a suspicious, misguided minority who have lost touch with America's inclusiveness, above all else I am a Muslim' (Yee 2005: 221).

'I am an American' deals in all sorts of distress. Perhaps it is not too much to suggest that the film itself is a distress signal. Out of many, one.

References

Agee, James and Evans, Walker (1988[1941]), *Let Us Now Praise Famous Men*, Boston: Houghton Mifflin.
Danchev, Alex (2008), 'Bad Apples, Dead Souls: Understanding Abu Ghraib', *International Affairs*, 84: 6, pp. 1271–1280.
Danchev, Alex (2009), *On Art and War and Terror*, Edinburgh: Edinburgh University Press.
Farber, Manny (1998[1962]), *Negative Space*, New York: Da Capo.
US Flag Code, available at: http://www.usa-flag-site.org/etiquette.shtml. Downloaded 28 January 2009.
Visser, Margaret (1992), *The Rituals of Dinner*, London: Viking.
Yee, James (2005), *For God and Country*, New York: Public Affairs.

'Do you know if your borders are secure?'

by Roxanne Lynn Doty

At this particular moment, this very long, eternally returning moment when uncertainties about who 'we' are hang heavy about us, voices echo from many directions disseminating messages about what it means to be an American, a citizen, and a good human being. These range from the relatively subtle and aesthetically articulated campaign of the American Ad Council to the dogmatic rants of media outlets such as FOX news and US talk radio. In the name of security, democracy, diversity and humanity itself we are encouraged/coerced into accepting an ultimately simplified understanding of our own identities, an understanding hinging on a certain blindness to the boundaries constantly being erected to circumscribe just what diversity can be allowed to mean and how much of it can be tolerated before it becomes threatening to the very idea of a unified identity and thus undermines the coherence of the statement 'I am an American'. However, as many have wrapped themselves in the myths of a popularly professed American identity, numerous situations and experiences illustrate the kinds and degrees of diversity that are at work, 'on the ground', outside the bounds of state generated proclamations. It is to these experiences that Cindy Weber's 'I am an American' turns. Through these films we hear statements about being an American that are not slick ad agency slogans but rather reflect the many silenced voices and situations which constitute the fragile fabric of who 'we' are.

For the most part, the stories in this video embody the values that the United States celebrates rhetorically, but so often negates in practices. The stories of each of the individuals in the film illustrate a complicated and rather uncomfortable relationship to the state, a state which is not in fact the final 'decider' when it comes to many of the real life situations that arise from and complicate the notion of being a 'good American citizen'. The state may have the authority to officially decide who can be an American citizen, but it cannot control the contradictions that incessantly circulate around the concept of citizenship itself, its relationship to morality, and the imperative to be a good human being. Ostensibly the state is supposed to make its citizens safe, but these stories show that the state can and does create unsafe situations – not unsafe because of an objective, external threat, but unsafe because of the state itself and its own simultaneously precarious and all powerful 'ground'. The people interviewed in these films pose a threat to the state because their stories render such a ground all the more unstable. Many of these individuals can never be considered 'safe citizens' (see Weber 2008) because their lives and experiences exceed the limits of national tolerance. I say 'many', but not all because I believe there is one story and one person/group in the films that actually embodies the state. This aspect of the film is significant in terms of illuminating the connections between the state and safe/unsafe citizens.

The disciplining of diversity, tolerance, and citizenship by the American Ad Council is mirrored in the words of Chris Simcox, founder and leader of the Minuteman Civil Defense Corp. There are a couple of ways one can interpret this particular segment in the collection of films and its place in the overall project. One is to understand the inclusion of Chris Simcox as simply one story amongst many whose 'I am an American' assertion highlights the diversity and tolerance presumed to define the United States. From the point of view of Simcox as citizen, just as for the others, there is no safe citizenship. Simcox too has a complicated and uneasy relationship with the state. He believes it has failed him and indeed has failed all US citizens by not fully exercising its sovereignty through its refusal to take control of its own territorial borders. His 'citizen political action group' seeks to right this situation. On this interpretation Simcox may be viewed with a certain degree of legitimacy, a man whose story deserves to be heard, a man who represents many other American citizens who share his frustrations. Indeed there is a risk that Simcox and the practices in which he engages will be lent a degree of legitimacy by virtue of inclusion in this project. But this project does not shy away from risk, and I would invite the viewer who leans toward this interpretation to rethink the film on Simcox and his relationship to the state, citizenship and humanity. Contrary to lending the practices of Simcox an air of legitimacy, I would suggest that the film actually highlights the ways in which Simcox repeats and reproduces the very myths propagated by the American Ad Council. The state lurks in the shadows of 'I am an American', and it is Simcox who throws light on it and gives it voice. He is in fact a crusader for the safe citizenship that has never existed. Simcox is the state's supplement patrolling the barren deserts and borderlands for those whose humanity must be denied for the sake of the compromise Weber (2010) refers to, i.e. citizen first, human second. The state, here the United States, but arguably any state needs people and groups like Chris Simcox and the Minuteman Civil Defense Corp just as it needs advertisements like the Ad Council's PSA. It is never completely decidable if these supplements are 'add-ons' to a pre-existing entity we call 'the state' or if, in fact, their presence marks an emptiness in 'the state' itself and thus a troubling aporia in any attempt to unproblematically define 'an American' (see Derrida 1976; 1993).

This second interpretation, I would argue, is more to the point. The other stories illustrate, as Weber suggests, that citizenship cannot guarantee one's humanity and that arguably citizenship as a concept and practice severely compromises humanity. This point is powerfully depicted in the stories of several of the interviewees, most notably Shanti Sellz who shows that humanitarianism is often criminalized in the name of misguided state security, or the story of American citizen Saul Arellano whose undocumented mother must be banished from the United States. The opposition between citizenship vs humanity looms large in these stories, the strong arm of the state obliterating the latter. Clearly these individuals have an extremely uncomfortable relationship with the state. In contrast, Simcox wants *to be the state* and reaffirm an understanding of citizenship, that the rest of the films brilliantly illustrate does not and perhaps never did exist. He wants to show the state how it *should* be, how it *should* exercise its sovereignty and protect its true citizens. He is the embodiment of injustice and violence that constitutes the 'modern compromise'. Simcox equates citizenship with humanity, with the right to have humanity, and he sets about to do his part to ensure that this idea of citizenship is not torn asunder and that the 'American-citizen-human' trinity remains intact. In doing so he explicitly articulates in a crude and direct way what the PSA must only imply and at a superficial level deny, i.e., that difference must be tightly controlled. Those who want to be citizens 'will assimilate' and 'leave behind unacceptable cultural practices', says Simcox in the film. He sees no need to specify particulars here; we all should just *know* what he means.

In the Phoenix, Arizona studio where his 'Radio Minuteman' program is broadcast, Simcox asks, 'Do You Know If Your Borders Are Secure?' It is a telling question and one that must be answered in the negative, though not for the reasons Chris Simcox would likely point to. 'Our' borders can never be fully secure not simply in the territorial sense but in the sense of the borders that would cordon off what the state would like the words 'I am an American' to convey and the inherent instability and open nature of what these words actually signify 'on the ground'. The diversity of American citizens portrayed in these films overflows anything that could be contained within the American Ad Council's campaign or within Simcox's undefined, but presumed to be always already known notion of 'unacceptable cultural practices'. 'And it has nothing to do with racism', says a voice in the background towards the end of the film. Oh, but it *does* have a great deal to do with racism – not in every single instance and often not in any straightforward, easily articulated way. Still, racism always has and continues to hover close to issues of borders, identities, and the saying of 'I am' this or that. '"White" has often been "the effective equivalent of 'American'"' (Nevins 2008: 13), and has been so thoroughly interwoven with culture, nation, and religion that it is virtually impossible for it *not* to be about racism.

Only someone who grossly misunderstands the invitation to critical, self-reflection offered in this film and in the films that constitute Weber's 'I am an American' project as a whole could find in them instead an opportunity to wave the flag of patriotism and good citizenship in a thinly disguised effort at self-promotion. In his smiling and smug arrogance, Simcox personifies the certitude that often characterizes the state itself. He is as oblivious to the film's questioning of his own brand of patriotism as the United States often is to the profound questions that experiences such as those depicted in Weber's films raise about exclusion, intolerance, and its own identity. In fact, Chris Simcox was so completely convinced of his righteousness in defending the myth of safe citizenship that on April 22, 2009, he announced that he would run for the position of United States Senator for the State of Arizona, and without the knowledge much less permission of Cindy Weber, appropriated her film 'Chris Simcox: "I am an American"' as an advertizement for his campaign (See Figure 147, page 187, Chapter 5).[2] Clearly, some borders between legal and illegal appropriation are not very secure or worthy of securing for Simcox.

References

Derrida, Jacques (1976), *Of Grammatology* (trans. Gayatri Chakravorty Spivak), Baltimore, Maryland: The Johns Hopkins University Press.

Derrida, Jacques (1993), *Aporias* (trans. Thomas Dutoit), Stanford: Stanford University Press.

Nevins, Joseph (2008), *Dying to Live – A Story of U.S. Immigration in an Age of Global Apartheid*, San Francisco, California: City Lights Books.

Weber, Cynthia (2010), 'Citizenship, Security, Humanity': Cynthia Weber's Multimedia Project "I am an American"', *International Political Sociology*, 4:1, pp. 80–85.

Weber, Cynthia (2008), 'Designing Safe Citizens', *Citizenship Studies*, 12: 2, pp. 125–142.

Missing citizenship

by Peter Nyers

Cynthia Weber has impressed upon us a formidable task: to unpack (briefly, no less) the statement 'I am an American'. It is a complex declaration, to be sure, as Weber illustrates in both her opening essay to this forum and in her multimedia project of the same title (Weber 2010). For all that is said and could be said about being American, what I find immediately striking about the statement is something that is left unsaid. An absence, something unspoken and unnamed, is at the core of 'I am an American'. After all, the statement 'I am an American' implies a claim to American citizenship. Citizenship is central, and yet it is missing within the statement. Citizenship is without presence, even though its absence can leave one to a whole host of everyday and exceptional forms of exclusion. Indeed, the stakes involved in one's relationship to citizenship are very high, something that Weber underscores when she notes how the 'good citizen' gets equated with the 'good human'. If what it means to be human is caught up in what it means to be a citizen, then the absence of the latter status should be cause for worry. And yet, as the category that formally binds the individual to the nation and the state (and, as Hindess [1998] emphasizes, to the international), citizenship is seemingly too obvious to be named. It is an extraneous disruption to the elegant flow of 'I am an American'. Its inclusion would risk reducing a sublime statement about belonging into a mere administrative detail.

Citizenship is missing from the original American Ad Council's 'I am an American' PSA because it is assumed that we know that nationality and patriotism are embodied by obvious subjects: citizens. By contrast, Weber's multimedia project refuses to leave citizenship unnamed, invisible, or missing; she asks each of her interviewees to reflect on citizenship in relation to their post-9/11 experiences. In this way, Weber suggests that there are other, not so obvious, subjects through which citizenship can be investigated. Recent scholarship in citizenship suggests that citizenship can be studied through its constitutive alterity (Isin 2002). Similarly, statements like 'I am American' can be investigated as claims made by obvious and not so obvious subjects. To understand citizenship it is not sufficient to despair over citizenship's exclusions; equally important is to investigate the claims about rights, membership, and belonging made by excluded populations.

Weber's 'I am an American' multimedia project demonstrates that there are, thankfully, plenty of examples from recent US history to inspire and sustain such investigations. For example, one of the most moving and politically suggestive film segments is the feature on the undocumented migrant Elvira Arellano and her US citizen son, Saul. Arellano took church sanctuary as a means to fight the deportation order that would break apart her family. Although her fight was in the end unsuccessful and Arellano was deported to Mexico, the massive community support for her case in Chicago and elsewhere played a role in inspiring the May 1, 2006 'A Day Without Immigrants' marches and demonstrations. The significance of this day of protest cannot be underemphasized, as Lomnitz (2007: 434) explains: 'If we interpret the marches as a form of labor protest, they constitute the largest mobilization of workers in the history of the United States. If we interpret them as civil-rights protests, they were the most important since the 1960s'.

While 'A Day Without Immigrants' clearly demonstrated the high level of social mobilization of migrant communities in the US, we have yet to come to terms with the full political implications of this event. For example, when millions of non-citizens take to the streets and demand recognition and a voice by saying 'We are America', does this count as a *demand for citizenship*, or as an *act of citizenship*? (Isin and Nielsen 2008) What becomes of citizenship when it is claimed and enacted by those without status or presence within the political sphere? Does it make a difference that citizenship is claimed through various absences, withdrawals, and refusals? These are not easy questions, especially given that citizenship is caught up in a tradition about thinking about politics that emphasizes vision, visibility and presence (Wolin 2004). Nonetheless, 'A Day Without Immigrants' can be analyzed as an example of how absence can be put into play in the mobilization and, indeed, creation of political subjects.

In the first place, the designation 'a day without...' signifies an intention to withdraw immigrant labor without calling the act a 'strike'. Rather, the mobilizations utilized a long held truism about undocumented migrants: they are a constitutive absence within the national community. Their presence is only worthwhile to the extent that it marks an absence. The 'a day without...' is also a temporal claim. The protests were to be temporary, lasting only one day. This is in contrast to the near permanent exclusion that exists for undocumented migrants, an exclusion that often persists, notably through racism, even after regularization and being formally recognized as 'legal'. While the terminology 'a day without…' underscores the absence of undocumented migrants from full participation in civil society, it is not entirely a lament. Rather, the absence is a symbolic resource to draw upon as a mobilizing tool. The dramatic, record breaking numbers of undocumented migrants and their supporters in the public realm underscored the reversal of the logic of absence. Undocumented migrants made an appearance; they occupied public spaces on an unprecedented scale; they constituted themselves as subjects capable of making claims about rights, belonging and membership. In short, they imposed themselves upon the political scene (Balibar 2002) – including, of course, by making an appearance in Weber's multimedia project.

Does utilizing absence to mark a presence not bind us into a tautological trap that is itself constitutive of sovereign power? Does the strategy of countering invisibility with visibility, speechlessness with voice, illegality with legalization, keep us trapped within the same framework of sovereign politics that is itself the source of the problem of invisibility, speechlessness, illegality and abjection? Todd May's (2008) work on democratic politics suggests an alternative to this cycle of capture and cooptation. Working with the political philosophy of Jacques Rancière, May suggests that reversing the logic of equality is a productive place to start a discussion about democratic politics. Instead of placing equality at the 'end' of our democratic politics (through, for example, an emphasis on expanding the rights of citizenship), May seeks to understand the implications of placing equality at the 'beginning' of the political process. May follows Rancière's (1999) understanding of equality as the 'presupposition' of democratic politics. The presupposition of equality can be explicit or implicit in democratic politics. When it is implicit, equality can remain unspoken and outside the discursive frame within which democratic acts of being political take place. Equality can be 'lived rather than spoken' and can appear as a form of 'intervention, not a discussion' (May 2008: 59, 49). If so, then public speech acts about equality need not be a necessary presupposition of equality. Explicit or implicit, either way to demonstrate equality is to engage a process of what Rancière calls 'subjectification' and, in doing so, to constitute oneself as a claims-making subject. As May (2008: 71) puts it: 'To engage in a democratic politics is not to discover a subject of politics; it is to create one. Equality is not received. It is made.'

May suggests that the politics of equality that lies at the heart of the democracy can be investigated in two ways, one negative the other positive. First, we can ask how democratic politics disrupts or challenges the various structures and practices of inequality within the social order. Democratic politics from this perspective *stops* certain things from happening (e.g. deportation, eviction, racism, sexism, discrimination, etc.). The second, more complex direction is to ask what new political possibilities emerge from democratic politics? What is created? What new citizenships are put into motion?

There is an emerging critical scholarship that approaches equality for undocumented migrants that speaks to the first direction of investigation that May identifies. By far and away the focus has been on debating the type of 'regularization' program that would provide an entry way for migrants into permanent residence and, eventually (perhaps) full citizenship. More provocative has been the emergence of de facto regularization regimes in so-called 'sanctuary cities' that offer municipal services to non-status migrants on a 'don't ask, don't tell' basis. In Weber's film, 'No More Deaths' activist Shanti Sellz resists letting a person's legal status affect her decision on how to treat them. In a similar way, sanctuary cities across the United States are seeking to build communities without reference to status. In a context where municipalities have experienced 'downloading' of the implementation of services by federal and state/provincial governments, it is noteworthy that many of these services constitute the core rights of social citizenship, such as welfare, housing, emergency services, and so on (Nyers 2008).

The second direction of May's analysis is more difficult to discern with any certainty. The demand that sanctuary cities provide the benefits of social citizenship on the basis of territorial presence alone – as opposed to residency, which introduces the inequality of access to proof of identity and residency – is a key site of contemporary struggles around democratic politics (Bosniak 2006). The subjects who are at the centre of such politics are yet to be named. But perhaps the title of 'citizen' remains a suitable, if provisional, designation. This is because citizenship is much more than legal status or the distribution of rights. It is about a struggle for what Arendt called the 'right to have rights'. That this is in fact a *struggle* is important to emphasize, because as 'A Day Without Immigrants' demonstrates the subject of citizenship can precede the formal designation of citizenship.

Should we be missing citizenship? The American Ad Council's original 'I am an American' PSA campaign left citizenship unnamed because it felt the links between citizenship, nationality, and patriotism are obvious. Weber's project focuses on this missing element and reveals citizenship as a complex and contested site where what it means, and does not mean, to be 'American' is enacted and performed. In this way, Weber's project makes clear that citizenship is fundamentally about political subjectivity. Her film features both citizens and non-citizens and their struggles for the right to have rights. Claims about the right to have rights end up being claims about citizenship because citizenship 'gives an account, and always creates an image, of the citizen with the right to have rights and obligations' (Isin et al. 2009: 1). If the utterance 'I am American' is an unspoken claim to citizenship, it is also fundamentally a claim about political subjectivity.

References

Balibar, Étienne (2002), *Politics and the other scene*, New York: Verso.

Bosniak, Linda (2006), *The Citizen and the Alien: Dilemmas of Contemporary Membership*, Princeton: Princeton University Press.

Hindess, Barry (1998), 'Divide and Rule: the international character of modern citizenship', *European Journal of Social Theory*, 1: 1, pp. 57–70.

Isin, Engin F. (2002), *Being Political: Genealogies of Citizenship*, Minneapolis: University of Minnesota Press.
Isin, Engin F. and Nielsen, Greg M. (eds.) (2008), *Acts of Citizenship*, London: Zed Books.
Isin, Engin F., Nyers, Peter and Turner, Bryan S. (2009), 'The Thinking Citizenship Series', *Citizenship Studies*, 13: 1, pp. 1–2.
Lomnitz, Claudio (2007), '2006 Immigrant Mobilizations in the United States', in Michel Feher with Gaëlle Krikorian and Yates McKee (eds.), *Nongovernmental Politics*, New York: Zone Books, pp. 434–45.
May, Todd (2008), *The Political Thought of Jacques Rancière: Creating Equality*, University Park, PA: Pennsylvania State University Press.
Nyers, Peter (2008), 'Community without Status: Non-Status Migrants and Cities of Refuge', in Diana Brydon and William Coleman (eds.), *Renegotiating Community: Interdisciplinary Perspectives, Global Contexts*, Vancouver: University of British Columbia Press, pp. 123–138.
Rancière, Jacques (1999), *Disagreement: Politics and Philosophy*, Minneapolis: University of Minnesota Press.
Weber, Cynthia (2010), 'Citizenship, Security, Humanity: Cynthia Weber's Multimedia Project "I am an American"', *International Political Sociology*, 4:1, pp. 80–85.
Wolin, Sheldon S. (2004), *Politics and Vision*, Princeton: Princeton University Press.

Who is an American?

by L.H.M. Ling

Cynthia Weber's documentary 'I am an American' is an audacious and creative intervention into the field of International Relations (IR). It bypasses the usual conceptual boxes that the discipline imposes upon us since day one of graduate school: e.g., only abstract arguments have force, only written articulations are acceptable, and only topics of 'high politics' matter. With her documentary, Weber shows that we gain richer debates and insights if we extend these maxims: e.g., abstract arguments *and* concrete emotions have force; indeed, one often informs the other; sometimes visual images articulate what the written form cannot; and topics of 'high politics' are not so 'high' or 'political' when ordinary lives are marked forever, like losing a loved one to war or the Immigration and Naturalization Service (INS) (viz. Weber 2005). In form alone, Weber's project shakes the discipline from its tendency to remain removed from and complacent about the very subject that accounts for it: i.e., relations international. But this documentary bears more import than mere form; its content blazes a pioneering path as well.

Weber's documentary conveys at least three layers of meaning.[3] The first offers a dissenting voice to a series of images produced by the American Ad Council to promote unity through patriotism in the US shortly after the 9/11 attacks in 2001. These, she felt, gave an incomplete understanding of what it meant to be an American, especially for those designated as 'unsafe citizens' (Weber 2008). The Ad Council's campaign, for example, did not include the poor, the illegal, the dissenting, the grieving, or the hateful in its multiethnic, multi-cultural pastiche of America. In omitting these Americans, Weber implies, the Ad Council risked propagating the very notion of an America that has no relation to the furies that unleashed 9/11. 'We are great', the images seemed to say. 'What's wrong with you?' Weber's documentary aims to set the record straight.

A second layer of meaning to Weber's project, however, can be read as conservative, even reactionary. Her interviews with 'unsafe citizens' seem to reinstate the same, establishment view of America and Americans from the Ad Council. That is, in giving the poor, the illegal, the grieving, the dissenting, and the hateful a platform to explain why they seek US citizenship or affirm it, even if it means being poor, illegal, grieving, marginalized, and/or hateful, Weber is underscoring the ultimate desire that 'America the Beautiful' evokes around the world and within its own people. Who doesn't want to be an American?, her interviewees seem to ask. America is the center of the world!

This conservative undercurrent applies even to those who reject their US citizenship. These include conscientious objectors who would rather endure political asylum in Canada than condone an unjust war; or those caught 'in-between' such as the native American whose nation is divided by the border between the US and Mexico, yet is demanded to declare fealty to one; or the grieving father who refuses posthumous citizenship for his son who died on the sands of Iraq. Weber's documentary itself could be counted in this category. These courageous acts of dissent indict the US government for failing to honor its founding principles of democracy, freedom, and justice for all. Nonetheless, these critiques still inscribe the myth of 'America the Beautiful' for, without the ideals of democracy, freedom, and justice for all, they suggest, where would we be? 'America the Beautiful' is not just a state or a government but an expression of desire, ranging from the geographical (e.g., I live/work in this space) to the legal (e.g., I have/want the papers) to the psycho-cultural (e.g., I am entitled to certain rights). To push this logic further, one could reason: Even if I have to suffer exile, indignities, and loss to be a *real* American, then so be it. In this sense, Weber's dissent could be seen as a more entrenched version of the narcissistic patriotism that she contests – were it not for the project's third layer of meaning.

A radical interrogation underlies this documentary. Asking who qualifies as an American also probes into the core concepts and institutions that make our contemporary world politics: i.e., sovereignty, citizenship, and the Westphalian inter-state system (Linklater and Suganami 2006). Sovereignty refers to the notion that each state, like the individual as defined by classical liberalism, inheres with an inalienable right to be, to act, and to control its own affairs, as demarcated by territory, without undue interference from others, whether states or individuals. Sovereignty has an internal purpose as well. It provides a legal-juridical status to individuals – i.e., citizenship – to ensure a social contract that the state will protect and nurture citizens in exchange for certain duties and obligations like obeying laws, paying taxes, and serving in the military. The Westphalian inter-state system imposed these notions and institutions on the rest of the world through colonialism and imperialism, starting some five centuries ago when Columbus sailed to the 'New World' and staked flags into the ground.

Yet the Westphalian inter-state system contradicts itself, Weber's documentary intimates, precisely due to its raison d'être. The Treaty of Westphalia (1648) aimed to end war in medieval Europe with commerce and trade, an activity thought to benefit all and harm none. Conventions like sovereignty, citizenship, and international law were developed to facilitate commerce and trade among the rival kingdoms of Europe. Citizenship achieved its modern form with the American (1776) and French revolutions (1789); nonetheless, the notion of citizenship began with the Westphalia Treaty. It sought to protect traveling merchants from undue taxation, piracy, or confiscation by local authorities.

Indeed, the British Parliament invoked sovereignty to justify the Opium Wars (1839–1842, 1856–1860) (Ling 2002). The Qing Emperor had banned opium from entering China and sanctioned the burning of British ships docked at the port of Canton with the intent of selling its addictive cargo to the Chinese heartland. Warmongers within the British Parliament chose to ignore this act of sovereignty on the Qing Dynasty's part to emphasize, instead, their outrage at the destruction of ships that belonged, technically, to the East India Company. To them, this violation of British property amounted to a violation of British sovereignty. Supported by other colonial powers in Europe, the British soon defeated the Qing and concluded a series of 'unequal treaties' in the name of sovereign equality (Liu 2004). Chief among the stipulations was a legal-military cordon of 'extra-territoriality' whereby citizens of a European (and later American and Japanese) colonial power would be exempt from Chinese law and tried according to their own laws, even in cases when a foreign national murdered a Chinese national on Chinese soil.[4] So began the era of 'Pax Britannica' and 'free trade', later inherited by 'Pax Americana' and its contemporary progeny, 'globalization'.

Two centuries later, the chickens have come home to roost. The US rules the globe economically, militarily, culturally and ideologically. But such hegemony comes with a zero-sum price in history, as demonstrated by the Opium Wars. That is, the hegemon's wealth and power *necessarily* impoverishes Others through subjugation (Rodney 1973; Escobar 1995; Chomsky 2003; Johnson 2003). For this reason, multitudes flock to the hegemon in search of a livelihood or way of life not available at home.[5] Weber's interviewees attest to these struggles and labors in their declarations that 'I (too) am an American'. Yet for those within the hegemon, these 'aliens', whether foreign-born or home-grown, must be kept out (jailed, deported or exiled), if not down (silenced, condemned or erased), to maintain the privileges of hegemony. Such are the internal contradictions of sovereignty and citizenship in the Westphalian inter-state system.

Here, Weber indirectly challenges the 'liberal-democratic-capitalist peace' school of thought (Gartzke 2007). It claims that liberal democracies are intrinsically superior, peaceful, and prosperous because they have representative governments, do not war against one another, and provide greater opportunities for prosperity and stability. For Francis Fukuyama (1989; 2006), liberal democracy brings an added bonus. It ends history by realizing nirvana on earth.

But no, Weber reminds us. Representative government may be a good idea but it cannot flourish when restricted to 'members only'. Liberal democracies may not war against one another (suspending, for the moment, the dubious definitions that undergird this claim), but they certainly war against Others precisely to gain the wealth and power that enable their liberalism, their democracy, and their capitalism. Where is 'the end of history', for instance, for the migrant woman from Mexico fighting to stay in a country whose economy disables her own from providing decent wages at home, forcing her to support herself and her son across the border? Or the radio talk show host in Arizona who enjoys enough material comfort and surplus, due in part to 'cheap labor' like that of the migrant woman's, so he could patrol the borders after work to keep out 'illegals' like her? How are future generations assured of prosperity with stability under these contentious circumstances?

What we have is an unsustainable world politics. Westphalia's inter-state system was designed to institutionalize commerce and trade as a means to peace but it banked on one assumption: i.e., 'they' will not come 'here' (Ashcroft et al. 1989). It was fine for the conquistadors to contaminate, rob, rape, enslave, and kill Others in places far away and unfamiliar, but the 'lords of all the world' (Pagden 1998) did not expect a return visit. Whether as slaves, servants, or subalterns, the Other came to the metropole and stayed. Nor did the 'lords' foresee that the colonizing Self, once in the colony, would go 'native' (Todorov 1984; Mignolo 2000). Indeed, this cross-traffic between Selves and Others began to blur the distinctions between sovereignties, citizens, and states, soon to be supplanted by an unexpected intimacy *across* borders of all kinds (Stoler 2006), proliferating subjects and subjectivities (Agathangelou and Ling 2009). Examples abound from the colonies (Nandy 1988; Stoler 2002), but Weber's documentary underscores such intimacies – and the complexities that come with them – apply today as well and inside the hegemon, not just the 'out there'.

References

Agathangelou, Anna M. and Ling, L.H.M. (2004), 'Power, Borders, Security, Wealth: Lessons of Violence and Desire from September 11', *International Studies Quarterly*, 48: 3, pp. 517–38.

Agathangelou, Anna M. and Ling, L.H.M. (2009), *Transforming World Politics: From Empire to Multiple Words*, London: Routledge.

Ashcroft, Bill, Griffiths, Gareth and Tiffin, Helen (eds.) (1989), *The Empire Strikes Back: Theory and Practice in Postcolonial Literatures*, London: Routledge.

Chomsky, Noam (2003), *Hegemony or Survival: America's Quest for Global Dominance*, New York: Henry Holt & Co.

Escobar, Arturo (1995), *Encountering Development: The Making and Unmaking of the Third World*, Princeton: Princeton University Press.

Fukuyama, Francis (1989), 'The End of History?', *The National Interest*, Summer, pp. 3–18.

Fukuyama, Francis (2006), *The End of History and the Last Man*, New York: Simon & Schuster.

Gartzke, Erik (2007), 'The Capitalist Peace'. *American Journal of Political Science*, 51: 1, pp. 166–91.

Johnson, Chalmers (2003), *The Sorrows of Empire: How the Americans Lost Their Country*, New York: Metropolitan Books.

Ling, L.H.M. (2002), *Postcolonial International Relations: Conquest and Desire between Asia and the West*, London: Routledge.

Linklater, Andrew and Suganami, Hidemi (2006), *The English School of International Relations: A Contemporary Reassessment*, Cambridge: Cambridge University Press.
Liu, Lydia H. (2004), *The Clash of Empires: The Invention of China in Modern World Making*, Cambridge: Harvard University Press.
Mignolo, Walter D. (2000), *Local Histories/Global Designs: Coloniality, Subaltern Knowledges, and Border Thinking*, Princeton: Princeton University Press.
Nandy, Ashis (1988), *The Intimate Enemy: The Psychology of Colonialism*, Delhi: Oxford.
Pagden, Anthony (1998), *Lords of All the World: Ideologies of Empire in Spain, Britain, and France c.1500–c.1800*, New Haven: Yale University Press.
Popper, Karl. (2004[1957]), *The Poverty of Historicism*, London: Routledge.
Rodney, Walter (1973), *How Europe Underdeveloped Africa*, London: Bogle L'Ouverture Publications.
Stoler, Ann Laura (2002), *Carnal Knowledge and Imperial Power: Race and the Intimate in Colonial Rule*, Berkeley: University of California Press.
Stoler, Ann Laura (ed.) (2006), *Haunted by Empire: Geographies of Intimacy in North American History*, Durham: Duke University Press.
Todorov, Tzvetan (1984), *The Conquest of America: The Question of the Other*, New York: Harper and Row.
Weber, Cynthia (2008), 'Designing Safe Citizens', *Citizenship Studies*, 12:2, pp. 125–142.
Weber, Cynthia (2005), *Imagining America at War: Morality, Politics, and Film*, London: Routledge.

Notes

1. 'Hauntology' is good, but at the risk of splitting hairs, it seems to me that 'hauntography' is better, agreeing as it does with biography and documentary.
2. Cynthia Weber published this film a year and a half earlier as part of a collection of films that put the Minutemen's project in a critical context. These films appeared on the website OpenDemocracy.net, on Weber's condition that they could not be downloaded or screened on other sites because she refuses to screen the film 'Chris Simcox: "I am an American"' in isolation. Weber insists that this film can only be screened as part of her whole 'I am an American' project so that if its critical content is overlooked by those who adhere to the Minutemen cause, the other films in the project make it clear that Weber in no way endorses the Minutemen project. When Weber discovered that her film had been appropriated by the Simcox For Senate campaign and appeared on the website www.simcoxforsenate.com, she immediately instructed OpenDemocracy to remove her film from the web and to send the Simcox For Senate Campaign a copyright violate warning.
3. Of course, there could be more. I state three only to give a sense of the intellectual journey that this project invites us to take: that is, to travel from 'surface', direct impressions to 'deeper', more complex interpretations.
4. This situation prevailed in all the 'treaty ports', of which Shanghai in the 1920s–30s was the most notorious.
5. A recent BBC report states that 1 of 35 persons in the world is a migrant and that the industrialized economies absorb 40 per cent of those who cross international borders to live and work (http://news.bbc.co.uk/2/shared/spl/hi/world/04/migration/html/migrant_labour.stm. Downloaded 14 June 2009). According to the National Public Radio (NPR), the US remains the final destination of the largest flow of global migration (http://www.npr.org/templates/story/story.php?storyId=10767136. Downloaded 14 June 2009).

www.ingramcontent.com/pod-product-compliance
Lightning Source LLC
LaVergne TN
LVHW071320310826
846742LV00022B/89
* 9 7 8 1 8 4 1 5 0 4 2 2 3 *